Understanding Scrupulosity

Understanding Scrupulosity

QUESTIONS, HELPS, AND ENCOURAGEMENT

Revised Edition

Thomas M. Santa, C.Ss.R.

LIGUORI, MISSOURI

Published by Liguori/Triumph
An imprint of Liguori Publications
Liguori, Missouri
www.liguori.org

Previously published in 1999 by Liguori Publications under the title *Understanding Scrupulosity: Helpful Answers for Those Who Experience Nagging Questions and Doubts.*

Library of Congress Cataloging-in-Publication Data

Santa, Thomas M., 1952–
    Understanding scrupulosity : questions, helps, and encouragement /Thomas M. Santa. Rev. ed.
        p. cm.
    Includes bibliographical references.
    ISBN 978-0-7648-1576-8
    1. Scruples—Miscellanea. 2. Christian life—Catholic authors—Miscellanea. I. Title.
    BJ1278.S37S26 2007
    241'.042—dc22   2006039564

Liguori Publications, a nonprofit corporation, is an apostolate of the Redemptorists. To learn more about the Redemptorists, visit *Redemptorists.com.*

Printed in the United States of America
14 / 6
Revised edition 2007

In loving memory of
Rev. Patrick Kaler, C.Ss.R.

Contents

Introduction

This is a pastoral book, not a professional tome; the difference is essential to note. I do not believe that I am qualified to write a professional work on scrupulosity because I have not received psychological training. However, I do have many years of practical and pastoral experience working with scrupulous people, and I have learned something from them that may prove to be useful.

Because of my work with the scrupulous, and my awareness of the almost daily situations of anxiety that are so much a part of this affliction, I perceived a need for a practical resource. Since this book was first published in 1999, the need has not diminished and warrants this current edition. I hope it continues to fulfill its primary purpose as a help for those who suffer with scrupulosity to use as a quick reference and a reassuring friend.

So very often when the initial anxiety of a scruple comes to a person's awareness it can often be dismissed with some reassurance. On such occasions the scrupulous person, seeking the reassurance he or she knows will help, turns to a priest or counselor—who, unfortunately, is not always available. It is my hope that this book, representative of more than thirty years of questions and answers about scrupulosity recorded in the pages of *Scrupulous Anonymous (SA)*, might prove beneficial at such a moment. In this sense I understand my effort in these pages as pastoral.

Although certainly not a professional work, it may still be helpful to the professional. I hope, too, that priests and spiritual directors who are often the first point of contact for the scrupulous person might find these pages useful in helping them understand exactly what they may be dealing with. In addition, I am very hopeful that this book will be required reading and required reference for seminarians and for others who are preparing for ministry. It would be a great gift to the scrupulous to have ministers prepared to listen and to understand. In this sense I understand my effort to be professional.

Two very fine books have been published that are essential to the understanding of scrupulosity, works that I have found helpful. Dr. Joseph Ciarrocchi's *The Doubting Disease* (Paulist Press, 1995) presents the psychological groundwork that is necessary for beginning to understand scrupulosity. In my opinion the work is extremely important and a welcome addition. In 1997, Dr. William Van Ornum made yet another significant contribution to our understanding of scrupulosity with *A Thousand Frightening Fantasies* (Crossroad). This book effectively combines the necessary psychological background and applies the psychological principles to actual case histories, enabling us, for the first time, to make the necessary connections to help people who seek out help and direction. I was so impressed with this effort that I used the pages of the *Scrupulous Anonymous* newsletter to review and to recommend it to our readers, the first time the pages of the newsletter were ever used for such a purpose.

I would like to believe that this edition builds on the efforts referenced and offers the potential for even more understanding. It is based on the questions asked about scrupulosity and features the consistent answers of the seven priest directors who have been dedicated to this ministry. The *SA* newsletter, published monthly and free for the asking, has tried to help the scrupulous by providing practical advice and guidance in a simple, unpretentious way. With very little effort, and minimum publicity, the *SA* newsletter has maintained a readership in the thousands. I am convinced that the number could easily increase five times; and still we would not begin to reach all those who suffer with this affliction. This statistic may surprise many people; I know it surprised me.

Before I accepted the position of editor of the *SA* newsletter, I was convinced that scrupulosity was dying out. I assumed that because there was less and less emphasis on the celebration of the sacrament of reconciliation and less and less emphasis on rules and regulations, there would be fewer and fewer scrupulous people to minister to. I assumed that scrupulosity was a problem for the elderly and those accustomed to the "way we used to do things." Unfortunately, this assumption proved to be inaccurate.

Although there has never been a study of the *SA* subscriber base to determine the age of the membership, the countless personal letters that I received each month came from people of all ages. In fact, the subscriber base is slowly growing, and the new members of SA are not the elderly—or at least my SA correspondence leads me to make this assumption. What very well might be happening is that the priest, because he is not in the confessional as often as he once was, is not necessarily the one whom the scrupulous person is talking to. My guess is that more psychologists, social workers, and spiritual directors are now ministering to these people.

There is also the issue of the scrupulous person giving up hope for any type of help or useful guidance and simply choosing to suffer quietly. I have received so many letters that express frustration at the inability to find anyone who is willing to listen. For a person suffering from a very active case of scruples, finding a person who seems willing to listen is like trying to find a lifeboat in the middle of the ocean in which you are floundering. Scrupulous people are so desperate for help that they cling to the person who is reaching out to them, and in their desperation they soon swamp the boat. There seems to be no end to the questions, the details, the exceptions, and then even more questions, details, and exceptions. More than one scrupulous person has experienced impatience in the confessional, avoidance in public places, and the occasional slammed phone in frustration.

I have tried to write this book with you in mind, the person who may be asked to help the scrupulous person. I have tried to choose language, examples, and experiences that will be helpful for you in coming to an understanding of the scrupulous.

In the pages that follow we will try and understand a little more about scrupulosity. What makes this book unique is that our understanding will come not from the insights and imaginings of a single person, but rather from people who suffer from this affliction. My contribution to the project has been to organize the questions and answers into a system that I hope proves helpful. In addition, I have provided some commentary and an introduction to each section in the hope that these few words will increase our understanding.

The other unique contribution of this work can be found in the answers that have been provided by the priest/directors of Scrupulous Anonymous who have joined me in this ministry. I am very grateful to Fathers Thomas E. Tobin, Don Miller, Dan Lowery, John Farnik, Louis Miller, and Joseph Nolen. However, in a very special way, I must single out Father Patrick Kaler. For many members of SA, Father Kaler was the only person they could turn to for help and understanding. In my opinion, Father Kaler "earned" sainthood because of this ministry. The many phone calls, always graciously accepted, the volume of letters meticulously answered, and the daily prayers and sacrifices he freely offered, were an inspiration to me. I have never pretended that I follow in his footsteps.

Finally, I must thank some very special people. The first is my sister, Theresa Czarnopys. Theresa is the person who took twenty-five years of questions and answers and made sense out of them. She was very patient with my many changes and with the unreadable scribbled notes that I made in the margin. In a very real sense her name belongs on the cover of this book.

I also wish to thank Patricia DeClue. Pat helped me prepare 125 issues of the *SA* newsletter. She made sure that what I wrote made sense; and if it didn't make sense, she gently brought it to my attention. She continues to be the person who organizes the correspondence of our SA members. I will always be grateful for all her help and assistance.

Hans Christoffersen, the former editorial director at Liguori Publications, invited me to offer this current revision and update. He has a keen pastoral sense and is personally concerned that the people who suffer with the affliction of scrupulosity have available to them the best possible resources to help in their recovery.

In closing, I need to thank the members of SA. I cannot begin to tell each of you how much I appreciate you. I hope, above anything else, that this book is a help to each of you. If, in some small way, this book contributes positively to your sense of peace, my work will be worthwhile. I know that you will join me in inviting any person who reads this book and who finds it helpful to join our group. To do so, all a person need do is send their name and address to

SA
One Liguori Drive
Liguori, MO 63057-9999

Your name will be added to the monthly mailing list. There is no charge for receiving the monthly newsletter, and there is no worry that your name will ever be sold or exchanged. If you prefer you may access the newsletters electronically at *www.liguori.org*. Simply click on the newsletter icon and you will be directed to the *SA* archives.

REV. THOMAS M. SANTA, C.SS.R.
TUCSON, ARIZONA
2007

PART ONE

Defining the Problem

Chapter One

What Is Scrupulosity?

hen I was a newly ordained priest and stationed at my first parish assignment, I received an unusual phone call within the first few days of my arrival. It was a woman who asked me a question I was totally unprepared to answer: "Should I serve tomato soup or vegetable soup for dinner?" I remember standing in the rectory, phone in hand, frantically trying to determine if this was a crank call, if this was some important question that only the pastor should answer, or whether there was something here that I was missing. I finally blurted out, "Make the tomato soup."

The only reason I had for this choice was my own preference. In fact, my own preference in soup was the only thing that I understood about the entire conversation. There was undoubtedly something going on, I reflected, but I was missing it.

Later, through the wise counsel of another priest, I discovered that I had experienced my first scrupulous phone call. The woman, well known in the parish by all of the priests on staff, had called me because she was "paralyzed" in front of her cupboard, trying to make a decision that she understood to be a serious choice that might offend God. Because I was the priest who answered the phone, I then became the person who was going to help her out of her predicament.

Later on, through many more such experiences, I have learned that the choice of "what soup might be more pleasing to God" would be understood as an extreme manifestation of scrupulosity. I have

3

also learned that there was probably more at work with the woman that day than scrupulosity, and if I were going to be an effective minister I would have to learn more about such an experience.

What is scrupulosity? The simplest answer may be to describe it as an age-old problem that has long been understood as an affliction most often manifested in the "tender conscience." Great saints have spoken about it and have counseled their followers about it. Still others, such as Saint Alphonsus Liguori and Saint Ignatius of Loyola, have suffered from it. For many people scrupulosity is understood as a religious problem, and for still others it is understood specifically as a Catholic problem.

For many years mental-health professionals dismissed scrupulosity as a symptom of neurotic behavior and treated it accordingly. Though not included as a specific entry in the *Diagnostic and Statistical Manual of Mental Disorders,* and although it has been long recognized by priests, rabbis, and spiritual directors, it has been only recently understood as a possible subtype of obsessive-compulsive disorder (OCD).

Perhaps the best way to understand scrupulosity is to recognize the manifestation of the affliction. For most sufferers the experience of scrupulosity is described as "thoughts that cannot be shaken." It has been variously described as being possessed by "a thousand frightening fantasies" or as "constructing a spider web in the mind." Others describe the affliction as being constantly and unrelentlingly "pricked by a pin."

Joseph Ciarrocchi, PhD, in an article entitled "Ministry to Scrupulous Persons" that appeared in the Jesuit journal *Human Development*, identifies the core experience of scrupulosity as "an intrusive idea, often associated with a sinful impulse, which the person abhors but cannot shake."

What the doctor is describing is the exact situation of the person who suffers from scrupulosity. Good people, from all walks of life, find themselves possessed by a thought or a desire that does not seem to want to go away. Even though they may realize that they are obsessing over a particular thought or idea, they can summon no amount of logic or rational argument that would help. They continue to obsess, and they continue to be robbed of the peace they long for. The thought continues to disturb them, through no fault of their own. In fact, that which the person desires is exactly the opposite of what they experience.

In addition to the "thought that will not go away," there is yet another manifestation of scrupulosity that might be even more paralyzing. Since the thoughts that obsess the person are often understood within the context of faith and spirituality, their experience of faith is marked with anxiety and fear instead of a source of peace and strength. They want to believe, they are doing all that they can to believe and to be hopeful, but they just cannot seem to shake a feeling of impending doom, disappointment, or eventual condemnation.

SYMPTOMS

QUESTION: I wonder if I am really scrupulous or if I am just using it as an excuse. How can a person really determine whether or not there is a real case of scruples?

ANSWER: There are no mathematical guidelines that can be applied, and the dividing line between scruples and ordinary garden-variety worries is sometimes hard to determine. It might help to compare yourself with relatives and close friends. Do you fret intensely about matters that don't seem to worry them? This may well be a sign that you do not have your conscience in a healthy, normal state of balance.

Father L. Miller, C.Ss.R.

QUESTION: Where does the word *scrupulous* come from?

ANSWER: It comes from a Latin word meaning a small, sharp stone. If you walk with a small stone in your shoe, it is annoying. Scruples can be annoying, too, and can cause open sores. They should not be neglected.

Father L. Miller, C.Ss.R.

QUESTION: What really is scrupulosity? Is it a mental or an emotional sickness? How does it differ from ordinary worry?

ANSWER: Many years ago my moral theology professor, Father Hugh O'Connell, answered a similar question in this way:

> Scrupulosity may be defined as a habitual state of mind that, because of an unreasonable fear of sin, inclines a person to judge certain thoughts or actions sinful when they aren't, or that they are more gravely wrong than they really are. Emphasis must be placed on the assertion that scruples involve an unreasonable fear of sin. If a person merely makes a mistake and thinks an action to be wrong that is not wrong, he is not necessarily scrupulous. Scrupulosity involves an emotional condition that interferes with the proper working of the mind and produces a judgment not in accordance with objective truth, but with the emotion of fear.
>
> *Father Kaler, C.Ss.R.*

QUESTION: How can a person be sure that he or she is scrupulous?

ANSWER: Scrupulosity has been termed "the doubting disease." In short, people who suffer from scrupulosity are people who find it difficult to trust in their own ability to make decisions. The inability to trust in my own decisions means that I constantly examine my motives, my thoughts, my feelings, and anything else that might come into play in the decision-making process. If a person who is scrupulous is in fact a person who doubts his or her ability to make a decision—about sin, for example—why wouldn't such a person also doubt whether he or she is scrupulous or not? It doesn't matter what the decision is about. The anxiety is created in the act of making a decision and trusting that decision. Persons who suffer from scrupulosity might sometimes wonder if they are scrupulous, just as they sometimes wonder if they are in serious sin, or if they have correctly performed a penance, or if they are indeed capable of praying a prayer that is acceptable to God, and so forth. In each instance it will be necessary to learn to trust the advice and the counsel of a single confessor or spiritual director. God bless you!

Father Santa, C.Ss.R.

QUESTION: How does a person know if he or she is really scrupulous or not?

ANSWER: The dictionary defines *scruple* as "(1) a very small quantity, (2) an ancient Roman weight equal to 1/24th of an ounce, (3) a feeling of hesitancy, doubt, or uneasiness arising from difficulty in deciding what is right, proper, ethical, and so on; qualm or misgiving about something one thinks is wrong." The adjective *scrupulous* is defined as "(1) having or showing scruples; characterized by careful attention to what is right or proper; conscientiously honest, (2) demanding, or characterized by, precision, care, and exactness." These dictionary definitions have to be quite general to cover all situations.

When we try to focus more specifically on religious scrupulosity, we detect a more somber mood. And with good reason. One author describes this religious scrupulosity as "a spiritual or psychological state of anxiety and fear about sin and evil in one's life; an abiding sense of guilt that one is practically always in the state of sin." We are no longer talking about mere perfectionism, concern about minutiae, or a preoccupation with neatness and order. No, the person who is religiously scrupulous finds himself or herself in a much more perilous situation. There is the dreaded fear that he or she may have offended God in the past or is offending him now or will offend him in the future. (There is also the accompanying fear that these sins of the past, present, or future will never be forgiven.) For a person who is sincerely religious, nothing could be worse. Self-loathing, as bad as it is, is nothing compared to the conviction that God loathes you. It is a living hell, a terrible affliction. It does not tell the truth about you or about God. Each person's scrupulosity has unique characteristics. But if you have some of the abovementioned traits, if you are terrorized by sin, then you are probably scrupulous. Do all you can to overcome it. Have confidence. It *can* be done. Despite your fears, the truth can set you free. Why? Because the truth is as Saint John says: "God is love" (1 John 4:8).

Father Kaler, C.Ss.R.

QUESTION: There is one thing that concerns me. You say "scrupulous people tend to multiply serious sins, to see serious sin in almost everything." If it is true that we human beings sin whenever we think we are sinning, then scrupulous people must be guilty of a multitude of offenses against God, and there is no hope unless they are cured of their scrupulosity. There must be some error in this reasoning, but I cannot find it.

ANSWER: The error may be in your understanding of the very nature of sin. We should keep in mind that sin does not happen "by accident." You will recall that there are several basic elements to a sin. One of these is often called sufficient reflection. This implies that a person is clearly aware of the seriousness of the action he or she is contemplating and the choice he or she is making. This knowledge or advertence implies the ability to evaluate and appreciate moral values. It is, as it were, "knowledge with a twist." It demands a certain insight into moral values. A scrupulous person is often not able to have such reflection or advertence. This is because the scrupulous person tends to evaluate moral questions not as the Church wants us to evaluate them, but in an unnecessarily strict manner. Some scrupulous people, in other words, do not have the kind of appreciation of moral values necessary to distinguish between what is sinful and what is not.

A second point is that sin implies full consent of the will. It is essentially a free choice. Without freedom, there cannot be guilt or moral responsibility in the proper sense of the word. It is important to realize that the exercise of freedom can be limited by many influences, and scrupulosity is one of these. Theologians commonly accept that scrupulosity can either diminish or destroy the exercise of moral freedom. When this occurs, there cannot be sin. In other words, if one does not have sufficient reflection and full consent of the will, one cannot truly commit a sin. That is why the great spiritual directors of the ages have advised scrupulous people to trust in the judgment of their confessors. Since scrupulous people's judgments are not accurate, they must rely on the judgment of another. In this way, they have a safe course for their consciences to follow.

Father Lowery, C.Ss.R.

QUESTION: Sometimes I wonder if I am really scrupulous or if I am just calling myself scrupulous to let myself "off the hook" in many cases. What do you think?

ANSWER: Since I do not know you personally, I cannot say whether or not you are scrupulous. I suggest that you ask your confessor. I do know that persons who are indeed scrupulous sometimes say the same thing you have said. This often comes up, for example, when a confessor tells them what they, as scrupulous penitents, should do. Later, they will sometimes decide that they should not do what the confessor has told them because "I'm not really scrupulous, I'm just taking the easy way out." The truly scrupulous should beware of this pitfall. It may sound good, but it doesn't help.

Father Lowery, C.Ss.R.

QUESTION: Is it possible for a person to be scrupulous in one area of life and lax in another area? Which areas cause scrupulous persons the most anxiety?

ANSWER: It certainly seems possible for a person to be scrupulous in one area of the Christian moral life and lax, or at least normal, in other areas. Scrupulosity does not always touch all moral matters. That is why it is important for a scrupulous person to have good self-knowledge and be able to distinguish the scrupulous areas from other areas. From my experience I would say that the areas most troubling to scrupulous persons are: (1) the sacraments of penance and Eucharist (Did I tell all my sins exactly? Am I committing a sacrilege? Am I receiving holy Communion in the state of mortal sin?); and (2) sex and chastity (so-called bad thoughts, TV shows, movies, and so on). While these two areas seem to be quite common, it is evident that scrupulosity can strike any area of life.

Father Lowery, C.Ss.R.

QUESTION: Basically, are a scrupulous person's reasoning powers as capable as a nonscrupulous person's?

ANSWER: Yes, basically, but since scrupulosity is a serious emotional disorder it can cloud reason in given situations. When that happens, it becomes almost impossible for the person to see clearly and thereby come to a proper decision. That's why scrupulosity is so disruptive. It ruins just about everything. Who needs that? Life is hard enough as it is. So do what you can to throw off this added burden.

Father Kaler, C.Ss.R.

QUESTION: How can I be sure that what bothers me really are scruples and not sacrileges in my confessions and Communion?

ANSWER: As long as you cannot swear on a stack of Bibles that you deliberately kept back a certain mortal sin or had absolutely no sorrow for what you told, then you are sure that you made a good confession. You can never make a bad confession without knowing it at the time. Also, unless you are absolutely certain that you were in mortal sin when you went to Communion, you did receive Communion worthily. All this is really a scruple or an unnecessary anxiety that has no foundation in reality.

Father Kaler, C.Ss.R.

QUESTION: Do you think scrupulous people are the way they are because of the sin of pride? Or, to put it another way, do you think pride plays a significant role in a person's scrupulosity or in his or her remaining in that state?

ANSWER: Not in my opinion. First of all, in itself it's not a sin to be scrupulous. Many wonderful saints have had bouts of scrupulosity. They bore these trials not only with deep humility but also with great hope that God would eventually deliver them from the darkness that surrounded them. It's true that some persons who are scrupulous have perfectionist tendencies that might give the impression of pride, but I don't think that's the truth. I don't see them nurturing these tendencies for their own sake. They don't insist on certain things because they consider themselves better than others. Rather, these are obsessions and compulsions that just plague them. They would get rid of them if they could.

With regard to a person's self-image, how many scrupulous people feel that they are the worst of the worst, that even God detests them? No one could have a lower self-image than that. That is why this affliction is a living hell. I can't think of one scrupulous person who wants to remain in his or her scrupulosity. They would love to throw it off forever and experience the unrestrained joy and freedom that is their heritage as the redeemed people of God.

Father Kaler, C.Ss.R.

QUESTION: Recently I heard about a sickness called obsessive-compulsive disorder, or OCD. There was some indication that scrupulosity might be connected with this. Is that correct?

ANSWER: In general, the answer is yes. Let's consider this obsessive-compulsive disorder as the main category, the umbrella that covers several chronic psychiatric problems. One group underneath OCD is "scrupulosity," taking the word in a broad sense. Underneath that, we have "religious scrupulosity," an affliction which certainly needs no introduction. But these categories are not airtight—oftentimes there is overlapping. Moreover, people can experience these disturbances in varying degrees, from mild to bothersome, to completely disabling.

The "obsessive" part of OCD refers to recurrent, persistent ideas, thoughts, or impulses that enter a person's mind. Some examples are fear of contamination by dirt, germs, bodily secretions, or environmental toxins. Others are apprehension that something terrible might happen to oneself or a loved one, preoccupation with symmetry, anxiety about unlucky numbers, or the stubborn presence in the mind of perverse images or impulses.

The "compulsive" part of OCD refers to the behaviors that are generated by these obsessive thoughts. These actions are usually performed in a repetitive fashion, or according to certain rules. Heading the list of compulsions is excessive hand-washing, showering, or grooming. Others are the repeated checking of locks, appliances, or car brakes, or the arranging of objects in an effort to ward off danger. How does scrupulosity fit in? Taking the term in its broadest general sense, some experts apply it to those thoughts and actions that have to do with cleanliness; or with the responsibilities thought to be part of one's duties; or with the efforts made to follow certain rules in their most minute detail. But how does all this apply to religious scrupulosity? We know from experience that many of the above examples were too close for comfort. But for victims of religious scruples, there is an added element always present, and it intensifies the suffering even more. For such a person everything comes under the dark shadow of SIN. This means that around every corner there is the possibility that he or she might offend God. For the deeply religious person nothing could be worse than that.

Sometimes this haunting fear focuses on the past. Then the mind is filled with obsessions, such as "Was what I did a sin? Did I confess it right, or did I leave out important details? Was I truly sorry? Did the confessor understand?" Strong compulsions follow immediately: "I will try to recall exactly what happened; I will check it out once more; I'll make another general confession; I'll find another confessor and confess it again, this time putting it in the worst possible light." Sometimes the fear of sin casts its shadow over the present and the future. Then the obsessions are the feelings, urges, or strange thoughts that invade the mind. The mere hint of a temptation panics the person. "That image, idea, or suggestion was so bad, I must have sinned! I probably didn't act fast enough." Or the thought of death terrifies the person. "What if when I go before the judgment seat of God, he condemns me?" The compulsions are "I'll pray continuously," or "I'll distract myself completely," or "I'll avoid that action." Soon the boundaries of a person's life are severely restricted. Holy Communion is no longer received (despite the confessor's admonition); many worthwhile endeavors are called off; needed recreations are avoided. Life becomes almost unbearable.

But not all is gloom. There is good news from the scientific front. Psychiatrist Judith L. Rapoport reports that a specific anti-OCD drug has been found, and it works. For the person suffering from religious scruples there is also good news. Real help has been found, and it, too, works. We'll let Saint Alphonsus report this good news: "Obey in all things your spiritual Father, for by the practice of obedience you will always be secure. And doubt not that if you practice it you will be saved, and will become a saint."

Father Kaler, C.Ss.R.

DOES GOD LOVE ME?

If persistent thoughts are not enough, if a life burdened with unwanted thoughts and details is not enough, there is even more, a question that plagues the scrupulous mind: "Does God love me?"

Most people, at one time or another in their life, find themselves asking the same question. There comes a time in any developing spirituality and awareness of God when it is necessary to ask the question and then come to a faith conviction that we are indeed loved.

When we ask ourselves the question, *Does God love me?* we are also asking ourselves, *Do I love me?* It is very hard for the average person to answer that question; but for the scrupulous it is even more difficult, if not seemingly impossible. "How can God love me when I have all of these thoughts and these feelings? Surely my life is displeasing to God."

QUESTION: My confessor tells me that God loves me, no matter what I have done in my past life. But this priest does not really know how bad I used to be. I wonder if God really loves me.

ANSWER: God loved you first. God's love started everything off. Because God first loved you, he gave you life. Your confessor is right: God does love you, no matter what you have done. There is nothing you can possibly do to make God stop loving you. When God loves, he loves for keeps. He will not change. He will always be faithful in his love for you. Keep thinking about that. That is why the Bible tells us: "God is love."

Father Farnik, C.Ss.R.

QUESTION: I have a constant fear that I could be living my life better than I am. I am always worried that God may not love me.

ANSWER: You could be living your life worse than you are doing, right? If you could be doing worse, would this be a reason for feeling proud and conceited and self-righteous? No, of course not! On the other hand, you could be living your life better than you are. If you could be doing better, is this a reason for feeling afraid and worried and anxious? Again, of course not! You need to be patient and gentle with yourself. Keep reminding yourself that you have a merciful Father. He loves you. Trust in him. Trust in God's love. Don't put your trust in yourself and in what you are able to do that is good and right. What you do and what you are is secondary. The all-important and primary matter is our loving God's goodness and love and gentleness and patience with us. Try to learn to say the beautiful prayer that we find on the lips of Saint John the Baptist: "He must increase; I must decrease."

Father Farnik, C.Ss.R.

PERFECTIONISM

The questions above vividly illustrate the anxiety and the concern that is devoted to answering the question, "Does God love me?" In the attempt to answer the question, the scrupulous person often determines that the best choice may be to move from a position of questioning to a position of perceived strength. "I will make God love me by becoming perfect. In this way God will have to love me." An enormous amount of energy is wasted by the scrupulous person trying to "fix" himself or herself or trying to become perfect. I often asked the person who comes to me with such a preoccupation to try and refocus one's energy and attention. Instead of trying to make yourself pleasing to God, imagine how much more hopeful it might be to try and accept yourself exactly as you are. Imagine yourself loved by God, not as you one day might be, but exactly as you are today, at this present moment, now, in love. Quite a challenge, and not just for the scrupulous person.

Most of us are willing to accept other people, with their faults, weaknesses, and other little irritations, but when it come to ourselves, we become perfectionists. Suddenly every little fault, every little weakness, and every little irritation becomes a major obstacle to self-love and acceptance of who we are. In such an instance, we find ourselves repeating, again and again, *if only I could become...*

For the person struggling with scrupulosity, there is oftentimes a conviction that everything needs to be perfect before God will accept him or her. Of course, this desire for an impossible perfection is a manifestation of scrupulosity and an indication of how the affliction affects the decision-making process. In this instance the time and energy spent trying to become perfect so that the person can be pleasing to God ultimately means learning *not to be scrupulous*, which is the ultimate "imperfection."

QUESTION: One great difficulty for me is that I must do everything perfectly. My prayers must be said perfectly; I must meditate perfectly without interruption. I am always asking, "How can I do everything more perfectly so God will be pleased with me?"

ANSWER: Perfectionism is an unrealistic expectation of what a human person is capable of in the moral order. It is simply not possible for a human person to do everything perfectly. It is very important that you try to accept your human condition and not place unreasonable expectations on yourself. Moreover, it is clear that you have a wrong image of God. God does not love you because you do everything perfectly. God loves you, in the words of Saint Paul, "not because of any works of righteousness that we have done, but according to his mercy..." (Titus 3:5). God's love for you is unconditional. Nothing can make God stop loving you, not even sin. Father John Powell, SJ, expresses God's unconditional love in this way: "I want to love you. That is all. I just want to love you. If you choose to leave me, I will not stop you. I will leave you free, but I will always love you."

Father Lowery, C.Ss.R.

QUESTION: My worry is that no matter how I try, and no matter how much I pray, I have the feeling that God will not forgive me for my past sins, which now appear to me as unforgivable. How can I ever get rid of these feelings?

ANSWER: There is no easy or magic formula. The act of faith and trust in God requires painful effort at times, because we are walking in darkness and the light seems far away. But by the very fact that you want to make an act of faith and trust, you are in fact making one. God is always pleased when he sees us making this effort in the face of great difficulty.

Father Kaler, C.Ss.R.

QUESTION: Whenever I talk to people, no matter how briefly, afterward I feel like I have said something stupid or wrong, or hurt someone's feelings. I am really uncomfortable and feel like I have to call or see this person again and try to make everything right. Please help.

ANSWER: These feelings you have are not rational and objective, but compulsive. They are not based in reality but in your obsessive fear of doing something wrong. Such feelings are very common among scrupulous persons. It is not possible for me to know why you have these frequent feelings of guilt, but I recommend that you act against them. Do not treat them as if they were rational and realistic. Treat them for what they are. Do not constantly try "to make everything right." It won't work. Try to put up with the discomfort you experience in the hopes of overcoming your compulsive need to apologize.

Father Lowery, C.Ss.R.

QUESTION: When facing a decision or a confusing matter of conscience, I sometimes ask a particular saint to inspire me with a specific sign. If I come across the sign within a certain period of time, I take that to be my answer. On several occasions, I have had questions answered through rather uncanny, and thus convincing, signs. But sometimes the signs seem contradictory or ambiguous. Is this a wise practice? Can these signs be trusted? If they can be trusted, how obligated am I to trust them? If I cannot look for signs, how can I obtain certain guidance in these matters since I have difficulty knowing and trusting my gut feelings?

ANSWER: No, this is not a wise practice—and from your questions, I think you already know that it is not. The Lord gave us the saints to inspire us and to be witnesses of his love, not to make up our minds for us or take responsibility for our decisions. It would seem that your effort would be better spent in dealing with the personal issues in your life that make you mistrust your gut feelings instead of running around in search of contradictory and ambiguous signs. God bless!

Father Santa, C.Ss.R.

QUESTION: Since scrupulosity is a form of sickness, does one have an obligation to tell a prospective marriage partner that he or she has this problem? It certainly would be difficult to explain to someone who has never experienced the problem.

ANSWER: It's hard to give a general answer to this question because scrupulosity can afflict people in various ways, some more serious than others. For some it is merely an occasional doubt or worry that bothers them a bit. They have discovered ways to handle these worries. For others it is a perfectionist attitude that makes them feel they are always failing. For some other people it is a full-blown neurosis that prevents them from living a normal life. Should the prospective spouse be told? Certainly in this last case the future husband or wife has a right to know. That would be true of any ongoing illness that greatly disturbs a person's mental, emotional, or spiritual welfare. One's spouse is bound to be affected by it also, so he or she should be told in advance.

Father Kaler, C.Ss.R.

QUESTION: Should anyone be ashamed of being scrupulous?

ANSWER: Of course not. We have Saint Paul's word that no one is tested beyond his strength. Scruples are a part of the human condition. Perhaps more people are affected by them than we realize. The thing to do is to be patient with this particular kind of cross, and try to be at peace in spite of it. That is not to say that we should not try to keep the scruples under control. God surely does not want them to make it impossible for us to do the good things during this short life that we should do. The embarrassment of having scruples and the pain that they cause will surely merit a high place in heaven. There can be no doubt about that. In the meantime the laughter should be kept in the heart and the song on the lips.

Father L. Miller, C.Ss.R.

AND IF ALL THAT IS NOT ENOUGH!

To one degree or another, most people, not just the scrupulous, struggle with perfectionism, with doubts about their relationship with God, and experience anxiety—even fear—about the choices and decisions they make. However, there is a difference that needs to be underlined because sometimes it may be missed. For the scrupulous person such doubts, feelings, and anxieties are an *everyday occurrence*, constantly present and always in the uppermost in their minds. It is not an occasional struggle, an occasional doubt or wonder, but rather is a state of mind, a state of being, that is present, at least as "background noise or static," day in and day out. And if that is not enough, there is even more.

The scrupulous person, possessed as he or she is by "a thousand frightening fantasies," doubts not only the big questions in life but also doubts even that which is genuinely helpful to them.

Over the years the pages of the *SA* newsletter have revealed concern on the part of some readers that the advice they are offered is suspect. In one sense the question is a good sign because it indicates that the person is arriving at a point in their development where they may be willing to try and make the beginning steps toward recovery. However, in yet another way, it is a question that reflects the complexity of the affliction and clearly reveals the multiple layers of doubt and anxiety that are present.

QUESTION: After several years of reading the *SA* newsletter, I detect a philosophy that all extremes are to be avoided at all costs. *SA*, fearful of aggravating any neurotic tendencies in its readers, advocates a middle-class, middle-of-the-road, conform-to-the-society-around-you type of Christianity. You want people to be "normal," but doesn't this often mean spiritual lukewarmness or, at best, very moderate zeal?

ANSWER: We certainly do not advocate a "normalcy" that means sitting in the middle without having any convictions or commitments. But scrupulousness ordinarily is an abnormality in the direction of overstrictness, and one of the purposes of SA is to help readers develop their native fund of common sense. There is a sense in which it is good to be scrupulous, if it means being conscientious and idealistic. But it is not helpful to be scrupulous if it means having a distorted outlook on life and going through the day without joy or peace. God surely doesn't want this.

Father L. Miller, C.Ss.R.

QUESTION: I have a confession to make. I am embarrassed to admit that the thought has occurred to me that the Redemptorists must be a liberal order of priests. Although you may specialize in helping scrupulous people such as myself, you may be letting us "off the hook" by excusing us of real sin.

ANSWER: Our attempt, through the *Scrupulous Anonymous* newsletter and through our other apostolic efforts, is not to let people "off the hook." Our goal is to preach the gospel of Jesus Christ and to let people experience it, not as a burden, but as good news. I'm sure that when the gospel was first preached and it was recognized, in the time and person of Jesus, as liberating, there were some who accused him of "letting people off the hook." Today I think we would recognize that what he was doing was announcing that the "kingdom of God is at hand." In our small way we, too, try to imitate the Lord. God bless!

Father Santa, C.Ss.R.

QUESTION: Can one regard that all answers in any of the *SA* newsletters are in accord with traditional Catholic teaching?

ANSWER: Yes, every answer that I give is in accord with traditional and orthodox Catholic teaching. If I have any doubt in reference to any question, I always check it out before I answer. I find, for example, that the *Catechism of the Catholic Church* is often very helpful. However, let me also state that "traditional Catholic teaching" is not always what scrupulous persons think it is. It is possible that what we might think is traditional teaching is, in fact, not traditional at all. We should always very careful and check out the necessary facts. God bless!

Father Santa, C.Ss.R.

DOES A PERSON EVER GET OVER SCRUPULOSITY?

QUESTION: Does a person ever "get over" scrupulosity?

ANSWER: Every day we receive letters from the members of SA. It is not unusual to receive a letter that asks us to remove a person's name from our list because he or she no longer suffers from scrupulosity. Each and every time this happens, I say a little prayer of thanksgiving because I have yet another example of the power of God's grace. How a person arrives at the conviction that he or she is no longer scrupulous is another question. One of the previous directors of SA, a director who I believe was most revered and respected, was Father Patrick Kaler, C.Ss.R. Father Pat answered such a question in this way:

> For some people, being able to manage their lives without excessive worry would be a real victory, considering where they have come from. For others, acquiring a certain sense of peace, even while life storms about them, gives evidence that they have, indeed, received many special graces. And for some, being scrupulous seems to have been only a temporarily painful period that they had to go through, but one that is now completely over. Once again, they are able to enjoy life.

If you do find yourself a member of these happy groups, it is not a sin. Some people are never freed of this affliction—they have had it for years, and they will carry it to their graves. We don't know the reason for this, but, I repeat, it is not a sin to be scrupulous and it is not a sin not to be able to "get over" it. All the same, we should try our best to rid ourselves of it. That is all the Lord asks of us. May God bless you.

Father Santa, C.Ss.R.

QUESTION: Once scrupulous, always scrupulous, right?

ANSWER: That's not the way it appears to me. Hardly a month goes by when we don't receive two or more letters stating something like this: "You can remove my name from your SA list. I've enjoyed your newsletter and it has helped a lot. But practically speaking, I've overcome my scruples. At least I feel they are 99 percent gone, or manageable to the point where they don't really disturb me." We love to get letters like that! Life has enough hills to climb without burdening oneself with a knapsack of heavy worries. Think of how great it feels to be relieved of that! So, even if you've been scrupulous a long time, don't give up hope. And even if you can't rid yourself of scrupulosity, you are not committing sin. God loves you just as you are.

Father Kaler, C.Ss.R.

QUESTION: You mentioned that some people write in and tell you that they no longer need the *SA* newsletter, that they have overcome their scruples. How does a person know when he or she is really cured of this affliction?

ANSWER: When he or she can distinguish between a temptation and a sin and not worry about confession, Communion, and already-forgiven sins.

Father Kaler, C.Ss.R.

LETTERS OF RECOVERING SA MEMBERS

QUESTION: All my life confessions and Communions have been a great burden for me. I saw serious sin in so many of my thoughts and desires and my failures to act. I never would let myself go to Communion without first going to confession. Even though confessors told me that I had not committed clearly evident serious sin, I always wanted to play it safe and go to confession first. Then I finally realized that other Catholics, no better than me, go to Communion every Sunday and many of them seldom go to confession, not even once a year. It somehow dawned on me that I could not possibly be as bad as I had always assumed I was. So at last I got up enough nerve to go to Communion without going to confession first. I received Jesus and felt a great weight taken off my shoulders. I felt so happy that I walked home with my head in the clouds. I need your honest opinion, Father. Did I do right?

ANSWER: You certainly did right! You confronted your fear head-on. You decided that *you*—and not your fears—were in charge of your religious life. If you keep on meeting your fears head-on, you will become more and more confident about the goodness in you, the goodness that is the work of God's hands, baptized in Jesus, a temple of the Holy Spirit.

Father Farnik, C.Ss.R.

QUESTION: Of late, I sometimes wonder at the joyful awareness of freedom from guilt which I have experienced. After so many struggles, this is almost a miracle to me! Am I deluding myself?

ANSWER: There is no reason to think you are deluding yourself. When it comes to spiritual "miracles," we can say with the old song: "A hundred million miracles happen every day!" Growth in the spiritual life is definitely possible. If the Lord could free people from the clutches of demons, he can certainly free souls today from the bonds of guilt and scrupulosity. I suggest that you feature a spirit of thanksgiving in all of your prayers. Praise and thank the Lord who has delivered you from bondage to true freedom as a child of God!

Father Lowery, C.Ss.R.

QUESTION: How can a scrupulous person learn to make his or her own prudent decisions concerning various courses of action that are open to him or her in his or her daily life?

ANSWER: There is no easy formula that can be made to apply here, but perhaps the most important factor is to begin building up self-confidence, and to do this by taking the bull by the horns, making small decisions first and then larger ones. There will be mistakes of judgment (no one can avoid them altogether), but you shouldn't waste time over these, nor will God hold them against you. The important thing is to make a beginning.

Father Kaler, C.Ss.R.

QUESTION: My greatest help in overcoming my scrupulosity was to use the conscience of my late husband who was a good, loving, moral person. I was given this advice by a wise priest who, of course, knew my husband. I have passed this advice on to my son, who also tends to be scrupulous, as he likewise has a good, loving, moral wife who can decide for him when he is in doubt. Do you agree with this?

ANSWER: I certainly do agree with it. It is excellent advice which I, too, have used on many occasions. Many scrupulous people, for example, get worried about financial matters—especially filling out tax forms and paying taxes. If at all possible, they should let their spouse or some other trusted family member take care of it. In a similar way, scrupulous people tend to get all hot and bothered about the morality of TV shows or the ways of dressing. If other good Christians are not disturbed by a given show or way of dressing, let the scrupulous person follow their example.

Father Lowery, C.Ss.R.

Chapter Two

Two Scrupulous Saints: Their Stories

Before we continue with the task of trying to understand scrupulosity I thought it might be helpful to read something of the lives of two people who suffered with scrupulosity. It can be helpful to reflect occasionally on the lives of others in order to help gain perspective in our own lives. Sometimes it helps to read the story of people who share some of the same characteristics and sufferings we have. It is especially gratifying to be able to recognize in the life of a saint the characteristics of who we ourselves are!

It has long been a tradition in the Catholic Church to read the lives of the saints. This is a practice that has been encouraged through the years because it is believed the lives of the saints can encourage and strengthen all of us. It is hoped we can discover in the life of the saint some particular inspiration, or perhaps a remedy for something that we might be struggling with, or even a solution to a problem, big or small.

I have chosen to include in this book the highlights, and some of the insights and teachings, from the lives of Saint Ignatius of Loyola and Saint Alphonsus Liguori (the patron saint of the Scrupulous Anonymous organization). Both of these men are considered great saints, and both of these men struggled with scrupulosity. Possibly through their example, and by a quick review of their insights into what might be helpful in the battle with scrupulosity, we might all learn something that could be useful. I am very hopeful that potential confessors and potential counselors of the scrupulous might pay close attention to their suggestions.

SAINT IGNATIUS OF LOYOLA

Saint Ignatius was born in the Castle of Loyola, Spain, in 1491. He was the thirteenth in his family, not at all unusual in that time and place. From our historical knowledge of life in a castle in Spain, we have some idea what his childhood might have been like; we have some idea about the food he ate, the games he played, the holidays he celebrated. Despite all this information, and the information we have about his family and his relationships, we nevertheless have no clue as to the cause of his scrupulosity.

Because of his great accomplishments and achievements, it is often surmised that his scrupulosity must have developed in an otherwise healthy mind. (This is an important and reassuring fact, I hope, for each of us.) Be that as it may, it would seem, from a careful reading of his life story, that the first spells of desolation he suffered might reveal that there seemed to be present, from a very young age, at least the beginning signs of the scrupulous mind.

Saint Ignatius reveals in his writings and reflections that when he recalled the doubtful sins of his past life, he could also recall his torment and unease almost from the very beginning. For the first twenty-six years of his life, because he was busy with many things, he did not seem to be dominated by these thoughts, but later, especially when he became silent and introspective as a recluse in a cave near Manresa, his scruples became the primary problem in his mind.

Saint Ignatius reveals that he made a general confession, feeling that by this act of devotion he would be able to combat his scrupulosity. Ignatius wrote out every sin he could imagine, in great detail, but he was still tormented by the thought that there might be something he had forgotten to confess. He relates that he convinced himself that if he could just find the right spiritual director and confessor, he would be at peace. However, he found himself not trusting what he was directed to do. He recalled the story of a saint who went many days without eating, and so he went an entire week without putting a morsel of food in his mouth. Nothing seemed to help.

One day, he relates, he was possessed with disgust for the life he was leading and a desire to be done with it. It was this thought that scared him more than any other. It was this thought that served as a turning point for him. He made up his mind that he never wanted to be possessed by this thought again. He further willed that he would never confess his past sins again. From that day on, he remained free of his scruples, holding with certainty that our Lord in his mercy had liberated him. At first glance, this might seem to be an abrupt turn of events, almost a miracle! When we examine this experience closely, however, we discover that although it would be true to state that Ignatius was cured from his scruples on the day he determined not to go over his past sins again, it would be important to point out that this was not the event that started him on his road to recovery. The single most important event that began his period of recovery happened much earlier, when he was being tormented by his scruples and when he was working with his confessor. In that process he came to an understanding and a belief that scruples are temptations. It took a period of time for this truth to sink it, but it was a truth that he learned through his practice of going to a regular confessor and slowly learning to trust that confessor.

It is also important to point out that in the midst of his suffering and torment, he was also able to compose the *Rules for the Discernment of Spirits* and the *Rules for Scruples*, which are considered to be essential components of *The Spiritual Exercises*. The legacy of Saint Ignatius to those who suffer from scruples may well be discovered through an examination of a very important question for which Saint Ignatius provides important insight and direction. That question is, "What is a scruple?" At first glance this may seem to be a silly question, but it is not. If a person believes that he or she is suffering from scrupulosity, but in fact is suffering from something else, the person will not be able to successfully come to a sense of peace and experience relief. Again, this is the primary reason why a spiritual director/confessor is so very important.

Father V. M. O'Flaherty, SJ, in a little book entitled *How to Cure Scruples* (Bruce Publishing, 1966), helps us understand the teaching of the saint. Saint Ignatius writes:

> After I have stepped upon a cross formed by two straws [for example], or after I have thought, said, or done some other thing, there comes to me from without a thought that I have sinned, and on the other hand, it seems to me that I have not sinned; nevertheless, I feel some uneasiness on the subject, inasmuch as I doubt and yet do not doubt. This is properly a scruple and temptation suggested by the enemy.

From this explanation, and from the rules for the scrupulous that are outlined in *The Spiritual Exercises,* Father O'Flaherty identified some rules about scrupulosity that may prove to be helpful:

- A scruple is concerned with an incident, thought, word, or deed
- The tendency to doubt is not a deliberate compulsion
- After the incident occurs, the thought comes that I have sinned
- The cause of uneasiness and distress is that I doubt and yet do not doubt
- The inclination to enter into the confusion of doubts and counter doubts is best understood as a temptation
- The argument between guilt and innocence never ends
- A scrupulous person is both obsessed and compelled by a need to settle the doubt about their eternal welfare

Saint Ignatius assumes that a scruple enters a mind that is healthy, normal, and free of pathological disorder.

Saint Ignatius and his struggle with scrupulosity are important for us. His realization that the scrupulous thought is a temptation, and not a sin, is something that all scrupulous persons need to remind themselves of. If we were left with nothing else, this insight and conviction of faith would be important. However, Ignatius left us with one more valuable insight. The struggle to overcome scruples demands a certain amount of faith and courage. Ignatius reminds us that it is part of the normal human condition to waver between the courage that is necessary to confront the scruples and the temptation to give in to the guilt and the anxiety that are hallmarks of the scrupulous conscience. Isn't this great news, to be assured by a saint of the Church that it is perfectly all right to struggle? I find this to be very hope-filled.

SAINT ALPHONSUS LIGUORI

Saint Alphonsus was born in the city of Naples, Italy, in the year 1696, the oldest of eight children. As with Ignatius of Loyola, we know many of the details of a life lived in the Neapolitan city of his time. But unlike Ignatius, we do have some direct insight into the cause of his scrupulosity. His many biographers usually make reference to the fact that Alphonsus was very close to his mother and she suffered from a tender conscience, if not from scrupulosity. We also know, from Alphonsus's own admission, that when faced with a choice or a decision he would exhaust most of the confessors in Naples trying to come to a decision with certitude.

Saint Alphonsus Liguori, in my opinion, was not just another saint who struggled with scrupulosity; he is much more. Unlike Saint Ignatius, Alphonsus was never able to completely conquer his scrupulosity. He suffered until his death, and his suffering had a major, central, and pivotal role in his life, his theology, and his relationship with God.

I believe, because of my work with the scrupulous and my

awareness of the effect that scrupulosity can have on a person, that the legendary illnesses and other physical sufferings that affected Saint Alphonsus were the direct result of scrupulosity, perhaps OCD. I believe that his emotional pain found an outlet in his physical person, probably as a result of the fact that this seemed to be the only expression of illness (psychological) he could not, or at least failed to, control or discipline. In short, the anxiety and stress of his scrupulous conscience did not always express itself in thought and word, but it did express itself through emotional and physical suffering.

In his lifetime, Saint Alphonsus suffered numerous periods of exhaustion and at least one episode that might be identified as a nervous breakdown. His biographers traditionally attribute this experience to his vow, "never to waste a moment of time." Personally, I am more inclined to attribute it to scrupulosity. In addition, there are many examples of torturous periods of indecision, sleepless nights, severe stomach ailments, and related physical suffering.

I could list countless examples of physical suffering, complicated no doubt by the severe penances he practiced, but complicated also by, and possibly even the result of, scrupulosity. People in his own time and history considered his many penitential practices to be severe, and there were many instances in his life when his confessor had to intervene in order to temper his choices.

It might be comforting for someone who suffers from scrupulosity to be aware of the fact that a great saint like Alphonsus was someone who suffered the same affliction. However, for me what is important is not that he somehow survived his scrupulosity, or even that he became a saint, but rather his experience of grace. I look to that for my inspiration.

The miracle of grace that Alphonsus experienced as he suffered with this affliction was that, in the midst of all of the ravages of scrupulosity, he was able to recognize the love and the forgiveness of God. And not only to recognize God's gifts and presence but also to respond to God's call—even in the midst of great suffering, suffering that was lifelong and never cured.

When we understand what Saint Alphonsus experienced in his struggle with scrupulosity, and then are able to read the rules and directions that he left us for our edification and healing, his words seem so much more powerful than the words of someone who did not know what they were really talking about.

Saint Alphonsus's teachings on scrupulosity are contained within his *Guide for Confessors*, or, as it is better known, the *Praxis Confessarii*. Unfortunately, the work is somewhat dated and not in general circulation. However, those sections that deal directly with scrupulosity are available to us and included here for our reflection.

1. The confessor must convince the scrupulous person that it is always safe before God to obey their spiritual director where there is no sure sin. In doing this, the scrupulous person is not obeying a man, but God, who says, "The person who hears you, hears me." This is the teaching of Saint Bernard, Saint Antony, Saint Francis de Sales, Saint Philip Neri, Saint Teresa, Saint John of the Cross, Saint Ignatius of Loyola, and countless others.

2. The penitents must be convinced that the only anxiety they should have is in not obeying. Scrupulosity exposes them to the danger of losing not only their peace of mind, their devotion, and their progress in virtue, but even their sanity, and above all, their soul. Scrupulosity can grow to such proportions that they are driven to despair, letting down all barriers against sin.

3. The confessor must try to get across to the scrupulous person that God does not weigh every last detail of our lives. We try as best we can not to offend God, and then leave the rest to God's mercy. We admit that we cannot save ourselves without the help of God's grace, and so we pray for grace with perseverance, confidence, and peace of mind.

Saint Francis de Sales once said, "It is a good idea for us

to close our eyes in the darkness and difficulties of life and walk through them under God's loving care. We should be at peace if our spiritual director tells us we are doing well and let it go at this. The obedient person will never be lost." Saint Philip Neri assures the scrupulous penitent that he will never have to give God an account of his actions if he obeys his confessor. Saint John of the Cross calls it a mark of pride and lack of faith for a person not to trust the advice of his or her confessor.

4. Because of all this, the confessor should speak very often to the scrupulous penitent of the confidence he or she should have in Jesus Christ who died for our salvation, and in his most holy Mother whose great power is at the mercy of those who come to her for help. The confessor should try to get the penitent to be convinced of the certainty of salvation whenever he or she runs to Jesus and Mary who are ready to hear every prayer addressed to them.

5. The confessor should forbid the scrupulous person to read books that increase anxiety and to mix with other scrupulous persons. If one of them is troubled with terrible guilt feelings, the confessor may even forbid attending sermons on terrifying subjects. The confessor may even forbid the scrupulous penitent to make an examination of conscience in regard to the things that cause irrational trouble.

6. If the scruple is nothing more than the fear of giving into bad thoughts (as for example, against faith or purity or charity), the confessor should not hesitate to disregard it and assure the penitent that these thoughts are trials and there is not consent or sin. In this matter the confessor should use the rule: When a person has a tender conscience, it should be presumed that the sins have not been committed unless the penitent is extremely certain that they have. As Father Alvarez says, "Such a terrible thing cannot happen to one who hates sin without it being clearly recognized." Consequently,

it is sometimes good to forbid penitents to accuse themselves of such thoughts again, unless they are sure and can testify under oath that they did indeed consent to them.

7. Some scrupulous persons fear that everything they do is sinful. In counseling persons like this, the confessor should command them to act without restraint and overcome their anxiety. The confessor should inform the penitents that their first obligation is to conquer their scruples, whenever what they are doing is not clearly sinful. This is what the moralists teach.

Chapter Three

Scrupulosity and Confession

Hopefully, with our introductory questions and answers and the story of the lives of two great saints, we are now beginning to better understand scrupulosity. At this point it is important to come to an appreciation of the state of mind of the scrupulous person. To understand the intensity of the feeling that is always present, to be possessed by the "thought that cannot be shaken," and to understand the resulting anxiety and fearfulness, helps prepare us to understand the types of questions that will therefore be asked.

The scrupulous question, the scrupulous detail, the scrupulous exception, is impossible to understand if it is not understood within the context of the "always present background noise and static" of scrupulosity. If we cannot somehow understand and arrive at some point of empathy, the result will invariably be frustration and impatience.

If you are reading this book and do not suffer from scrupulosity, it is helpful to understand that the scrupulous person does not desire to be the source of your impatience and frustration. It may at first be difficult to fully grasp this notion, because if you are working with a scrupulous person you have probably already experienced what seems like never-ending questions and clarifications. Regardless, I assure you that it is true. I cannot begin to recount the numerous scrupulous people I have counseled and who have shared with me their concern for what they are inflicting on their confessor, their spouse, their friend, or confidant.

The scrupulous person desires, above all else, a healthy relationship with God. However, in the grips of the manifestation of scrupulosity this seems unattainable, and so they seek instead the peace and tranquillity that comes from another person's reassurance and certitude. The cruelty of the affliction is that even a confessor's most forceful certitude may not be enough. Moments after you respond to one question or clarify a doubt, another question and another doubt will rise to take its place. It is in the doubt and the questioning that scrupulosity is manifested and the helper's impatience and frustration is experienced.

A CATHOLIC PROBLEM?

Although not a Catholic disease, scrupulosity is often associated with confession, the sacrament of reconciliation, as it is practiced in the Church. (See appendix 1 for "The History of Confession.") Because of this it is therefore assumed that scrupulosity and Catholicism must somehow go hand in hand. While this is an understandable assumption, it is also an unfortunate one.

There are countless non-Catholics who suffer from scrupulosity. Their basic struggles, which include anxiety about pleasing God, problems with decision making, and other issues with a possible religious interpretation, are just as real and just as painful as those of their Catholic counterparts. The only component that does not come into play with these people is the confessional component; but every other fear and anxiety is the same.

It may be easier for a Catholic who struggles with scrupulosity to receive help because he or she has the confessional contact point. Unfortunately, this opportunity is sometimes wasted by the priest who may be unprepared or unaware of the problem, thus missing a chance for intervention and guidance. The non-Catholic person who struggles with the affliction has the added burden of seeking help and guidance in waters that are unknown, uncharted, and unfamiliar. His or her single greatest challenge will be to find a counselor or a therapist who is willing to accept and work within the religious parameters of the struggle. (Fortunately, such people are easier to find today because of a growing awareness and respect.)

QUESTION: Are Catholics more prone to be scrupulous in regard to their religion as opposed to those in other religions?

ANSWER: It seems clear that scrupulosity is not confined to those of the Catholic faith. I myself have met scrupulous persons of other Christian faiths, as well as the Jewish faith. It may be, however, that because the Catholic faith places a strong emphasis on externals (for example, the sacraments), and because there is a clear and definite body of Catholic laws (canon law), Catholics are more often troubled by scruples than persons of other faiths.

Father Lowery, C.Ss.R.

CONFESSING SINS

Realizing that the struggle with scrupulosity is not manifested completely within the Catholic world, it is nevertheless true that the most obvious manifestation of scrupulosity is associated with the Catholic practice of the private confession of sins to a priest. It is within the preparation for the reception of this sacrament—an exercise traditionally understood as the examination of conscience—and the actual confession of sins, that scrupulosity is obviously and painfully manifested. Equally painful is the period immediately after the confession of sins, when the scrupulous person leaves the confessional and reviews his or her confession. In fact, that is one of the first practices that a priest/confessor will try to end. Often this is a first positive step toward recovery, enabling the scrupulous person to begin to trust their confession and not engage in fruitless and painful reexamination of the confession. It is an important and a difficult first step.

Because of the relationship between scrupulosity and confession of sin to the priest, many questions present themselves. The questions, which are usually different variations on a theme, or limited to a favorite area of concern and anxiety, are as persistent as they are predictable.

TYPES OF CONFESSION

The usual practice for confessing sins to a priest requires that all mortal and serious sins be detailed (it is not unusual for the priest to ask clarifying questions for the purpose of offering advice and counsel). Venial sins may be mentioned, but no detail is necessary. The scrupulous person has problems determining if a sin is serious (which we will cover in detail in chapter 4) and is often unsure if enough details have been provided (it is the responsibility of the priest to ask for clarifying details if he does not understand what is being confessed).

Confession is a source of great anxiety to the scrupulous person. Instead of being a help—as it is meant to be—it becomes a hindrance, another source of worry. Because of this, the confessor may suggest a confession of devotion or a generic confession as appropriate for the occasion.

QUESTION: What is meant by confession of devotion? Does one have to have permission to use this? I was told to do this because I am always nervous and upset at confession, and I can't remember anything the priest tells me.

ANSWER: Confession of devotion simply means a confession in which no serious sins are confessed. If the confessor tells you to mention only one or the other small fault, and not to go into any detail, you must try to obey. And you need not do this very often if it causes you such great distress.

Father L. Miller, C.Ss.R.

QUESTION: In the August 1978 issue of *SA*, Father Louis Miller wrote that a person who has great difficulty in going to confession should restrict himself or herself to a generic confession. I am scrupulous, under the care of a psychiatrist, and have a confessor who has offered to help me from a spiritual standpoint. I go to confession and only say, "I am a sinner." Now I doubt if I am taking advantage or committing mortal sins because I can make a generic confession. What should I do now?

ANSWER: Father Miller's advice is very sound. Your confessor obviously agrees with him. Continue to confess in this manner. Try to ignore your fears and the constant questioning of your motives. If you stay with your present practice, you may find some measure of peace.

Father Lowery, C.Ss.R.

QUESTION: Sins of my past—especially of adolescence and young adulthood—often come back to my mind. I asked my confessor if I could make a general confession so as to find peace of mind. He said that a general confession would not bring me peace of mind, but only keep me on the treadmill of scrupulosity. What do you think?

ANSWER: I think your confessor is very wise. I also think that your question clearly illustrates yet another reason why a scrupulous person should choose a regular confessor. Let me explain. Your confessor knows that another general confession will not help you because, after a brief interlude, the same old doubts and fears will return. The challenge for the scrupulous person is to place absolute trust in the forgiveness of Jesus as celebrated in the sacrament of reconciliation. Anything short of that will not bring peace.

The second point is the wisdom that is found in having a regular confessor. If you persisted in jumping around from one priest to another, instead of following the advice of your confessor, you would never be able to come to a point where you could learn to trust in the absolute power of forgiveness. You would be self-condemning yourself to a life of brief interludes of peace but never the opportunity for sustained healing. Only a regular confessor makes this possible. God bless!

Father Santa, C.Ss.R.

QUESTION: I find myself unable to wipe the slate clean. I made a general confession some time ago. The priest told me that all my sins, confessed or forgotten, were forgiven and that I must not repeat any of those sins again. But now past sins pop into my mind and I can't remember if I committed them before or after my general confession, or if I ever confessed them. I have no peace of mind. What should I do?

ANSWER: Your basic problem is that of most scrupulous persons: You want to "wipe the slate clean," you want to have mathematical certainty about the forgiveness of your sins. But such certainty is not possible. Your only chance for some measure of peace is to follow the confessor's advice: Forget about your past sins. Forget about all the details of when exactly you committed them and how exactly you confessed them. Believe me, you could confess them a million times and still not be satisfied. Trust in the advice of your confessor and in the Lord's absolute love for you.

Father Lowery, C.Ss.R.

QUESTION: I have been wondering about something. Please don't laugh. Is it possible to make a confession through the mail and have it count? I just feel that you understand scrupulous and fearful people and it would be easier to make my confession to you.

ANSWER: I am certainly not tempted to laugh at your question. In fact, theologians have posed the same question many times. The clear discipline of the Church, however, is that the sacrament of penance (including the confession of sins and also the absolution by the priest) cannot be administered by mail.

Father Lowery, C.Ss.R.

FORGETTING OR BECOMING CONFUSED

Yet another common problem, not to be understood as a symptom of scrupulosity but rather as the result of the panic and anxiety that often accompanies it, is the experience of forgetting or becoming confused. This experience is common to the actual confession of sins to the priest, where the penitent may stumble over words, repeat the same perceived sin and the details associated with it over and over again, or repeatedly ask the confessor, "Did I mention that I...?"

The other manifestation of this type of anxiety is also commonly experienced immediately after the confession when the scrupulous person returns to the pew and begins a detailed examination of the confessional experience. It is in this detailed examination, something certainly not required as a condition for celebrating the sacrament, where the scrupulous will more often than not convince themselves of some kind of shortcoming in their confession, some detail missed, or some perceived sin not sufficiently explained. This discovery will often lead to the erroneous assumption that the confession was invalid or even sacrilegious. As a result of this false assumption, even more anxiety is experienced and the scrupulous person becomes convinced that he or she must repeat the confession.

If the scrupulous person is somehow able to make it successfully through the detailed examination of the confessional experience and conclude that he or she made a valid and pleasing confession, there is still one more hurdle to be navigated: the penance given by the priest and the absolution prayed.

QUESTION: What should one do if he tries to make a good confession, says his penance, and then on arriving home cannot remember receiving absolution? This has happened to me more than once. Do other people have this problem?

ANSWER: For the consolation of this questioner, yes, they do. Our memory can easily play tricks on us, especially if we are preoccupied about something. In this case you *can* and *should* proceed on a presumption: What ordinarily happens has happened *this* time also. The priest regularly gives absolution when he hears your confession, and therefore, even though you don't actually remember it, you can take for granted that he gave absolution to you this time also.

Father L. Miller, C.Ss.R.

QUESTION: If, after going to confession, you remember a sin you forgot to confess, should you go back to confession before you leave the church or wait until your next confession?

ANSWER: There is no need to go back to confession before you leave the church or to mention the sin in your next confession. Your sins are forgiven. Everyone, if they would enter into an examination of their confession, would remember something they did not mention or something they feel they did not clearly state. The difference is that most people do not examine their confession once it is over; they simply accept their penance and the fact that they are forgiven. Scrupulous people, on the other hand, as a symptom of their disease, often examine—and judge—their confession. In the process, they oftentimes forget that their sins have been forgiven by a loving God who is not demanding perfection, but rather who is gracious with his grace and with his forgiveness. May God bless you!

Father Santa, C.Ss.R.

QUESTION: If I forget what the penance is that the priest gives in confession, have I still made a valid confession? Am I obliged to go back to the priest and tell him that I forgot my penance?

ANSWER: Your confession is still valid and there is no need to go back to the priest. Simply do your best to recall what the penance was. More often than not, the penances we receive are pretty standard. What I do, if I forget my penance, is simply recall a penance that I received at a previous confession and I perform that penance. I believe that what God desires from his people is the willingness to be reconciled, the firm purpose of amendment, and openness to do God's will. May God bless you!

Father Santa, C.Ss.R.

QUESTION: It seems to me that I read in one of your answers that a sin is forgiven, regardless of how it is presented in confession. In addition, I believe that you stated that a person does not have to go into detail. Is this right?

ANSWER: Yes. When a person goes to confession he or she is required to name one's sins to the best of his or her ability and with a heart that is open to God's forgiveness. It is the responsibility of the priest to ask any questions that he feels are necessary in order for him to understand what the person is confessing. As long as the penitent is not deliberately withholding essential information, the assumption should always be that the priest correctly understands what you are confessing. I have listened to many confessions, and I have heard sin identified in many different ways. If I do not understand what the person is talking about, I will ask. However, because I have heard so many confessions in my life, I have developed the ability to quickly grasp the length and breadth and depth of the subject at hand. It is my experience as a confessor that leads me to believe that other confessors have the same experience. Please be at peace and try to learn to trust your confessor. God bless you!

Father Santa, C.Ss.R.

REMEMBERING PAST SINS

There is a formulaic prayer that is often prayed at the end of the confession of sins. "I am sorry for these sins and all the past sins of my life—especially..." The penitents then name a sin they are grateful that the Lord has forgiven, or a sin they are still struggling with and for which they would like a little extra grace or even encouragement. This prayer was intended to be devotional in character, and millions of people routinely pray it without difficulty. However, for the scrupulous person, it is not a devotional prayer but more often than not yet another hurdle to be conquered.

Past sinfulness plagues the scrupulous. Perhaps it is the fact that the sin happened so many years ago, and the exact *circumstances* of the event are so hard to remember. Perhaps it is the difficulty of accurately and perfectly recalling the *moment* that a perceived unconfessed sin must have occurred. Perhaps it is the inability to recall the *details* that somehow convinces the scrupulous person that, in the forgetting, something suspicious and unforgiven must be present.

QUESTION: Many years ago when my sister and I were quite young, we were not allowed to go to Mass one Sunday. I don't think we were ill; and I don't remember if it was the weather or what the reason was. After all these years it came back to me. Should I tell it in confession?

ANSWER: No. Let this incident of the past rest quietly in the mercy of God.

Father L. Miller, C.Ss.R.

QUESTION: What is a scrupulous person to do when out of the clear-blue sky a sin is remembered that happened forty years ago? I can't remember if I confessed it or not.

ANSWER: Trust in the mercy of God and don't dig up the past. Those sins of so long ago are long since forgiven.

Father L. Miller, C.Ss.R.

QUESTION: I am sorry for all my sins, but I am worried that I may have committed some sins in the past which I have never confessed or, if I did confess them, maybe I did not confess them in the right way and I may have left out important details.

ANSWER: The sacrament of penance should include two things. By far the more important of these is inner sorrow within one's heart. Without sorrow for sin and purpose of amendment, our confession would be hypocrisy. We would be telling God that we are sorry for what we did in the past, while intending to keep right on doing the same things in the future. You were sorry, and you continue to be sorry in your heart for all your sins. This is the all-important aspect of confession. This contrition of yours received God's instant and complete forgiveness.

The second thing that should be included in confession is to accuse oneself as a sinner. With our lips we humbly admit, as well as we can, what our deliberate failings were. If we are aware of serious sins, and if we are certain they were serious sins, then we must acknowledge them. But absolute perfection and accuracy are not demanded. God accepts our human and imperfect memories. God does not expect the impossible. You have doubts and misgivings, but you have no certainty that you failed to confess some serious sin or sins in the past. You have no certainty that you confessed sins incorrectly. Therefore, since you lack such certainty, you have nothing to be afraid of. Forget it. Leave it all in God's hands. That is all that God expects of you.

Father Farnik, C.Ss.R.

QUESTION: If a person goes to confession and says something from the past is still bothering him or her but cannot remember whether it was ever confessed, and the priest tells the person to "forget the past," does that mean even if it was never actually confessed, it is still forgiven?

ANSWER: Yes, it is still forgiven. God forgave it at the moment when this person became sorry and repented. Telling the sin in confession is always a secondary and relatively less-important matter. Repentance within the heart is the primary and all-important consideration: internal sorrow and purpose of amendment. In these cases of worrisome doubts about having confessed sins from the distant past, one may certainly "forget the past." God's forgiveness is linked with our inner repentance and purpose of amendment, not with the externals of self-accusation in confession. The self-accusation has its place. If we are certain we did not confess a serious sin of the past, we should do so at the time of confession. But if we are not certain about this, if we have doubts, if we have vague anxieties about it but not clear-cut certainty, then we should simply "forget the past." Leave it all in God's hands. Always remember that inner sorrow and purpose of amendment are the all-important considerations here, not the external confessing or self-accusation. Confessing is always a secondary and less important matter.

Father Farnik, C.Ss.R.

QUESTION: I want to make a general confession every time I go. My past sins keep coming back. I make up my mind to forget them, and I try to, but they keep coming back.

ANSWER: Wait a minute. Let's be more precise here. Is it really your past sins that keep coming back, or is it your *memory* of past sins that keeps coming back? How can your past sins themselves come back? Those sins no longer exist. God forgave you for them a long time ago when you first were sorry for them. It is only your memory of those past failings that keeps coming back. But what's wrong with remembering? There's nothing wrong with having a good memory. Each time you remember those past sins of yours, try to think of how good and merciful God has been to you. He forgave you for all those past sins.

Father Lowery, C.Ss.R.

QUESTION: I am getting older and my memory is not so good anymore. I worry about past sins and how many times I did them and whether I ever confessed them. What shall I do?

ANSWER: No person can remember the past perfectly. But it doesn't matter, because God does not require that you have a perfect memory. God asks only that you be sincerely sorry for having offended him and that you sincerely strive to love and serve him better in the future. God cares about your future, not your past. You should try to do the same. Leave all the past in God's hands. Tell him you are sorry for every way you may have offended him, for everything remembered and everything forgotten. Tell God that you will try to love and serve him well this day. That alone is what really matters. You cannot relive the past and do it differently now. You can only live today the way God wants. So forget the past and give to God your gift of today.

Father Lowery, C.Ss.R.

QUESTION: My whole life is always before me, it seems. All the terrible sins and mistakes are torturing me. I go to confession; but then I start thinking of these awful things and I don't know if I confessed them, or did I forget one? It's an awful feeling. What can I do?

ANSWER: Your brief letter describes the feelings of many scrupulous people: mental torture about past sins and no relief from the sacrament of penance. I can only encourage you and others to "let go and let God." Your emphasis is entirely wrong. You turn the spotlight on yourself: Did I do this or that? The spotlight must be turned on God. His mercy is infinite, his forgiveness is absolute, and his love is unconditional. Keep trying to believe that.

Father Lowery, C.Ss.R.

QUESTION: For the past two years I have been focusing on sins of the past. I confess them, but continue to experience guilt over them. I feel I have not fully confessed them or been fully forgiven for them and have difficulty forgiving myself. On an intellectual level I am aware of God's generous forgiveness, but on an emotional level I have great difficulty with applying this to myself.

ANSWER: Your letter is a good description of how many scrupulous persons feel. Note that the repeated confession of past sins does not bring peace. That is why wise confessors forbid their scrupulous penitents to confess past sins. Note, too, the split between your intellectual conviction about God's mercy and your emotional experience of it. No one can guarantee that you will *feel* forgiveness, but both the Lord and the Church assure you that your sins *are* forgiven. The only way to peace is to believe in God's mercy and to place your absolute trust in him. "Let go and let God!"

Father Lowery, C.Ss.R.

QUESTION: What can I do? I've been scrupulous for many years. Going to confession has always been a torture for me. Sometimes I have found a little peace for a while after confession—but then some sin of the past comes up, usually something that happened many years ago when I was a child, and once again I panic. Now I have to go back to confession! Oh, how I dread that! Please help me. It seems like it will never end.

ANSWER: Dear reader, you are right about one thing: It will never end if you continue in the present pattern. There will always be one more "sin" that will move into your consciousness, one more specter arising from the misty past to haunt you. What should you do? You should accept what your confessor has told you many times, what Saint Alphonsus and other spiritual advisors have stated over and over, what the *SA* newsletter has recommended again and again: Forget the past! All your past sins have been forgiven. You do not have to go back and examine them, and you certainly do not have to confess them. This is a perfectly safe way to act. In doing that, you are not offending God. Rather, you are obeying your confessor, which is what God wants you to do. This is very pleasing to the Lord. He loves you very much.

I would also like to suggest that you get an appointment with the priest (outside the confessional, if you wish) and tell him how you feel about confession. He will probably have some ideas that will make the sacrament less of a burden to you. I'm pretty sure he will recommend that you don't go to confession very often. Whatever advice he gives, try to follow as well as you can. It will take some courage to confront your fears, but it is well worth the effort. It is the way to peace and happiness.

Father Kaler, C.Ss.R.

QUESTION: If you remember something in your past that might have been a sin but you're not sure if it was, and you don't know if it was ever confessed, what should you do? Should you ask about it in confession or should you just forget about it?

ANSWER: Forget about it. There is no obligation to bring doubtful sins to the sacrament. That holds whether the doubt is about the sinfulness of what happened or about whether it was ever confessed.

Father Kaler, C.Ss.R.

QUESTION: My confessor told me, "Don't bring up your past sins." But every now and then something reminds me of them and I find myself thinking about them, sometimes at considerable length. I know this is going against my confessor's advice, but it keeps happening. Am I sinning again when I do this?

ANSWER: No. What your confessor was telling you was that you shouldn't worry about your past sins or consider them as unforgiven or try to confess them again. Like everyone else, you have a memory. You will at times recall your past sins, as well as many other matters. There's nothing wrong with that. In fact, you could use that opportunity to remember how merciful God was in forgiving you. The memory of past sins and God's goodness to you can inspire you to renew your sorrow and your determination never to offend him again. It can also help you to be humble and keep you from having a "better-than-thou" attitude toward others.

Father Kaler, C.Ss.R.

QUESTION: Suppose a person has led a very sinful life for many years. I've repented now and confessed several times all the sins I can remember. But the past keeps coming up. Did I tell all my sins? Suppose I forgot some? My confessor has told me to forget the past completely, that all my sins are forgiven, and that I should concentrate on leading a good life now. Can I safely follow my confessor's advice?

ANSWER: By all means! And when thoughts of the past come up, simply thank God for his loving mercy!

Father Kaler, C.Ss.R.

NECESSARY AND UNNECESSARY DETAILS

The confession of sins to a priest presumes a certain amount of detail. To simply confess a sin such as lying may not be enough; for example, if the lying that you have in mind is perjury, falsely testifying in a court case, which results in the unjust conviction of an innocent person, more detail is necessary. The confession of the act of lying demands an explanation in this instance, so that the priest/confessor understands the seriousness of the sin that is being confessed.

Unnecessary detail is to confess the sin of lying, and in the confession of the sin explain to the priest that it was on a Sunday afternoon, that you may have been a little upset, and the neighbor's dog was barking. It is enough in this instance to simply confess that "I lied."

The scrupulous person finds it very difficult, if not impossible, to distinguish between the details that are necessary and details that are not necessary. For the scrupulous person, every detail may be "necessary." There is no presumption that the priest/confessor, who has undoubtedly celebrated many occasions of the sacrament of reconciliation, may be capable of understanding the serious sin or the venial sin without detailed explanation. There is also a reluctance to trust that the confessor will ask for the necessary details if he does not understand what is being confessed. Obviously, the need to provide so much detail increases the anxiety and the frustration of the scrupulous person who is confessing. It also has the potential of increasing the impatience of the confessor, making it all but a remote possibility that the scrupulous person will leave the confessional having a real sense of not being listened to and understood. The result is frustration—for both the confessor and the penitent.

QUESTION: Sometimes after I go to confession I begin to worry about the sins I have confessed. I wonder if I have told them clearly enough, with enough details, or if I had enough sorrow. The more I think about this, the worse it gets. What should I do?

ANSWER: The one thing you should do is stop worrying. All your sins have been forgiven. There is no need to repeat them in another confession. Your confessor is well trained, has had much experience in the confessional, and could ask questions if he felt it necessary. Besides, and most importantly, God gives special graces to both the confessor and to the penitent at this time. That means our Savior lovingly fills in all the human "gaps" our confessions may have. There is no need for worry before, during, or after receiving this sacrament.

Father Kaler, C.Ss.R.

QUESTION: If a sin is told in confession but afterward the person feels that it was not really understood by the confessor, should the sin be told again?

ANSWER: No. The sin was forgiven, and it should not be repeated. Because of their fears, many scrupulous people experience very strong urges to reconfess their sins. But a line must be drawn. They must be firm with themselves about this. According to Saint Alphonsus, their fears are groundless. It is a perfectly safe way to act, and it is what the Lord wants. If they give in to this urge to reconfess, it will never end. There will always be one more sin that was not told properly, clearly, or in enough detail. Then this sacrament will become a torture chamber rather than what it was meant to be: a place of great blessings and consoling peace.

Father Kaler, C.Ss.R.

QUESTION: I've been scrupulous for many years. I wonder if some of my past confessions were good. Here's what I did sometimes. I would confess things as sins, and I don't know if they really were sins. I would do that just to make sure. I would portray matters in the worst possible light, figuring it would be better to err on that side than on the other. Now I'm worried that what I did might have been lying to the priest. Were those confessions sacrilegious? What about other real sins that I confessed during those years—were they forgiven? What should I do now? It's impossible for me to remember all the details of those confessions of many years ago.

ANSWER: You don't have to do anything. All those past confessions were good. You weren't trying to lie or do anything sacrilegious. Quite the contrary. Scared and worried, you did everything possible to be on the safe side. This way of acting is typical of scrupulous people. Some experienced counselors believe that the root cause of all scrupulosity is this very strong need to feel secure. That's why scrupulous people want to make one more general confession, repeat prayers over and over, reexamine their consciences a thousand times, agonize over the reception of the sacraments, et cetera, et cetera. How can such a person find security? Saint Alphonsus Liguori, a great moralist who had struggled with scrupulosity himself, gave this advice:

> This instruction to be obedient to one's spiritual director in doubts of conscience is given by all the doctors of the Church and the holy fathers as well. In short, obedience to one's confessor is the one safest remedy which Jesus Christ has left us for quieting the doubts of conscience, and we ought to return thanks for it.

Father Kaler, C.Ss.R.

QUESTION: If you confess a mortal sin do you have to think further thoughts like these: "Did it occur on Sunday? Did you make another person commit sin?"

ANSWER: You have to confess only what you realized at the time that you did it. A mortal sin on Sunday is no different from a mortal sin on any other day, unless done deliberately just to profane the Sabbath. God holds us responsible only for the knowledge we have at the time we do something. Any knowledge that comes to us after the sin is done does not, and cannot, add to the sinfulness of the action. Foolish guilt feelings should be disregarded, since they lead only to more foolish guilt feelings and do not lead to God.

Father Kaler, C.Ss.R.

THE SCRUPULOUS CONFESSION: A CLASSIC EXAMPLE

In the pages of the *SA* newsletter one of our readers asked a question that included many of the ingredients of a scrupulous confession. The question clearly illustrates the anxiety that is present, the concern for details, including the details of ritual and form that are proper to the priest/confessor, and the ever-present scenarios of what could possibly go wrong. Father Kaler patiently answered the question and provided the necessary direction.

QUESTION: My worst problem at the moment is confession.

1. Must the sacrament of reconciliation always be approached with prayers on the part of both priest and penitent? Many priests do not pray before the sacrament.
2. Sometimes the priest doesn't raise his hand to make the Sign of the Cross. Is my confession valid?
3. If I don't hear the words "I absolve you" loud and clear, I worry, are my sins really forgiven, even then?

4. If a priest does not want to forgive a person, is it his duty to tell the person?

5. Do I always have to tell when my last confession was? What if I have forgotten?

6. Sometimes I say the given penance over and over. Also, I have confessed the same sins over and over, just to make sure. Have I committed new sins by doing either of these? All the above are driving me crazy. Please help me.

ANSWER: My heart goes out to you. The sacramental rite of reconciliation was never meant to be the instrument of torture it has become for you. Rather, it's supposed to be a loving encounter with a forgiving Savior. I'll try to help you think of it that way by answering each of your questions as clearly as possible.

1. The prayers that are suggested as the introductory part of this rite are surely recommended, but they are not essential for validity.

2. The priest's absolution does not hinge on whether the confessor raises his hand while making the Sign of the Cross. Even if he doesn't, your sins would still be forgiven.

3. For validity, the words "I absolve you" do not have to be spoken in an audible voice. Whether you hear them or not is not essential.

4. Yes, if a priest refuses absolution he must tell the penitent what he is doing. Pastorally, I'm sure he would also make a great effort to explain why he considered it necessary. He would be pleading with the person to change so that absolution could be given. There would be no ambiguity about the conversation. A scrupulous person should not worry about this at all.

5. It is not an essential part of the sacrament that you tell when your last confession was. It's a good thing to do when you remember, but it would not affect the sacrament itself. If you

can't remember the actual time that has gone by, just give an approximation.

6. Say the given penance only once. If you have forgotten what it was, say the penance that you usually receive. If you are still not sure what to do, tell the Lord to count some of your everyday prayers as equivalent to your penance. In every case, the forgiveness you have already received would still hold. With regard to repeating sins over and over in other confessions, "just to make sure," this is not recommended. It was not a sin to do that, but repeating only feeds your scrupulosity. The sins were already forgiven; they do not have to be told again. It is all right to mention them in a general way, as already forgiven, but it is not necessary.

I recommend very strongly that you talk over with a priest your many fears concerning this sacrament. You might want to do this outside the confessional. He'll probably tell you not to go to confession very frequently at present. Whatever other advice he gives you, follow to the best of your ability. If you do, I'm sure you will experience the loving encounter with your forgiving Savior that I spoke about.

Father Kaler, C.Ss.R.

THE SEAL OF CONFESSION

One of the first things young children learn when they are preparing for their first reception of the sacrament of reconciliation is that the priest will not, under any circumstances, break the seal of confession. In other words, what is confessed in the confessional stays in the confessional. The priest will never identify the sin with the sinner, under any circumstance.

I can remember as a young boy being told heroic stories of priests who faced torture, imprisonment, and even death because they were unwilling to break the seal of confession. These stories stirred within me a great admiration for the priesthood and a confidence in the sacrament.

As inspiring as these stories were to a young boy, what probably helps guarantee the seal of confession more than anything else is the fact that priest confessors—like all other Catholics—are at different points in their lives also penitents, people who confess their sins to a priest. The confidentiality of the confessional is important to everyone, including the priest. That being said, there is nevertheless a concern among some of the scrupulous that the priest will break the seal of confession and repeat his or her confessed sins to another.

QUESTION: Would you please discuss the seal of confession? I have always heard that priests, or anyone who overhears a confession, are forbidden to mention it to others. If they would do so, they are guilty of breaking the seal of confession. I attend Mass where a community of priests lives in the same building. During a priest's homily, and for other reasons, I believe my confession was discussed with other priests.

ANSWER: Priests are forbidden to discuss a particular confession in any manner that identifies the sin with the sinner. In other words, I cannot say to someone that John Doe committed the sin of adultery. In the same way, I cannot talk about John Doe in a manner that someone might assume that there is any connection between adultery and John Doe. In addition, I cannot even speak to John Doe, outside of the confessional, about his confession, in a particular *or* general way, unless he introduces the subject first.

With the above in mind, however, there are some things that I am permitted to do. For example, I am not forbidden to talk about the sin of adultery and even, in a prudent way, illustrate the sin with examples, some of which might have some reference to the confessions that I have celebrated. Such a discussion does not identify the sin with the sinner, which is the key concept here. On a practical note, the majority of priests whom I know protect the seal of confession by simply making it a practice not to discuss, at any time, any subject that others might even remotely assume might be of a confessional matter. At the very most, they might discuss with other priests, in a very general way, particular examples of sins that they may have heard in confession in order to seek guidance and direction. When this happens, it is always done with the utmost respect and care.

My guess would be that the priest whom you suspect of discussing your confession with others did not do what you suspected. At the very most, he may have sought the advice and guidance of another priest, as I have previously mentioned. Could it be that you are very sensitive about the subject which you confessed? Could it be, because of your sensitivity about the subject, you might be inclined to jump to a conclusion that the priest was talking about you? Have you considered that you may not be the only person with such difficulty and that you may share some characteristics with others? Could this not be the reason why you were able to resonate with what the priest spoke about? My advice to you is to resist the urge to jump to the conclusion that the priest in question broke the seal of confession. It might be more beneficial to give him the benefit of the doubt. God bless!

Father Santa, C.Ss.R.

Chapter Four

What Is a Sin and What Is Not?

Determining what is a sin and what is not a sin is the source of great anxiety for the scrupulous. The difference between a mortal sin and a venial sin is often blurred. Strong feelings of displeasing God, as well as one's self-esteem and self-worth, all come into play. The direct result is an ever-present feeling of anxiety and dread, "the background noise" that we have previously referred to.

Possibly the best way to illustrate this feeling is to list the everyday concerns and doubts that plague the scrupulous mind. For those who do not suffer from scrupulosity a quick review of this listing might provoke a feeling of disbelief: "How can anyone be concerned about such little things?" But that is exactly the point. It is the "little things," the thousand frightening fantasies, the lingering doubt, and the thoughts that cannot be shaken that define scrupulosity.

When you read these questions try to imagine thinking *all day* about the question that is asked. Not just once in a while, but all day. Try to imagine what it might feel like to know that what you are spending your time and energy on is probably unimportant and probably a manifestation of scrupulosity. Try to imagine what it must be like to know what is going on but not be able to stop it.

THOUGHTS THAT CANNOT BE SHAKEN

QUESTION: Is it a mortal sin to laugh at someone?

ANSWER: No. It is a healthy thing for friends to laugh at one another and to be able to accept good-naturedly the kidding that goes on among friends, even when it is directed at one of our own foibles. But there can be something a little unkind about laughing at others if it is done in a cruel and cutting way. A sense of charity should help us distinguish between kind laughter and cruel laughter.

Father L. Miller, C.Ss.R.

QUESTION: Is it a sin never to smile?

ANSWER: I would not call it a sin, but it is decidedly unhealthy and not to be recommended under any circumstances.

Father L. Miller, C.Ss.R.

QUESTION: Is it a sin to take laundry off the line after the clothes are dry and put them away on Sunday? It rained on Saturday, so I wasn't able to do it then.

ANSWER: No sin here. This was clearly a case of necessity. A little common sense goes a long way in such a situation.

Father L. Miller, C.Ss.R.

QUESTION: Is it a sin to be a perfectionist?

ANSWER: Not unless you are a malicious perfectionist, deliberately going out of your way to annoy people. Perfectionism is often a temperamental trait. Some people can't rest easily unless everything around them is neat, tidy, and in perfect order. Others seem to thrive on chaos in their households. Neither side should harshly judge the other. Each side should beware of pushing their tendency to extremes that will make people around them uncomfortable.

Father L. Miller, C.Ss.R.

QUESTION: Is it a sin to lose something?

ANSWER: If it were, very few of us would have much chance of getting to heaven. Losing things seems to be a common human trait, and I am sure God understands this very well and makes big allowances for our foolishness.

Father L. Miller, C.Ss.R.

QUESTION: Would it be considered a sin to wipe up cigarette ashes on the rug and chair on Sunday?

ANSWER: No, but don't do it while the guest is still standing there holding his or her cigarette, unless it is someone you are sure won't be embarrassed.

Father L. Miller, C.Ss.R.

QUESTION: Is it a sin not to make a will? I own a house with another person who isn't in favor of wills. What should I do?

ANSWER: To make a will is certainly an act of charity, because you will save a lot of trouble for your family. If you die without a will and leave an estate, the state takes over and divides it up, maybe in a different way than you would have wanted. I don't say it is a sin not to make a will, but it is a wise thing to do. In the case of our questioner, of course, there seems to be a human problem involved. You can't force people. You can only try to persuade them.

Father L. Miller, C.Ss.R.

QUESTION: It is embarrassing to me to make the Sign of the Cross before and after meals in restaurants, and so forth. So I have denied my faith in such public places, and I am worried that this might be a serious sin.

ANSWER: No, it is not. To make the Sign of the Cross is good, but not to make it is no sin.

Father L. Miller, C.Ss.R.

QUESTION: At this time of year people often are dressed in scanty bathing suits, shorts, and so forth. Is it a mortal sin to look at them?

ANSWER: One can scarcely avoid looking at them, and there is no sin involved in this. But don't keep looking at them in such a way that it becomes a kind of fixation. It is best not to get tense and uptight about this matter. Saint Alphonsus used to say, "Don't meet a temptation of this kind head-on, but run around it by occupying your mind with something else."

Father L. Miller, C.Ss.R.

QUESTION: I am elderly and live alone, except for my dog. I love my dog but sometimes he just won't obey me and I get furious at him. Is this a serious sin?

ANSWER: No sin whatsoever. It is what God expects us to do, as human beings, when we feel frustrated and helpless. The same thing is true if we accidentally drop and break a dish or painfully stub a toe. We are bodily beings. We are emotional beings. God deliberately made us so. God is not in the least offended by anger or frustration we sometimes feel and express. No sin whatsoever.

Father Farnik, C.Ss.R.

QUESTION: Please write something about the sin of overeating. I never know for sure when this is a serious sin and when it isn't. This bothers me.

ANSWER: Gluttony is the disordered or unreasonable desire for food and drink. The great Saint Thomas Aquinas tells us that gluttony is a serious sin only when a person places this disordered desire on a pedestal in his or her life, "being ready to disobey God's commandments in order to obtain the pleasures of the palate." He adds that gluttony is a venial sin "when a person has too great a desire for the pleasures of the palate, yet would not for their sake do anything contrary to God's law." It is clear, I believe, that most sins of gluttony would be venial sins.

Often, however, overeating is not a sin at all, but a compulsion. Eating disorders often stem from deep emotional problems over which a person has little, if any, rational control. The challenge here is to try to deal with the emotional roots of the problem rather than merely with the symptoms. Fortunately, there are many self-help groups, such as Overeaters Anonymous, which provide a great deal of practical help in dealing with these problems.

Father Lowery, C.Ss.R.

QUESTION: I have a brother-in-law who frequently tells off-color stories and double-meaning jokes. I don't mean to laugh, but sometimes I can't help myself. The other day he told a joke and I let out a guffaw. Did I commit a sin when I did that?

ANSWER: No, you didn't commit a sin. While it's not good for us to encourage this kind of talk by laughing, sometimes there is not much we can do when suddenly something strikes our funny bone. Humor is built on incongruity, and an off-color joke can be genuinely funny. Don't repeat the joke (unless you can "clean it up"), and don't worry about the fact that you laughed.

Father Kaler, C.Ss.R.

QUESTION: Is it a sin not to have trust in the mercy of God?

ANSWER: Despair is objectively a sin. But usually the scrupulous person is not capable of handling this situation properly and hence is not guilty of despair. He or she is not guilty of any serious sin. Part of the nature of scrupulosity is not to have enough trust and confidence in God.

Father Kaler, C.Ss.R.

QUESTION: I hope you do not think this question is frivolous. Is it sinful to step on insects for no other reason than that you don't want them (spiders, for instance) making webs in your garage or home? I started thinking about this when I realized that everything in nature is God's creation.

ANSWER: No, it would not be sinful to step on insects, to brush away webs, or to swat mosquitoes or flies. We should respect all of nature, be ecologically conscious, and be protective of our environment. But there is a hierarchy in nature, and we human beings, whether we deserve it or not, are at the top.

Father Kaler, C.Ss.R.

QUESTION: Is it a sin to exaggerate? Sometimes I stretch the truth a bit when telling stories of the past. This seems to happen especially when others are telling their stories. I certainly don't mean to hurt anyone by these exaggerations, but maybe simply add a little color or humor to the tale.

ANSWER: I don't see any sin here. It sounds like this storytelling getting-together has become a type of recreation for all concerned. I bet the participants are all aware that some of the stories will "grow in the telling," as the saying goes. It's sort of a "Can you top this?" game. As long as it is looked at in that way, I don't think there is a breach of truth or charity involved.

Father Kaler, C.Ss.R.

QUESTION: Is it a sin for me to lend a tool to someone on a Sunday when I know it is to be used to perform service work on Sunday?

ANSWER: No, it is not a sin. You can perform an act of charity by lending a tool. It is not your responsibility to decide whether the other person is justified in working on Sunday. You can leave that up to his or her conscience and you need not worry about it.

Father Lowery, C.Ss.R.

WHAT IS SIN?

A priest friend of mine has a sermon about sin that I have heard him preach on a number of occasions. He begins the sermon by asking people to recite answers to questions posed by the *Baltimore Catechism*. For any Catholic over the age of fifty-five, there seems to be a lingering ability to answer questions from the catechism, even after years of not thinking about the questions or the answers. This is probably a tribute to the nuns who taught us our catechism!

My priest/friend begins by asking the first question from the catechism, "Who made you?" Without usually a moment's hesitation the congregation will respond in unison, "God made me." He then asks the second question, "Why did God make you?" And again they reply, "To know him and love him and serve him, in this world and in the next." By this time the congregation is usually in the spirit of the day, and so he poses the next question, not found in the catechism, and it catches them off guard. "What are the two types of fun that God made?" The congregation stares at him and you can see them straining to remember. After a few moments he replies, with a straight face, "mortal sin and venial sin." Usually the congregation explodes in laughter.

Most people can laugh about sin. It is not that we don't take sin seriously or, as some commentators would have us believe, that we have lost a sense of sin in our lives. Rather, as in anything else, a sense of humor about the subject, especially a subject that is all too familiar to most of us, is probably a healthy sign.

For many scrupulous people sin is no laughing matter. It is a very serious matter, and more often than not, is *always* a serious matter. The struggle for the scrupulous person is the struggle to come to an understanding and acceptance of human weakness and imperfection. The tendency is to assume that any manifestation of weakness is seriously displeasing to God.

QUESTION: To me, every sin I commit seems serious. How does one make a decision as to whether a sin is serious enough to be mortal?

ANSWER: A good common-sense rule for scrupulous people to follow: Unless you are so absolutely sure that you have committed a mortal sin, that you would without hesitation swear to it on a stack of Bibles, you should presume that you have not committed a mortal sin. If you had done so, you would know it without any doubt whatsoever.

Father L. Miller, C.Ss.R.

QUESTION: I have trouble sometimes in determining if such-and-such is sinful or not. If a certain act stands out in all innocence and ends up on a doubtful note, how do I go about determining whether or not the act was sinful?

ANSWER: What is known as a reflex principle can be applied here. If anyone who is conscientiously trying to lead a good life were to commit a mortal sin, it would be clearly recognized. As the saying goes, it would stick out like a sore thumb. Therefore, if there is any doubt in your mind as to whether some act was seriously wrong, you can presume that it was not seriously wrong.

Father L. Miller, C.Ss.R.

QUESTION: I do not know for sure if these sins are venial or mortal. Now and then I use God's name in vain at work, and many times I hear other workers using blasphemous language. What is the Church's teaching about using the name of Jesus and of God in this way?

ANSWER: I think that every human being has at times used unbecoming language. The classic cases are when one accidentally hits one's thumb with a hammer, or breaks a shoestring when one is in a hurry, or bangs one's head against a pipe or other protruding object. Out pours a string of words that express rage in no uncertain terms.

And God's name is often a part of those words. The words come out automatically. After they are spoken, the person may be shocked at what he or she has uttered. In such a case, no sin was committed, not even venial. There was no deliberation and forethought. There was no free and deliberate choice to do wrong rather than right.

At other times, the person may realize that this language does not show God much respect, but he or she is angry and wants to say these words anyway to vent and express the anger inside. By deliberately doing so, the person can commit a *venial* sin of disrespect for God according to how much deliberateness was present beforehand.

Finally, a serious sin is never committed in these circumstances. There is lacking the clear and deliberate intention of insulting God, and there is present the mitigating factor of strong emotion. But, as Christians who profess our faith in a loving Father and a Savior who gave his very life on the cross for us, we should keep trying to make ourselves aware of how unbecoming such language is on our lips.

Father Farnik, C.Ss.R.

QUESTION: I have no doubt that things like murder, torture, bank robbery, prostitution, and drug peddling are seriously wrong. But what about the countless mortal sins that are less serious: hatred for others, gossiping and thereby in some way hurting reputations, anger, using foul language, resentful thoughts toward God for what he allowed to happen to me, immodest looks and desires and thoughts— even about married men and about priests, and so forth?

ANSWER: Notice that you have no doubt that certain ways of acting are seriously wrong. Your inner wisdom tells you that. But that same inner wisdom gives you doubts about the seriousness of many, many other thoughts, words, and deeds, what you call "the countless mortal sins that are less serious." Your inner wisdom can't exactly weigh how serious are those other "countless" wrongdoings. The reason you find it hard to weigh the gravity of those many wrongdoings is simple. They are all what you should be calling venial sins or venial wrongs. Venial sin refers to all the things that are less serious than those really big sins, which your inner wisdom tells you are clearly and certainly serious. Venial sins are the many, many wrongdoings that are unclear and vague in their importance and weight and evilness. They do not have to be confessed.

Father Farnik, C.Ss.R.

QUESTION: For years scruples and confession have troubled me. I was once told that there are just four serious sins. Is this true, and if so, what would they be?

ANSWER: I don't believe that such a mathematical approach to sin is helpful. No one, to the best of my knowledge, can give such a list of serious sins. Serious sin depends on (a) the nature of the act [grave matter], (b) sufficient reflection [true knowledge], and (c) full consent of the will [human freedom]. Scrupulous people tend to multiply serious sins without good reason. They tend to see serious sin in almost everything. In moral matters, the scrupulous person does not have a balanced judgment. That is why the saints suggested that scrupulous people abide by the judgment of their confessors. This is still the best advice for the scrupulous.

Father Lowery, C.Ss.R.

QUESTION: I have great trouble understanding what constitutes serious or grave matter. For instance, after giving an adverse opinion or complaining about someone, I can't help thinking my words have "seriously" affected that person's career or friendship or whatever. It has been suggested to me that unless I carried on some lengthy vendetta or had some special power over those to whom I was speaking that I was crediting myself with too much importance. What do you think? How can one judge serious or grievous harm?

ANSWER: I think the suggestion already made to you is very sound. Just because you express "an adverse opinion" or complain about someone does not imply any serious harm to that person's good name or reputation. We have to give some credit to our listeners! They are ordinarily capable of making up their own minds, despite our astute observations. The eighth commandment forbids us to tell lies about others or to reveal secret truths that would truly be harmful to them in their family life, their work, and their public reputation. The fact that you don't like the way a person eats, dresses, sings, types, or whatever—and express your opinion to that effect—does not constitute a sin against the eighth commandment. Common sense and your own experience of life should provide a good handle on what is "serious" in this area of Christian morality.

Father Lowery, C.Ss.R.

QUESTION: With regard to sin, do moralists ever take into consideration the state of mind of a person? I mean, does everything have to be just black and white, or would the Church make allowances in certain situations?

ANSWER: The general answer is yes. To understand why, let's go back to the basics—the three elements involved in mortal sin: (1) serious matter, (2) sufficient reflection, and (3) full consent of the will. Moralists have always taught that certain conditions could substantially alter any of these.

Regarding the first element, some matters are serious by their very nature, for example, the honor due to God, the integrity of a person's life and limb, his or her eternal salvation, and similar matters. But other matters aren't that weighty, such as failure to do a small favor for someone, a lapse in etiquette, a feeling of irritation, and so forth. Often scrupulous people try to make these minor matters into grave offenses. Their troubled consciences simply cannot be trusted to make valid judgments in this area. That's why these good people must turn elsewhere for guidance.

Regarding the second element, a person can be completely or partially ignorant about what he or she is doing. The ignorance (in whatever degree) can be about the morality of the action, its consequences, and so on. Another factor is how much knowledge should the person have had, considering his or her age, upbringing, and position in life? Also, some people really are victims of events that have happened to them (such as abuse), of their present surroundings, and so on. So much confusion in their minds could mean that their guilt is greatly diminished. The extreme case would be insane people. They are not sinning, mortally or venially, even when they do terrible things like commit mass murders.

Regarding the final element, think of what happens when a very strong emotion overwhelms a person. A person whose life is being threatened certainly is not as responsible for an action as someone who is not under duress. In fact, physical, mental, or emotional stress can sometimes completely deprive a person of his or her freedom. Other emotions can also come into play. For example, a cold-blooded murderer has sinned more grievously than has someone who killed in a fit of passion. In lesser degree, even such a thing as habit can reduce a person's responsibility. The same could be said for actions done by a person who has an obsessive-compulsive personality. In a word, anything that diminishes a person's freedom also diminishes that person's guilt for what was done.

In real life, number 1, number 2, and number 3 are often mixed together.

Father Kaler, C.Ss.R.

QUESTION: If you feel many sins are mortal, although they are not, are they considered mortal sins for you—since you think they are?

ANSWER: No, because you are scrupulous and cannot really judge.

Father Kaler, C.Ss.R.

QUESTION: Recently I heard a sermon in which the priest said he suspected that there were many more sins of omission (failure to do what one should have done) than sins of commission (actually doing something wrong). That's all I needed! Now I'm worried that I may have failed to carry out many serious obligations that I hadn't even thought about. Can you help me, please?

ANSWER: You've already answered your own question. Remember what has to be present for a mortal sin: (1) serious matter, (2) sufficient reflection, and (3) full consent of the will. But you said you were worried about obligations that you hadn't even thought about. Therefore you were not leading a double life, unwittingly committing all sorts of sins along the way.

Father Kaler, C.Ss.R.

QUESTION: In order to have committed a mortal sin, one of the criteria is "sufficient reflection." What does this actually mean in terms of time? One minute, or what?

ANSWER: Regarding "sufficient reflection," we can't come up with a specific amount of time, such as one second, one minute, or one hour. Rather, the questions that should be asked are more along these lines:

- How aware are you of the gravity of what you are about to do?
- Do you realize how terribly this offends God?
- Do you understand what this will do to the tender relationships you are meant to have with your loving Lord and with your neighbor?
- Is what you are tempted to do worth the price?
- What about the consequences of your action?

In any given case, a number of things can inhibit this type of "sufficient reflection" and thereby lessen a person's guilt. Sometimes there's certain ignorance. How much knowledge should a person have, considering age, upbringing, and position in life? Some people are victims of traumatic events in their life, such as childhood or spousal abuse. Others are so immersed in their present surroundings that they are confused and unable to make a sound moral judgment. An extreme example would be an insane person. He or she would not be guilty of any sin, even if a terrible act such as a murder had been committed. Remember also that for a mortal sin—besides "sufficient reflection"—there must also be "serious matter" (scrupulous people are poor judges of this) and "full consent of the will" (physical, mental, and emotional stresses can sometimes deprive a person of this).

Father Kaler, C.Ss.R.

QUESTION: Is every sin against purity a *mortal* sin?

ANSWER: Not necessarily. As you know, for a sin to be mortal there must be three conditions present: (1) serious matter, (2) sufficient reflection, and (3) full consent of the will. This holds for all sins, sins against charity, sins against the faith, sins of dishonesty, and so on, as well as sins of impurity.

Father Kaler, C.Ss.R.

QUESTION: I was taught that for mortal sin there must be serious matter. But doesn't wrongly thinking a thought or an act is serious matter fulfill that condition for mortal sin?

ANSWER: No. Serious matter does not change. Either it is serious matter or it is not. Something cannot be serious matter for you and not be serious matter for another person. Perception plays an important role in judgment and decision making, but it cannot change matter. For example, I may think a table is a chair and even go so far as to personally use it as a chair. However, no matter what I do, think, or perceive, the table is a table and not a chair.

The "matter" of serious sin is always serious; it is never not serious. You cannot be "tricked" into committing sin, and you cannot do something that is not serious and be held liable for it when you are in error. God bless you!

Father Santa, C.Ss.R.

QUESTION: Father, you are wrong. It is not merely the substance (serious matter) but also the conviction of the normal individual involved that constitutes mortal sin. We have been correctly taught that "a mortal sin, in the formal sense, is an action, which in itself is seriously wrong or is judged by the doer to be so, and which, nonetheless, is performed knowingly and deliberately." Even my mentally sick mind can comprehend "and accept" such a simple explanation.

ANSWER: Thank you for your research and your willingness to bring something to my attention, but I stand by what I have written. The key words in your answer that support my statement are "formal sense," "knowingly," and "deliberately." When a scrupulous person makes a decision, within the scrupulous condition, they are the furthest possible distance away from the experience of a formal sense of sin, and are simply not choosing to perform the act either knowingly or deliberately. In such a state they are indeed capable of turning something into a mortal sin, at least within the experience of the scrupulous mind, that is neither mortal nor even serious for that matter. That is why we understand scrupulosity as an illness; it affects our ability to knowingly and deliberately choose. God bless you.

Father Santa, C.Ss.R.

ACCIDENTAL SINS

In order to commit a sin a person must be fully aware that they are choosing to do something that is displeasing to God. It is not possible to commit a sin accidentally. The idea that sin may be accidentally committed is revealing: It suggests an image of God that is at best unfortunate and not helpful.

I don't believe the fear of committing an accidental sin is necessarily a common experience of scrupulosity. I believe that the operative image of God that is necessary in order to arrive at such a conclusion probably has more to do with personal experience than with scrupulosity. If a person experienced a type of parenting, complicated by the presence of alcoholism for example, it would not be difficult to imagine that a learned behavior might include "that I am responsible for everything, because my parent is not." To make such a conclusion, learned through the experience of living in an alcoholic home, and then to theologize the experience, is understandable.

Regardless of where it might come from, a percentage of scrupulous people are concerned with accidental sin.

QUESTION: When I'm on the fence about confession I fall back on the principle, "I cannot have committed a mortal sin unless I know with absolute certainly that I did so." Am I doing the right thing?

ANSWER: Bravo! You are doing the right thing. I wish more scrupulous persons would follow this principle!

Father Lowery, C.Ss.R.

QUESTION: Can one be guilty of scandal or serious harm to others without realizing it?

ANSWER: The answer to this question should be self-evident to anyone who looks at it closely. No one can ever be counted as guilty of a sin if he does not know at the time that he is committing a sin.

Father L. Miller, C.Ss.R.

QUESTION: How easy is it to slip into mortal sin? Does it happen without a person clearly knowing it?

ANSWER: How easy is it for a husband or a wife to lose all love for his or her spouse in marriage? Does it happen without their knowing about it? Of course not! Love can only be lost by disregarding it and letting it waste away. This is true about love for God, as well as love for other human beings. Any person who has deliberately chosen to reject God is completely clear about it: by robbing a bank, planning a murder, and engaging in other such serious matters. But love is not wiped out by the little faults of everyday life.

This, however, should not leave us feeling smug with ourselves.

God is so good that he deserves all our love. We need to keep trying to love him more deeply. But we need not fear that we are separated from him. A person who has separated himself or herself from God is clear about it. Serious sins stand out in a person's life like a crushed car in the middle of an intersection.

Father Farnik, C.Ss.R.

QUESTION: If you suddenly realize after reading something that you committed a mortal sin, but did not give it a thought at the time you were reading it, must you confess this?

ANSWER: No, you cannot commit a mortal sin without knowing it at the time.

Father Kaler, C.Ss.R.

QUESTION: Sometimes I do something and it seems appropriate at the time. Then later I think maybe it was a sin, even though I didn't think it was a sin while doing it. What should I do now?

ANSWER: This type of thinking, of reexamining past actions, is part of the affliction of scrupulosity. It has no validity. You don't have to do anything. You didn't commit any sins.

Father Kaler, C.Ss.R.

QUESTION: When a sinful thing happens, but it is not deliberate or premeditated, is this considered sinful?

ANSWER: The answer to this one is easy. You cannot commit a serious sin unless it is deliberate and done with sufficient reflection.

Father Kaler, C.Ss.R.

QUESTION: What if you just recently learned certain actions were sinful and you had performed these actions frequently in the past? Were those sins or not?

ANSWER: No, they were not sins. Sin is a fundamental choice against

God, a free and willing turning away from his love and his law. One of the conditions for mortal sin is sufficient reflection or advertence or awareness of the seriousness of the choice one is making. This condition was lacking in your case.

Father Kaler, C.Ss.R.

SIN AND DOUBT

A variation on the theme of accidental sin is the relationship between what is potentially sinful and what may well be just a doubt. The best advice I'd offer in such a situation is this: If you are doubtful about something, don't risk it; you may be uncomfortable about your decision if the doubt is confirmed. A simple example would be the decision on whether or not to take an umbrella with you to the baseball game. You may well doubt the weather report because it looks so nice outside, but you are risking that the meterologist could be correct in the forecast. If you don't really mind getting wet, then it is worth the risk. If, on the other hand, you desire to avoid getting wet, no matter what the circumstances, you may find it to be a better choice to take your umbrella.

Unfortunately, we are not here considering the risk of rain but rather the risk of sin, and that does seem to complicate the situation. The basic rules still apply, but we may well feel differently about the potential results.

QUESTION: I was told once that if you act in a state of doubt, then you commit sin. In my life, it seems to me that almost everything is a doubt, and, therefore, almost everything is sinful.

ANSWER: Life for all of us is full of doubts and uncertainties. In this you share the human condition with all other men and women. For whom should you vote? To which charities should you contribute? How much should you give? The list goes on and on. You cannot expect to live real life with clear-cut certainties in the many daily decisions that you have to make. Ambiguities, trade-offs, and compromises are certainly a necessary part of living and working together with others whose values and priorities are not exactly identical with your own. So what do you do? You do the best you can. You choose the least evil option. You choose what you think will do the most overall good when everything has been balanced out and taken into consideration. Even in your private decision making, which does not involve other people, you often have to choose less than perfect options.

But don't confuse good with perfect. A less-than-perfect decision can still be the only good decision in certain circumstances. Keep in mind the expression, "The perfect is the enemy of the good." If you do only that which will be perfect, you will fail to act when good actions are needed, when less than perfect decisions are called for. God does not want you to cringe and agonize over your decisions. God alone is omniscient. He alone knows everything. He knows that you are imperfect. He accepts you as he made you. God just wants you to do the best you can in your circumstances and then leave it in his hands. You cannot do any better than that.

Father Lowery, C.Ss.R.

QUESTION: Does not the Catholic Church teach that it is a sin to act in doubt?

ANSWER: At first glance it would seem that the answer is yes. But a better response is: "That depends." Normally, more information is needed. What kind of doubt are we talking about? Is it about whether a certain law exists? (This is called a *de jure* doubt.) What kind of law is it, divine or human? And what are the consequences if it is broken? Also, how far does this particular law extend? Let's say that the law is clear and the action surely comes under it, are we then in a doubt-free situation? Perhaps not. It's possible to have a doubt about whether the action was actually performed. (This is called a *de facto* doubt.) People can have a genuine doubt about whether they were fully conscious and completely free at the time. This is especially true with regard to whether certain thoughts were conscious. As you can see, all this is rather complicated. A brief answer cannot do it justice. Practically, we have to come back to what the *SA* newsletter has stated frequently: When in doubt, a scrupulous person should follow the advice of his or her confessor. There can be no safer route.

Father Kaler, C.Ss.R.

SINS OF YOUTH

I think it would be rare for a person to look back on his or her life, especially when very young, and not find something that would be a source of embarrassment.

For scrupulous people, remembering something from their past that they consider embarrassing or something they wish they had not done, often turns into more than just an unpleasant memory. Often, because of the feelings that are associated with the memory, especially the feelings of embarrassment, anxiety, or guilt, the assumption is made that sin must have been present. Acting on that assumption of sin, the person then considers it necessary to "root it out," thus making the self more pleasing to God.

How many of us can remember a general event or circumstance, but unfortunately find ourselves short on the details?

QUESTION: Twenty years ago, when I was a youngster, I stole money from my parents. I don't know if I ever confessed these thefts. I do know I used to sometimes avoid confessing things that seemed embarrassing. Should I confess them now? I don't know if I considered it serious or venial at the time I was doing this. Am I obliged to restitution—and how much restitution, since I don't know the amount I took?

ANSWER: Catholics must confess and own up to what they know for sure they did, what they know for sure was of a serious nature, and what they know for sure they never confessed already. You are sure only of the fact that you did steal, but you are not sure how much, whether it was serious, or whether you ever confessed it before. These are classic scruples. You should firmly put them behind you. Focus your energies in the present. What ways can you better show your parents the love and gratitude and appreciation you have for them? Why not do some little thing for them today?

Father Lowery, C.Ss.R.

QUESTION: When I was in third grade, an item on a book bill that I received was marked as "paid in full," but it was not. I cheated. I did not intend to steal, and I do not recall confessing this sin, so down through the years I have committed sacrilegious confessions and Communions. God help me! Realizing this, I have on numerous occasions donated to charities with the intention of paying the book bill. I know I did wrong, but now what?

ANSWER: Please be at peace. You are not guilty of sacrilegious confessions and Communions; you are in fact not even guilty of sin. You have no way of knowing why your book bill was marked as paid in full—it might have been an error, or it might not have been. Regardless, it is not a serious matter, it was not done willfully, and you did not do it in order to mortally offend God. Therefore, by no stretch of the imagination can you be guilty of serious sin. Since you are not guilty of serious sin, there is no way that you can be guilty of the presumed results of serious sin.

Father Santa, C.Ss.R.

QUESTION: Sins of my past—especially of adolescence and young adulthood—often come back to my mind. I asked my confessor if I could make a general confession again so as to find peace of mind. He said no. He said that a general confession would not bring me peace of mind but only keep me on the treadmill of scrupulosity.

What do you think?

ANSWER: I think your confessor is a very wise man. From experience he knows that another general confession will do no good at all. After a brief interlude of peace, the same old doubts and fears will come back. The challenge for the scrupulous person is to place absolute trust in the forgiveness of Jesus as signed forth in the sacrament of penance. Anything short of that will not bring peace.

Father Lowery, C.Ss.R.

Chapter Five

The Priest as Confessor: What Can Be Hoped For?

The priest/confessor is the listening ear, the gentle guide, the informed helper. Or at least that is the constant hope of those who come to him for advice and help. In the tradition of the Church, it is the priest/confessor who is central to any hope for recovery of the scrupulous, or at the very least, the peaceful maintenance of the scrupulous condition.

The priest enjoys a privileged relationship with the scrupulous, although I am not sure that all priests would consider such relationships in this light. The relationship is privileged because the scrupulous person is open to the possibility of trusting the confessor and following his advice—most other counselors have to earn this trust. However, the priest, because he is perceived as a true mediator between God and humankind, has the capacity at least to lessen one's anxiety and turmoil, if not actually effecting some positive change (See appendix 2 for "A Letter From a Priest").

If the priest is privileged, the priest is also challenged: The scrupulous person presumes that the priest knows what he is talking about, is prepared to deal patiently with the nuances of the questions and details, and will be, above all, patient and understanding at all times. The relationship, therefore, has many of the ingredients necessary for a disaster, which oftentimes is the case. The SA mailbox is filled with letters from the scrupulous who have been disappointed by a priest, and when I read the letters, I recognize the effort that is being committed to the relationship, and the disappointment that results because of a single slip-up or failure.

The main skill the priest/confessor needs in order to effectively minister to the scrupulous person is patience. Patience, of course, is a gift that is treasured and a requirement for the successful growth of any type of relationship. All relationships grow at different paces, have good moments and bad moments, and, when examined, will be recognized as maturing and life giving, even when some moments in the relationship may be less than perfect.

The priest who every day slides back the screen of the confessional or who welcomes the familiar penitent into the reconciliation room and hears the same litany of presumed sin, filled with questioning and detail, may well find it difficult to feel that any progress or growth is taking place. It would be a very unusual person who would not feel some sense of frustration, at the very least, when confronted with the same experience, perhaps questioning, "Am I accomplishing anything useful here?"

Once the priest/confessor is able to identify his own weakness and sinfulness, his own fears and anxieties, there is the possibility for effective ministry to the scrupulous. As priest/confessor, when the screen slides open and the familiar litany begins yet again, it is most helpful to recognize that moment as a potential moment of grace, and not as just one more moment that needs to be endured.

OBEDIENCE TO THE CONFESSOR

The initial step in the slow healing process is for the scrupulous penitent to come to an acceptance of the need to obey the directives of the confessor in all matters. All the great saints in the Church are in absolute agreement on this crucial point. There is no possibility for healing if the scrupulous person cannot learn to trust his or her confessor implicitly. Any confessor who wishes to enter into a relationship with a scrupulous person must also understand this essential point. The key to begin building the basis for becoming free from scrupulosity, or at the very least maintaining some semblance of peace, is the formation of this trust relationship.

QUESTION: In my recent confession, Father said, "I command you to do two things: (1) Do not bring up your past and (2) remember the goodness and mercy of God." I realize I should do what my confessor tells me, but does this bind under pain of mortal sin if I bring up my past? Don't I have to be sorry for past sins if I don't have any present ones to confess?

ANSWER: Your confessor gave you excellent advice. Bringing up the past would not be a mortal sin, but I certainly urge you to obey his instructions, for your own peace of mind. If you refer to the past, do so in the most general terms, such as "I am sorry for all sins against charity," and don't go into any detail beyond that.

Father L. Miller, C.Ss.R.

QUESTION: My present confessor has told me not to confess sins of my past life but to confess only those since my last confession. Yet, I worry about some of my past sins and feel that I should confess them again. How can I find peace?

ANSWER: You can find peace by humbly obeying your confessor. You will certainly not find peace by constantly rooting around in your past life and constantly bringing up past sins. The scrupulous person must learn to trust: Trust God's mercy and trust the confessor's direction. Trust leads to peace.

Father Lowery, C.Ss.R.

QUESTION: Years ago, when I made a confession of sins against purity, the confessor had me promise not to bring them up again. I have done so several times. Recently I asked my confessor if he could help me. He allowed me to confess them but said that I was never to bring up the past again. I failed to tell this confessor that I had previously promised not to confess them again. My question is, should I tell in my next confession that I broke my promise not to confess these sins again?

ANSWER: No. Once and for all, forget about these past sins. It is unfortunate that you, like many scrupulous persons, did not obey your first confessor. You could confess these same sins a thousand times, but you would not find peace. Your compulsion to confess them again and again is simply that: a compulsion. Act against this compulsion. In the future give absolute obedience to your confessor. If you do, you have a chance of finding peace. If you do not, you can be sure that your torment will go on and on.

Father Lowery, C.Ss.R.

QUESTION: Saint Alphonsus states, "The confessor may command the scrupulous to conquer their anxiety and disregard it by freely doing whatever it tells them not to do." But aren't all persons supposed to follow their consciences all the time? How can that be reconciled with the saint's advice?

ANSWER: Can someone make an apple pie without using apples? The very meaning of scrupulosity is that the person so afflicted simply cannot trust that part of his intellect which serves as his conscience. The aphorism about following your conscience applies to one that is in reasonably good working order. But in the case of the scrupulous person, that's not true. Something has definitely gone awry. What do you do with a compass that can no longer find true north? You have to put it aside (at least temporarily) and find some other way to get your bearings. Otherwise, you will never be able to move. Scrupulous people tend to see sin everywhere. They cannot make balanced judgments in moral matters, try as they may. They are hounded by a thousand doubts, and sometimes their compulsive nature drives them to bizarre actions. How can they trust a conscience that treats them this way? That is why Saint Alphonsus and other spiritual writers have always asked scrupulous people to seek help from their confessor. He can point them in the right direction so that they can get on with their life. This has proven to be wise advice. And for many, it has been the way out of the confusion and misery of scrupulosity into a place of peace and happiness.

Father Kaler, C.Ss.R.

QUESTION: My confessor tells me that I should receive Communion no matter how I feel. I am never sure that I am worthy to receive. What do you think about this advice?

ANSWER: You are right in going to Communion and not worrying about it. Your confessor gives you the right advice, and I think your effort should be in trying to follow him. Tell yourself that your problem is an emotional one and not a moral one. The confessor has handled the moral problem; you must handle the emotional one. So you are perfectly right in not giving in to yourself, but acting against your fears. In acting against them you will overcome them.

Father Kaler, C.Ss.R.

QUESTION: You frequently mention the need for complete obedience to one's confessor. Now this is my problem. Although my confessor has told me very firmly not to think about sins of the past, I can't seem to help myself. They keep coming back. Maybe something I hear in a sermon or read in a book upsets me and I get worried. What I want to know is, am I committing serious sins of disobedience when this happens? Do I have to confess them? Please help me.

ANSWER: I think you misunderstood what your confessor was telling you about past sins. He really wasn't saying, "Never think about sins of the past!" That would be impossible. All of us have memories, both good and bad, and unless we are victims of amnesia, these memories will come to mind at times. Many things can trigger them.

Perhaps we hear certain words or find ourselves in certain situations or experience certain feelings, and suddenly a vivid memory is there. It is not a sin to have that memory pop into your mind. What Father was talking about was the concern and worry that are associated with that memory. He doesn't want you to be asking yourself questions like, "Did I tell this sin in confession in the right way? Did the priest back then understand me? Was I clear enough? Did I paint the picture black enough? Was I truly sorry for the sin?" All these doubts and worries should be put aside. Try to be obedient about that. You may not succeed completely, but do your best. It is never easy, but it is the way to peace and happiness.

Father Kaler, C.Ss.R.

QUESTION: One bit of advice frequently given in the *SA* newsletter is that a scrupulous person should always obey his confessor. But suppose the confessor makes a mistake or gives the wrong advice, what then? Will the Lord take that into account on the Day of Judgment?

ANSWER: I'm glad you've stated your concern about confessors openly because I suspect there are people who have this worry in the back of their minds but don't quite know how to express it. Let me begin my answer by repeating the old advice: If you are scrupulous, your own conscience is temporarily out of gear. It isn't working right, so you need another guide to help you in your moral decisions. Try to find a wise spiritual advisor or confessor and submit yourself to his authority. This is a safe, tried-and-true way back to peace of soul. But how about your question? Father Hugh O'Connell, a moral theologian of note, answered in this way:

The only responsibility before God a scrupulous person has is that of obedience to his confessor. No act performed under this obedience is a sin. Even though the confessor makes a mistake, though this is hardly likely, the scrupulous person would commit no sin in obeying. Hence if the confessor tells the penitent not to repeat past confessions, he should obey, even though he fears these confessions have not been complete. If told to go to Communion, he should obey, even though he is afraid that he is in the state of sin. If advised not to spend more than five minutes in the examination of conscience, he should not spend an instant more. And so, with regard to all similar cases, there is but one rule: Obey, no matter what doubts, fears, or circumstances may be present.

Father Kaler, C.Ss.R.

QUESTION: Should one continue to follow the advice on scruples from a confessor, after one has lost him to death or transfer—for example, such advice as "don't look back, or confess from the past"—or should we open up all of these old problems with a new confessor? Logic tells me the suggestions of my former confessor on this subject should be followed through life, but the "problem" side of me keeps doubting.

ANSWER: It's perfectly all right to follow all the advice, suggestions, ideas, and permissions of your former confessor. Should you happen upon another confessor you would like to talk to, I would suggest you take a few minutes, if possible, to give a general idea of your relationship with the former confessor. It's not necessary to go into detail about the past or to renew any permission.

Father Kaler, C.Ss.R.

QUESTION: I feel guilty that I stuck with my previous confessor even though he made some statements that were contrary to Church teaching. Also, he may not have done a good enough job advising me about some things I was doing. Please comment.

ANSWER: Guilt is the result of many things. In this particular instance, you experienced some guilt because you chose to be loyal to your confessor, a confessor you believe may have been "disloyal" to the teachings of the Church. Your guilt is the result of the conflict that you feel. My comment is simple. If you feel that you are getting bad advice, why stick with it? Choose a confessor in whom you have confidence. A note of warning, however: Make sure that you don't use these feelings of guilt, and my advice, as a reason to switch from one confessor to another. This will do you no good in the long run. The situation that you described is not an everyday occurrence and should be understood as an exception, not the rule. God bless!

Father Santa, C.Ss.R.

QUESTION: Is it ever required to get a second opinion (moral judgment)? If so, and the opinions differ, which one should a person follow? For example, my former pastor gave me an unexpected "liberal" answer to a question about marriage. Must I ask the new pastor the same question?

ANSWER: What you are actually asking me is, "Is it necessary to seek a third opinion?" You made the first moral judgment, the second judgment was made by the person you asked, and yet another judgment would be made by a third person. Is it necessary to ask all of these opinions? The answer is a resounding *no.* This is the single most important reason why it is required that a person who suffers from scrupulosity confine himself or herself to the advice of a single trusted confessor or spiritual director. In order for healing to begin, he or she must resist the impulse to keep "shopping around" for an answer. God bless you!

Father Santa, C.Ss.R.

QUESTION: Would you explain the Church's teaching that one should follow his or her conscience, even if it is in error? I've come across this teaching in 1 Corinthians, chapters 8 and 10 and in *Crossing the Threshold of Hope* by Pope John Paul II, but the advice we scrupulous people receive involves ignoring and/or correcting our consciences.

ANSWER: This is one more example of a question that underlines the importance of a scrupulous person having a regular confessor. What sounds like a question that deserves a straightforward answer needs special attention, because a scrupulous person asks it. I am not stating by this answer that scrupulous people have "special" answers or "different" answers to such questions, but rather that there must be a pastoral sensitivity to the moral state of the scrupulous person who is asking the question. The reason for this pastoral sensitivity is that a scrupulous person often asks a question, with a particular circumstance or action in mind, that directly relates to the question—in other words, the question is not usually the "real question." Oftentimes there is much more behind it. A regular confessor immediately recognizes this because of his familiarity with the person and therefore is able to provide an answer that is helpful. I would ask that you refer this question directly to your confessor. May God bless you.

Father Santa, C.Ss.R.

QUESTION: I read somewhere that a scrupulous person should receive Communion when his or her confessor has told him or her to do so, even though he or she has a doubt or fear of being in mortal sin, because such a person cannot go wrong or commit a sacrilege in obeying. What do you think?

ANSWER: I am in entire agreement. Obey your confessor. This is a sure and safe path.

Father L. Miller, C.Ss.R.

QUESTION: My confessor has told me to go regularly to holy Communion. But I am always worried that I might not be worthy to go. I am always mixed up about what is a mortal sin and what is a venial sin. But then I wonder what a seventy-three-year-old widow like me could do that would be mortally wrong. I have been receiving Communion regularly since Christmas, but I always worry.

ANSWER: As we have said many times in these pages, a scrupulous person must be resolved to follow the directions of his or her confessor. Otherwise, there is little hope that such a person will find peace of mind and heart. Therefore, continue to follow the advice of your confessor. Your common sense shows itself when you wonder what a person at your age and in your circumstances could do that is seriously sinful. There is no reason to assume that you have committed mortal sin. Mortal sin, after all, does not "sneak up" on a person. Saint Alphonsus says that a person will know quite clearly when he or she has committed a grave sin. Be at peace!

Father Lowery, C.Ss.R.

QUESTION: I made a general confession about two years ago and really felt at peace. But now I am again disturbed by some of the serious sins I confessed at that time. I fear that I did not explain myself clearly enough. My confessor has forbidden me to confess these past sins again, but I am so afraid I may be damned.

ANSWER: In response to your situation, I want to share with you the advice of Saint Alphonsus Liguori when a similar problem was expressed to him. This is what he said:

> I tell you that you ought more implicitly to trust in obedience to your confessor....This instruction to be obedient to one's spiritual father in doubts of conscience is given by all the doctors of the Church, and the holy fathers as well. In short, obedience to one's confessor is the one safest remedy that Jesus Christ has left us for quieting the doubts of conscience, and we ought to return him the greatest thanks for it. For how could a scrupulous soul, in its doubts, find perfect rest otherwise?

Father Lowery, C.Ss.R.

QUESTION: It had been eight years since I received the sacrament of penance. I felt joy and happiness after I had gone. Now I recall things I forgot to mention and it troubles me. At my last confession my confessor said that all of my sins were forgiven. He said that in future confessions I should just say, "For these and all the sins of my past life, I ask forgiveness." He said that I shouldn't go digging into the past, but that my sins are forgiven. Are they?

ANSWER: I don't like repeating myself so often, but as I've said before, the only hope for a scrupulous person in regard to the sacrament of penance is to obey one's confessor. This is the teaching of the Church and the advice of the saints. Your confessor is well trained for his task. You are spiritually safe in following his advice. If you follow it, you will gain some measure of peace. If you don't, you will never stop going around in scrupulous circles!

Father Lowery, C.Ss.R.

QUESTION: I can never seem to find peace with regard to my past confessions. My confessor tells me I have nothing to worry about. But I do have a lot of worries. I'm not sure I've told all my sins properly. I'm not sure I was truly sorry for them or had real purpose of amendment. But no matter what I say, Father won't let me bring up these matters in confession. I'm really in a bind. Can you help me?

ANSWER: I urge you to follow your confessor's advice completely. Saint Alphonsus said many times that a person does not have to confess doubtful sins. (The "doubtful" adjective can be understood in two ways: The doubt can be about the action or about the thought itself—*Was it a sin?*—or it can be about whether the sin was ever confessed.) A person does not have to confess doubtful sins taken in either sense. That means that if you are worried about some sins that might have been confessed in some way (even in a general, partial way), there is no obligation to bring these matters to confession. You don't even have to go back and check it out one final time. You can close the book on it forever. This is a perfectly safe way to act. Remember, Saint Alphonsus, Patron of Confessors, said that the penitent CANNOT GO WRONG if he or she obeys the confessor. He said that a person is more certain of being in God's grace by obeying the confessor than if an angel appeared to that person with the news that everything was all right. So, there's every reason to put aside your fears. Be assured that good Saint Alphonsus is looking down from heaven and praying that you will be able to do just that.

Father Kaler, C.Ss.R.

FINDING THE RIGHT CONFESSOR

Scripture teaches, in the Book of Sirach, "A good wife is a great blessing" (26:3). For the scrupulous person, that teaching might easily be applied to a good confessor. To actually find a confessor who is willing to be patient, kind, and understanding, while at the same time demonstrating the necessary skill to effectively work with a scrupulous person, is the single most expressed frustration of the scrupulous.

Though many obstacles enter into the search process that makes it difficult, two seem most important to me. The first obstacle is the low self-esteem of the scrupulous person who is looking for such a relationship; the second obstacle is the lack of understanding and proper training for the priest who is asked to serve in the role of confessor.

Scrupulous people expect rejection, impatience, and expressed frustration. Because of their experience, and a mindset that easily jumps to the conclusion that another rejection is possible, any expressed impatience, sharp questioning, or even a response that sounds tired and perhaps disinterested, is immediately interpreted negatively. Since there is very little room for imperfection in the mind of the scrupulous person in his or her own judgment of self, there is even less room for imperfection in the response from another person to the scrupulous question, confession, or even casual conversation.

From my own experience of priests, and because of the many conversations I have had with priests about scrupulosity, I have concluded that few priests have ever been adequately trained to minister to a scrupulous person. Nonetheless, I have met very few priests who are not willing to work with the scrupulous person or who would reject them out of hand. More often than not, though, the lack of training, the inability to understand what is operative, and even the inability to offer beginning practical advice and consultation, leads to frustration. After a few failures, the priest's anxiety level increases, which unfortunately is interpreted by the scrupulous as agitation and/or rejection.

WHO CAN HELP ME?

QUESTION: Do you know any priest to recommend in my area of the country who deals with scrupulous people?

ANSWER: Your best bet is to telephone a priest and ask him for a recommendation. A priest in your own area will be able to direct you toward some priest who is especially gifted in this regard.

Father Farnik, C.Ss.R.

QUESTION: What should you do when you cannot find a confessor who is willing to work with you on your scruples?

ANSWER: This whole problem of finding the right confessor is very difficult. I often wish I had a list, covering the whole country, of names of priests I could recommend wherever the scrupulous person lived. But, of course, I don't have such a list. All the same, I keep saying, "Obey your confessor," knowing that this will not be possible for some people. But for those who are able to find one, it is a real blessing, oftentimes bringing much peace into their life for the first time. When that happens, quite often we'll get a glowing letter informing us of the "good news."

But what about those scrupulous people who haven't been that fortunate? Occasionally help comes from another quarter: the discovery of a "spiritual friend." Clearly ordination is not required in this case (unless, of course, there's the question of actually receiving the sacrament of reconciliation). What the role of "spiritual friend" principally calls for is a willingness to listen and to offer wise guidance, where appropriate. Or, to put it another way, what is needed is a friend's enlightened perspective of faith and an understanding heart. If you are blessed with such a "spiritual friend," hang on to him or her...and thank the Lord for a real treasure!

Father Kaler, C.Ss.R.

QUESTION: Why is it so hard to find a confessor who is willing to counsel and guide scrupulous people? It's been my experience that they are few and far between. Some priests act like they had never heard of scrupulosity. Others quickly become impatient or show very little compassion for the suffering the scrupulous person is undergoing.

ANSWER: I'm not making excuses, but I think a large part of the problem lies in the nature of scrupulosity itself. As you know so well, dealing with this illness is a very frustrating experience. Some priests feel inadequate when faced with it. Perhaps they tried to help certain scrupulous individuals in the past and, as far as they could tell, they "failed." They were unable to free those people from the many fears that dominated their lives. So it's not necessarily a lack of compassion. Rather, it's more a feeling that scrupulous people might be better served by other confessors or counselors who apparently are more skilled in these lines.

Scrupulosity can be thought of as a religious version of OCD (obsessive-compulsive disorder). Professional counselors, psychologists, and psychiatrists know how resistant that illness is to therapy. It's not surprising that religious scrupulosity would be equally, or perhaps even more, difficult to handle. It deals with the most fundamental relationship of all: the person's relationship to the Supreme Being. The overriding and ever-present fear is that he or she may have offended God in the past, or is offending God now, or will offend God in the future. To the scrupulous person the mere possibility that such might be the case is so important that all else fades into the background. It's no wonder that victory over this emotional, psychological, and spiritual illness is difficult to accomplish. It takes much hard work and patience. But it happens. Scrupulosity can be cured. And oftentimes a big help in achieving this is an understanding confessor. So the search should go on. Even if it is unsuccessful, it's a move in the right direction.

Father Kaler, C.Ss.R.

QUESTION: How do I go about finding a priest who understands scrupulosity? Are priests given special training for this? I really need some good advice, and I just don't know where to look. Please help me.

ANSWER: The scrupulous person and the scrupulous conscience are central issues in the training of many priests. There is not a priest ordained who does not have at least a rudimentary understanding of the problem. However, from my viewpoint, there are priests who seem to have a particular grace that helps them in this special ministry. My advice would be to ask your parish priest, within the sacrament of confession, if there is a priest he might recommend for the scrupulous. Most priests would not at all mind being asked this question, would not consider it inappropriate, and, in fact, would be grateful for being asked. Priests recognize, for the most part, their own particular talents and gifts and will not hesitate to recommend you to someone else if you feel they are not helpful. God bless!

Father Santa, C.Ss.R.

ATTACHMENT TO THE CONFESSOR

QUESTION: One of my greatest worries concerns a growing attachment to my spiritual director. I worry about whether it is not actually an occasion of sin for me to continue to seek his help. What should I do about this?

ANSWER: It is not surprising that such an attachment can spring up. You would be less than human if the danger were not there. If it seems that your relationship is getting a little too emotional at times, it is important to bring some sternness with yourself into the picture. Be on your guard against idle daydreaming about your director. As to possible impure temptations, make an end run around them. Don't clench your fists and furrow your brow. Gently distract yourself with a quick little prayer as you do so. But I repeat: The mere fact that an attachment springs up should not in itself worry you.

Father L. Miller, C.Ss.R.

DIFFERENT ANSWERS

All people, at one time or another, wish there would be more clarity in life. There probably isn't a single person alive, when faced with the complexity of life, who doesn't desire a simple answer, a black-and-white directive. Usually we find ourselves hoping for such clarity and a firmness of direction when we are faced with a question that we find particularly perplexing or a question that causes us some anxiety and concern.

For the scrupulous person all questions demand clarity and firmness of intention. For the scrupulous person there is nothing more fearful than "not knowing for certain," and, unfortunately, those moments are an almost everyday occurrence.

A solution to the feeling of uncertainty, or, more accurately, a perceived solution to the feeling of uncertainty, is to ask the same question of different people, and hope to receive the *exact* same answer. Of course, it is impossible to receive the same answer from any two people to the same question, for the simple reason that two people will perceive the question in different ways, answering with a different nuance or emphasis. The result is only more anxiety and restlessness rather than the clarity that was hoped for.

QUESTION: If you get a different answer from different priests when you pose a problem, which advice are you to follow?

ANSWER: It seems to be a frequent temptation of the scrupulous to "shop around" for counselors. But if you do this, it should not be surprising that you do not always receive the same kind of advice. A counselor to whom you put a spur-of-the-moment question does not know your background and the state of your conscience and may give an answer that a regular confessor, for the good of your soul, would not give. This points up the importance of staying with one director, if at all possible.

Father L. Miller, C.Ss.R.

QUESTION: My confessor told me I should never cut grass on Sundays or do any unnecessary housecleaning. He said that this is servile work and is forbidden. Then, in the *SA* newsletter you said that it was OK. My confessor told me to bury in the ground or to burn up old worn-out scapulars. The *SA* newsletter said it was OK just to throw them into a trash can. This confusion is what upsets me most. Priests don't agree. Which priest is right? Which priest do I believe? Why can't there be clear rules that all priests will follow so that they all give the same advice?

ANSWER: Priests and bishops, too, are in the same boat that you are in. We don't have all the answers. We each try to do our best to give prudent and wise advice. We have studied and continue to study the Church's long traditions and teachings, all the wisdom from two thousand years of history. But often we disagree with one another about practical solutions. Saint Paul told us that our knowledge of God and of the things of God is not at all clear in this life. In heaven, we will see God face to face, but now we see him only as in a blurred reflection. This is what God intended for us. There is nothing wrong with this. God just wants us to keep trying to do the best we can.

We should put our trust and our confidence in God and in God's limitless love for each of us. We should not pin our hopes on ourselves or on our own good actions. We don't save ourselves. God saves us. So we do the best we can, trusting in God and praying that special prayer that Jesus taught us at the very end of his life on earth: "Father, into your hands I commend my spirit."

Father Farnik, C.Ss.R.

QUESTION: Father, I asked a priest who taught at the seminary if a certain matter was a sin, and he said it was not. Then I asked another priest the same question. According to the Church, and for a right conscience, is one priest sufficient to consult? What if the priest was wrong and I followed his advice; would I then go to hell?

ANSWER: It is not necessary, and, in fact, not at all advisable, for a person who suffers with scruples to ask more than one priest for advice in matters of conscience. Recall, if you have any doubt in this matter, that seeking advice from the one priest more than fulfills the obligation to form a right conscience. Any other effort will probably not be at all helpful for you. If the priest gives you wrong advice, you would not go to hell for following it. You are not responsible for his actions and words; the priest is responsible for them. God bless!

Father Santa, C.Ss.R.

QUESTION: I once told Father Kaler I did not always know if my thoughts were serious sin. I was never sure if I should go to Communion or not. He said if there is doubt, I should go ahead and receive Communion. Recently, another priest told me that I should never do anything when in doubt. What should I do?

ANSWER: I would suggest that you try very hard to listen to the advice that you have received from Father Kaler. He would never give bad advice, and he would constantly pray that the advice he would give would be helpful. I don't think you could ever have better advice than the advice you received from him. Please be at peace.

Father Santa, C.Ss.R.

A REGULAR CONFESSOR

In order to try and address the problem of the scrupulous person seeking advice and counsel from a variety of people, confessors usually insist that the scrupulous person establish a relationship with one confessor, and one confessor only. In this circumstance the confessor will insist that the scrupulous person follow his advice exactly—in effect, turning over the decision making and discernment about sin to a single, trusted friend.

A confessor will insist on this strict relationship, because it is the experience of those who work with the scrupulous conscience that this is the first step to effectively controlling scrupulosity. If the scrupulous person can establish a trusting relationship with a confessor, it is possible he or she may begin to learn to trust themselves and their own ability to make a good decision. However, until some pattern of trust is established, and regularly experienced, there is little hope for recovery.

Without a regular confessor, the scrupulous person is doomed to a life filled with anxiety, restlessness, and frustration, plagued by a feeling of failure and a pattern of making decisions that are not helpful.

QUESTION: I have suffered from scruples since childhood (I am now fifty-eight). My confessions are a torture and have been years apart. I regret this very much, since I have not received Communion very often in my life. What should I do?

ANSWER: It saddens me that you have not received Communion very often in your life. This is certainly not the Lord's will. I can only encourage you, as I have encouraged so many others in these pages, to try to find a regular confessor, explain your dilemma to him, and abide by his advice. You should be at the Lord's table.

Father Lowery, C.Ss.R.

QUESTION: I make a generic confession each week. My pastor and sometimes the visiting priest also accept my confession with no difficulty. However I worry that some confessor will not accept my generic confession. From the time that I get up in the morning on Saturday until my confession is over I feel fear, dread, and slightly ill. I am grateful for the opportunity to go to confession and I wish that I could go every day.

ANSWER: You are experiencing scrupulosity and one of the manifestations of the scrupulous conscience. If it isn't one thing, it is another thing. Scrupulous people can always find something to worry about. With the manifestations that you experience each Saturday, I cannot imagine why you would want to go to confession every day. I can almost assure you that you would begin to feel the same symptoms every day that you now experience only on Saturday.

My best advice to you would be to see if you could not go to confession every Saturday and try going every other Saturday. In addition I believe that you should determine that you will celebrate the sacrament only when your pastor is in the confessional or when there is a visiting priest that you know is comfortable with people suffering from scrupulosity. Our Lord does not require that you go through this kind of agony week after week. God bless you.

Father Santa, C.Ss.R.

QUESTION: Some of your correspondents speak highly of confessors they have found who have special knowledge in dealing with scrupulous persons. How does one find these priests? Is there a "network" one can refer to?

ANSWER: I'm sorry I know of no such network. I do think that most confessors are sufficiently trained and willing to help scrupulous persons, provided those persons are willing to follow the confessor's direction. I suggest that a scrupulous person talk to a confessor first, preferably outside of confession, explain his or her problems, and reach a decision about frequency of confession, method of confessing, and the like. This kind of understanding tends to lay the groundwork for a good relationship.

Father Lowery, C.Ss.R.

QUESTION: The parish where I usually go to confession does not have a set schedule where the same priest always hears confessions at the same time. This makes it impossible to have a regular confessor, as I know I should. Under these circumstances, is it permissible just to follow the advice given in the *SA* newsletter without the additional guidance of a regular confessor?

ANSWER: When it is impossible to have a regular confessor, one can only do one's best. But because a regular confessor is so important for a scrupulous person, I would encourage you not to give up your search too easily. When I was a parish priest, I always had several scrupulous penitents who would come to see me outside of the usual confession times. For example, we would agree to get together on the first Tuesday of each month at 4:00 PM. If for some serious reason either the priest or the penitent would have to cancel the appointment, we would immediately make another one. You might think about asking your parish priest about some such setup. Believe me, it is worth the trouble!

Father Lowery, C.Ss.R.

QUESTION: I have had a scrupulous conscience for the past fifty years. I am now seventy-one years old and still have such problems. I used to go from one confessor to another, but now I have discontinued that practice. I rely on the help given by *SA* and the guidance and the example of our patron, Saint Alphonsus. My question is, can I use him as my counselor and director, since I feel such agony and torture in the confessional?

ANSWER: Yes, you may certainly use Saint Alphonsus as your guide. I do not think it would be unreasonable to pray to him and to ask for his blessing and his guidance. Certainly, as a saint who also suffered from scrupulosity, he would be very compassionate and understanding in this matter. May God bless you and keep you!

Father Santa, C.Ss.R.

WHEN A CHANGE IS NECESSARY

There are many reasons why a scrupulous person may be faced with a necessary change in his or her regular confessor. The most common reason is the transfer of the confessor to another assignment, a not-uncommon occurrence in the experience of parish life. Such a change will affect all parishioners on one level or another, but for the scrupulous person it can prove to be traumatic.

The best advice that I can give when the scrupulous person is faced with such a change is to suggest that the scrupulous person ask their present confessor to introduce them to the new confessor. This would not be an unusual request, and most priests would welcome the opportunity. This would also provide the opportunity for any questions to be answered so that all could be assured that the important relationship between the confessor and the scrupulous person is respected and honored.

QUESTION: When a scrupulous person has to change confessors, does the new one have to know all the rules and answers to questions the previous one handed out?

ANSWER: I suggest that a scrupulous person who is starting with a new confessor take a few minutes, if possible, to give a general idea of his or her relationship with the former confessor and to answer any questions the new confessor may have.

Father Lowery, C.Ss.R.

PART TWO

Questions and Dilemmas

**A REPRESENTATIVE SAMPLING
OF THIRTY-FIVE YEARS
OF SCRUPULOUS ANONYMOUS**

A NOTE TO THE READER

In the first section of this book, I felt it necessary on occasion to add my own comments to each question. This was to provide a framework for understanding and, hopefully, a guide for the reader just beginning to become acquainted with the scrupulous condition.

In this part of the book, it is my intention to permit the questions and answers to speak for themselves. I will provide an introduction to each section that I hope may prove useful in framing the question, but I will not comment on each grouping of questions. I have chosen this approach because I believe that part 1 provides the necessary insight into a basic understanding of the condition. The questions in part 2 are examples of the manifestation of scrupulosity to a specific question and set of circumstances.

I had hundreds of questions to choose from and could not have included all of them here. I have, however, made it a point to choose those questions that have consistently appeared over the last thirty-five years in the *SA* newsletter. My assumption was that if something appears to be a preoccupation for a significant group of people it should be included in these pages if this book is to fulfill its purpose. Other questions that seemed particular to a certain time in history, such as those questions that were asked because of the changes brought on by the Second Vatican Council, have not been included. There have been the occasional questions that seemed to be peculiar to a particular time and place in history. However, as time marched on, what once seemed to be a great concern no longer troubled the members of SA, and so those questions are also omitted.

Chapter Six

Questions About Holy Communion

Even though it was many years ago, I can remember many of the details about my first Communion. I remember the classes in preparation. I remember the celebration of first penance. I remember the practices that we had in preparation for the actual celebration. We practiced walking down the aisle, and we practiced genuflecting with our hands folded in prayer. We even practiced receiving the host so that the feel and texture of it would not surprise us on first Communion Sunday.

My most vivid memory of my first Communion had to do with my front teeth and Sister Mary Francesca, OP, my second-grade teacher at St. Alphonsus in Grand Rapids, Michigan. Sister constantly reminded us that we were not "true second-graders" until we had lost all of our baby teeth. For some unknown reason I was still retaining my front baby teeth, and this was a cause of concern. I desired, more than anything else, to be a "true second-grader," and I was hoping that this blessed event would soon happen. I did not want to disappoint Sister Francesca!

Just days before the scheduled event, it finally happened. My front teeth fell out—a fact obvious to all as soon as I smiled. I was so happy, and I wanted to share the great news with Sister Francesca. She was not going to have to worry about me any longer. She could concentrate her efforts on someone else. I was surprised when she did not share my joy. Although it was true that she wanted me to be a true second-grader, what she desired even more was a good picture of her first Communion class. With my teeth newly out, I was going to ruin the picture.

Somehow, with no front teeth, and with a less-than-happy nun, I got through the big day. I received my first Communion, thus taking another step into full sacramental initiation into the Church. In addition, I was able to receive the full sacramental graces of union with the Lord.

For most people, there are good memories associated with events such as the reception of their first Communion. For Catholics it is the moment when Jesus is welcomed into their heart and soul for the first time in a sacramental way. Although Catholics believe that they experience the presence of the Lord in many different ways throughout life, they nevertheless give special meaning and attention to sacramental moments. It is a spiritual event and a moment, although repeated often throughout life, which remains special because of the significance and emphasis that is given to the first experience of the sacramental union.

For the person who suffers with scrupulosity, this first reception of Communion is often not remembered in a positive way. For some, it is a vivid memory of the first pangs of scrupulosity, the first experience of the fear of making a sacrilegious Communion, because of the presence of serious sin, not properly confessed and not forgiven. Some scrupulous people recall the reception of their first Communion as the beginning of a lifetime of questioning, wondering, and anxiety.

The reception of Communion, the first time and each time thereafter, is a defining moment for the scrupulous person. If the confession of sins is an experience of anxiety, it is the reception of Communion, and the ritual, rules, and conditions that are a part of the experience, that provides the fuel that feeds the scrupulous conscience.

CONFESSION BEFORE COMMUNION:
IS IT NECESSARY?

QUESTION: I really want to know where I stand on receiving the sacraments. I repeat the same old offenses all the time and then I go without the sacrament of penance until I get enough courage to face my confessor again. I have been taught that one must go to confession before one is able to go to holy Communion. Consequently, I can go for weeks, even three or four months, between Communions.

ANSWER: It is not true that one must go to confession before one is able to go to holy Communion. Only if you are certain that you are in the state of serious or grave sin must you confess before receiving Communion. In regard to our daily offenses, a simple Act of Contrition is sufficient to obtain the Lord's forgiveness. Every Mass begins with such an Act of Contrition. There is no objective reason, I am quite sure, for persons like you to stay away from the Lord's table for such long periods of times.

Father Lowery, C.Ss.R.

QUESTION: For many years I would not let myself go to holy Communion without first going to confession. Even though confessors told me that I had not committed serious sin, I always wanted to play it safe and go to confession first. But finally when I saw other Catholics, some of whom I think go to confession only once or twice a year, going to Communion every Sunday, it dawned on me that I could not possibly be as bad as I thought I was. So I got up enough nerve to go to holy Communion without first going to confession. It felt wonderful. But now I'm having some doubts. Father, tell me honestly, was that the right thing to do?

ANSWER: Yes, it certainly was! Congratulations! You were able to face your fear head-on. You decided that you, and not your fears, were in charge of your life. If you can continue to do this, your confidence will grow. You will discover more and more how much God loves you, what blessings he has given to you, and how he wants your reception of him in holy Communion to be a wonderful experience of peace and joy.

Father Kaler, C.Ss.R.

QUESTION: I've always considered the receiving of holy Communion sacrilegiously as one of the worst sins. I can't imagine a greater insult to our loving Lord than this. Because I fear this so much, I don't think I should go when I might possibly be in sin. So, to make sure I won't receive our Lord unworthily, I stay away from Communion most of the time. I go only twice a year—at Christmas and during the Easter season—and only after I've made a very thorough confession of my sins. I know I agonize over this too much, but what can I do, since the danger of sacrilege is so real? Can you help me? Thank you.

ANSWER: I can understand your feelings and your fears about even the possibility of committing such a terrible sin. It would seem to be the prudent thing to do—to stay away from holy Communion—when there is the slightest risk of offending God in this way. However, we receive different advice from Saint Alphonsus. This doctor of the Church states that scrupulous people *should* receive Communion, unless they are absolutely certain they have sinned mortally. As you can see, the doubt is placed at the other end of the line. Remember, this advice is coming from a saint who loved our Lord in the Blessed Sacrament very much. He wrote a beautiful little booklet entitled *Visits to the Blessed Sacrament.* He often spoke of the dispositions necessary for a devout and fruitful reception of holy Communion. He would never give advice that would endanger the respect and reverence due this wonderful sacrament. Saint Alphonsus lived in an age when Jansenism was rampant. The rigors expounded by this heresy kept many people, especially those who were scrupulous, from receiving the Eucharist. In the saint's eyes, that was one of the worst things about scrupulosity. It kept them from going to their Lord who is the Divine Healer they need so badly. So, take the saint's advice and start going to Communion as frequently as you can. You can be sure that this is perfectly safe advice to follow.

Father Kaler, C.Ss.R.

QUESTION: If a scrupulous person wants so desperately to receive Communion and takes it upon herself to do so without confession, because confession aggravates her worries and scruples, and everything is a sin to her anyway, has she committed a mortal sin?

ANSWER: My answer is no. A scrupulous person should always give himself or herself the benefit of the doubt and receive Communion regularly. It may indeed be best for such a person to go to confession infrequently, if it is such a source of aggravation and fear. But in this you should follow the advice of a trusted director.

Father L. Miller, C.Ss.R.

QUESTION: Is there any occasion on which a person can receive Communion without going to confession? Especially a scrupulous person? I like to attend Mass often, but often hesitate to receive Communion because of some doubt.

ANSWER: I think you should receive Communion every time you attend Mass, even though you have doubts in your mind. The only time you should stay away is when you are so sure you have committed a serious sin that you could swear to it under oath. You need holy Communion. Don't stay away.

Father L. Miller, C.Ss.R.

DID I MAKE THE RIGHT DECISION?

QUESTION: Do you ever feel that some people may be making the correct moral decision by deciding not to receive holy Communion? In my case, I really believe I am taking responsibility for myself and am making the right moral decision. I stopped receiving holy Communion two years ago after I started having obsessive blasphemous thoughts, and since then my fears have grown. I don't confess past sins anymore, but just remembering them makes me doubt that I will ever be able to receive Communion again.

ANSWER: It is certainly possible and reasonable for a Catholic to make a correct moral decision to abstain from holy Communion because of serious sin that has not yet been repented. But to make such a decision because of "obsessive thoughts" or because of past sins that have already been confessed is not a correct or right moral decision. Jesus has given us the Eucharist as spiritual food for the journey of life. He wants us, indeed commands us, to "take and eat." To refuse his invitation because of scrupulous fears and false guilt is not, in my opinion, a correct way of acting. I believe that the scrupulous should approach the Eucharist with great trust and confidence, despite their morbid fears and worries.

Father Lowery, C.Ss.R.

QUESTION: I have a problem I've been putting up with for two years. When I go to confession I try real hard to remember all my sins. I even ask the help of the Holy Spirit. After confession everything is fine until it's time to receive Communion. Then, bam! I'll remember a sin (like taking the Lord's name in vain) and, of course, I don't receive Communion. Part of me says go ahead, and part of me says no way. Which should I do?

ANSWER: I say go ahead! Scrupulosity (as many readers can testify) often strikes at Communion time. It is very important for a scrupulous person to "act against" the scruple and receive Communion.

Your confession was a good one, even though you forgot to confess a particular sin. That sin, if serious, should be included in your next confession, but there is no need to refrain from receiving Communion.

Father Lowery, C.Ss.R.

SPECIAL PREPARATIONS FOR COMMUNION

QUESTION: Can you help me with my scrupulosity regarding the reception of holy Communion? I know that some of the things I do are extreme but I can't seem to stop, even though I realize that my actions are unreasonable. For example, I even have a special set of toothbrushes, cosmetics, and so forth, that I use only on Sunday. If I don't do this I feel that I am being disrespectful. I feel even more unworthy of receiving our Lord than before. I would appreciate any help you could give.

ANSWER: With regard to your Sunday preparations (special toothbrushes, and so forth), I have to admit that is the first time I have heard of that! However, I am not too surprised because I know that the reception of the Eucharist is a source of quite a few worries for some scrupulous people. Believe me, it isn't necessary to have a separate set for the day you receive holy Communion. Prepare yourself just as you would to meet a very special friend. You certainly would want to look nice, but at the same time you would have happy thoughts of anticipation, not worry, as you got ready. One reason for the happiness would be that you know that your friend accepts you just as you are. Say a prayer like, "Dear Lord, I know you love me just as I am. You love me even though you know I am very imperfect. You said it was the sick who needed the doctor. I am one of those sick people. I come to you to be healed. You can read my heart and see that I want to love you." This is just a suggestion, but I hope it helps.

Father Kaler, C.Ss.R.

COMMUNION PARTICLES—
LEAVE IT TO THE ANGELS

QUESTION: Sometimes, when I go to holy Communion, I see little white particles on the floor right at the place where the people just received. Maybe they are fragments of the sacred host. Undoubtedly they will be stepped on. Must I tell the priest right away or go into the sacristy after Mass and let him know?

ANSWER: No, you should do neither. The Lord knows how to take care of himself if he is actually on the floor. Anyway, the white particles may be lint or paper or almost anything. Don't worry if you should see the floor so covered. Do nothing about it.

Father L. Miller, C.Ss.R.

QUESTION: What about the fragments of the hosts that I see on the floor at the very spot where holy Communion is given out? I do not want to criticize my pastor. But apparently he doesn't believe in using the Communion paten. I'm the worrying sort. Every time I go to Communion I see small white things on the floor right where the people walk and on the very spot where they receive. Should I tell Father? Should I wait until everybody is out of church and then go up there and pick up the pieces of whatever they are and put them on the altar? I'm really worried.

ANSWER: No, do none of these things. You have no certainty that the little white specks you see are a part of the host. Even if they are, as far as you are concerned, forget your worries. Christ has a million angels surrounding him on the floor just as he has in a golden tabernacle. Remember, he was born in a stable. You never heard a word of complaint from him about that. The same about the floor, he doesn't mind as long as he's not thrown down there in disbelief and hatred and culpable carelessness. As to your pastor, let him be, too. He has his own conscience. He has his own accounting to make someday, the same as the rest of us. Don't make any judgments about him.

When you go to Communion, go about your business of talking to Jesus as he rests in your heart. Let that be your only consideration. There's no sin in regard to the other thing.

Father L. Miller, C.Ss.R.

QUESTION: After coming home from Mass, my children sometimes chew gum. My constant worry is that tiny pieces of the host may have remained between their teeth and later became mixed up into the gum that they chew. Then when I see what looks like remnants of gum on the refrigerator door or elsewhere, I am afraid to scrape it off for fear of getting part of the host under my fingernails or on the knife. Also, I have blessed candles that were given out after Mass. I worry that possibly particles of the host may have come out of my mouth when I coughed and embedded themselves into the candle wax. Since I keep the candles in a chest of drawers, I am afraid that pieces of host may now be in the wood. When I take clothes out of the drawers, I am afraid that if they touch the wood, they, too, will get particles of host on them.

ANSWER: A very wise priest used to tell people with such worries about particles of the host, "Leave it to the angels. They have to have something to do." He meant that human beings have no way of knowing for sure where particles of host might end up. And God does not expect us to worry about this. If there is a problem, it is God's problem, not ours. He will let his angels handle it. God expects only that we act "in a human way." He did not give us x-ray vision. He does not want us to get uptight and make a burden out of his gift of the Eucharist. By all means, we are to be reverent and take ordinary care not to scatter fragments of the host. But we should do this "in a human way," with all the limitations of being human, and leave the rest in God's hands. God knew what he was doing when he gave us the Eucharist. He does not expect the impossible from us. Let his angels have something to do.

Father Farnik, C.Ss.R.

QUESTION: As the priest was giving holy Communion to the person in front of me, I thought I saw something like a particle of host fall. I wasn't sure, but there was the possibility. The priest and the person receiving Communion didn't act in any unusual way. Then it was my turn to receive, so I tried to put it out of my mind. It probably wasn't a sacred particle because someone else would have noticed it. But I worried about it the rest of the Mass. After Mass I made it a point to go look, but I found nothing. But this doesn't mean it wasn't there. Now I feel a little guilty that I didn't do something at the time. Did I act correctly in this matter, or should I have stopped the oncoming line to look? By the way, I distribute Communion at times and I don't want to give up this beautiful privilege because of scruples.

ANSWER: I think you acted correctly. Chances are, it wasn't a piece of the sacred host—it could have been a piece of lint or a dust particle. If it had been a sacred particle the priest or someone closer would most likely have noticed it. I feel that your own reception of Communion and your role as eucharistic minister is so important we don't want a lot of scruples coming in and robbing you of the joy that should come to be yours at Communion time. Of course, reverence is very important also. But we are not speaking here of any deliberate irreverence or carelessness. In fact, in situations like this I feel that the good Lord would rather have a tiny particle inadvertently lost than have good people constantly worrying about it. He became one of us and was willing to put up with the limitations of earthly existence. He determined that he would give himself to us under the appearance of bread (he knew there would be crumbs) so that he could be food for our souls. So, please, fight off scruples along these lines.

Father Kaler, C.Ss.R.

QUESTION: I wear dentures and lately have been concerned about brushing my teeth on Sundays for fear that bits of the holy Eucharist may be stuck to my dentures and I may rinse them out. Am I doing something wrong? Should I worry about this?

ANSWER: No, you are not doing anything wrong. And no, you should not worry about this. I can assure you that this is one of the classical worries of scrupulous persons. Try to ignore it. Receive the Eucharist as usual. Brush your teeth as usual. Do not get tied up in unnecessary worries and fears.

Father Lowery, C.Ss.R.

COMMUNION IN THE HAND

QUESTION: I prefer to receive Communion in the hand but then I carefully examine my fingers for any particles of the host that may be lodged in the skin. This disturbs my meditation. I wish my conscience were as flexible as those who don't seem to worry at all.

ANSWER: Receiving holy Communion is a human act. We need only approach it in a human and reasonable way. I pass on to you the advice of Saint Alphonsus to a young priest who was scrupulous about cleaning the chalice and paten at his Mass: "Take ordinary and reasonable care to clean the sacred vessels, but let the angels take care of the rest!"

Father Lowery, C.Ss.R.

QUESTION: I am having difficulty with Communion in the hand. While I realize that the more customary option of receiving the holy Eucharist on the tongue is still available, I would like to begin receiving in the hand. However, I perceive the hands as instruments used in committing sin (such as theft, uncharitable gestures, impurity, and so on) and therefore feel it may be somewhat blasphemous to receive the holy Eucharist in the hands. Perhaps you can offer some advice that will help clarify my thinking.

ANSWER: If one wanted to think in this way, one could also make a case that the tongue is an instrument of committing sin (such as perjury, slander, and obscenity). But why put the emphasis on sin? Why not stress the positive? Both the tongue and the hand may also be instruments of prayer, praise, kindness, and assistance to others. For the first half of the Church's existence, Communion in the hand was the normal practice. For the second half (the past thousand years), Communion on the tongue was the customary practice. The Church now allows a choice to the individual communicant. We should not try to be "holier than the Church," nor should we condemn one practice or the other.

The following passage may help you appreciate in a positive way the beautiful symbolism of Communion in the hand. It is taken from a fourth-century catechetical instruction: "When you approach Communion do not come with your hands outstretched or with your fingers open, but make your left hand a throne for the right one, which is to receive the King. With your hand hallowed receive the Body of Christ and answer 'Amen!'"

Father Lowery, C.Ss.R.

PURIFICATION OF THE COMMUNION VESSELS

QUESTION: I am a eucharistic minister and recently our duties have been expanded to the purification of the chalices after Communion. We have been told to wash the Communion cups and to pour the water used in the washing into the sacrarium (a special sink in the sacristy especially constructed for this purpose). I have been thinking of dropping out of the ministry because I feel very anxious about doing this. A related question is, "How many times do I have to rinse the sacrarium itself after purifying the chalices?"

ANSWER: When a person is faced with anxiety, there are usually two choices: (a) confront the anxiety head-on, identify the fears, and learn to live with uncomfortableness until the anxiety lessens; or (b) avoid that which causes the anxiety. This is good advice. If your role as a eucharistic minister causes you anxiety, you can withdraw from the ministry or you can ask another minister to perform the task that causes you anxiety. In this case, ask to be excused from the purification process—I am sure that this would be very acceptable. If, on the other hand, you choose not to avoid that which causes anxiety, but rather confront it, then you must be willing to live with a certain uncomfortableness. You are following the directions and traditions of the purification procedure. You are not being careless—in fact, this is something you are trying to avoid.

Learn, then, to trust what you are doing. If you are unsure, ask a priest or another minister if you are correctly performing the task. If they assure you that you are, then try and learn to leave the matter at rest. The discomfort you first feel will begin to lessen as you learn to trust your decision-making process. God bless.

Father Santa, C.Ss.R.

THE COMMUNION FAST

QUESTION: I am very nervous and tense about receiving holy Communion because I worry about powder, lipstick, and hair spray breaking my fast. Should I worry about this?

ANSWER: Definitely not. Even if some small portion should get on your tongue, it would not break your eucharistic fast.

Father L. Miller, C.Ss.R.

QUESTION: When I receive Communion, I always worry about licking my lips or allowing any saliva to pass an imaginary line. Is this worry natural and normal?

ANSWER: No, it is not, and I think you can prove this to yourself by noting that your friends and relatives, even those you admire most as good people, do not give in to such worries. Don't worry about your saliva, in or out of your mouth.

Father L. Miller, C.Ss.R.

QUESTION: The Communion fast is a problem for me. Can you really be sinning in God's sight if your fast isn't exactly one hour? I'm trying to move from a religion based on rules and regulations to a relationship of love and trust, but trusting my own judgment is very difficult.

ANSWER: First of all, three cheers for you! You are certainly moving in the right direction! I believe that all Catholics (particularly scrupulous people) should aim at moving from a religion based on rules and regulations to a relationship of love and trust. The Communion fast is not meant to make us clock-watchers! The purpose of it is to help us prepare our minds and hearts for participation in the offering of the eucharistic sacrifice and for the reception of the body and blood of Christ. The Communion fast is a sign of reverence, a time for prayerful attention. All we are asked to do is make a reasonable judgment about the hour before Communion. If on occasion we are off by a few minutes, so be it! We have done our best, and that's all the Lord asks of us. The important thing is the spirit of the fast.

Father Lowery, C.Ss.R.

QUESTION: If we purposely lick our lips when we have on lipstick, can we still go to Communion?

ANSWER: Yes, yes, a thousand times yes! Lipstick is not food.

Father Lowery, C.Ss.R.

QUESTION: Whenever I am to receive holy Communion, I have a fear of not being worthy, and also I worry about fasting. Is taking aspirin or medicine of any kind before Communion the right thing to do?

ANSWER: Taking any kind of medicine, if it is prescribed, needed, or recommended, should not be dispensed with and should cause no hesitation; this has nothing at all to do with the worthiness of the Communion. Christ wants us to approach him above all with trust and love in our hearts. I know this worry affects many of our readers and is a source of anxiety. I suppose it is an example of one of those little "gnawing" doubts that are so much a part of scrupulosity. It is necessary, in order not to let scrupulosity control us, that we pray to God for the courage to confront such doubts. The best way to do so is to continue to be resolute in your desire to receive holy Communion and to continue to receive the sacrament, even if you are in doubt. This is one of the best ways to practice loving and trusting the Lord. May God bless you!

Father Santa, C.Ss.R.

Chapter Seven

Questions About
Prayer and the Mass

There is a great concern for physical health and the maintenance of a healthy lifestyle among people of all walks of life. Some attribute this concern to a growing awareness and commitment to healthy living, spurned on by the graying of the baby-boom generation. We are told that whatever concerns this generation concerns all of us because they are such a significant group within our society. Others are convinced that health consciousness is the result of better education for all people or simply better marketing efforts by the health industry. Whatever the primary driver might be, I think it would be agreed that healthy living is a concern.

As a result of this concern, we have come to an understanding that thirty minutes of aerobic exercise, at least three times a week, is necessary for good health maintenance. It doesn't matter what form the exercise takes—some might prefer a brisk walk, still others a cool swim, and others something even more athletic—but it is important that it is done on a regular basis.

In exercise we understand what the minimum is and what are the maximum benefits that the minimum will produce for us: such things as lower cholesterol, reduction of stress, maintenance of weight, and an overall feeling of confidence and peace.

The benefits of exercise and healthy living are measurable. There are no guarantees or warranties, but there is at least demonstrable and significant data to show why a person should commit to at least the minimum.

Most things in life, most of the choices and decisions we are asked to make each day, are not always as easily measured. Some of the things we choose to do, just because we think they're good for us, cannot be proven to be significantly helpful. Other choices and actions that we perform each day fall in the spiritual realm. Even though good for us, they cannot be proven to be helpful or even necessary.

There is no perfect prayer to pray. There are preferences and there are options, but there is no one prayer form that is perfect for everyone. There are no hard data to prove that thirty minutes of prayer, three times a week, is what is necessary for a healthy spiritual life. It would be nice if there were, but there is no such proof. There doesn't seem to be a minimum spiritual response that produces the maximum benefit we all seek. Some may argue that there is a minimum response and may argue forcefully for their opinion; but when all is said and done, we know that all we are, and all we ever hope to be, comes to us from God as a gift. We cannot earn it. We cannot demand it. We cannot manipulate it. All we can do is choose to accept or to reject the gift that is offered.

It is difficult for anyone to come to an understanding and acceptance of who they are before God. It is difficult for anyone to imagine that day when they will stand before God with open hands, alone, weak, sinful, and deserving of nothing, but expecting everything. It is difficult for anyone; for the scrupulous person it is terrifying. Any slip, any distraction, any action not perfectly performed is "sinful"; the only question is whether or not the sin is mortal sin or possibly a little less than mortal sin. To imagine standing before the Lord, in their perceived notion of sinfulness, is almost more than they can bear.

Spirituality demands trust. At the heart of all spirituality is the ability to trust in the witness of others who first introduced you to your faith and belief. For still others, further on in the spiritual journey, it is the ability to trust that which you have personally experienced, to trust that which can so easily be explained away, misunderstood, or not fully appreciated.

The scrupulous person struggles with trust. At the heart of scrupulosity is the inability to trust personal decisions and to have the necessary confidence that the choice was the best that could be made. As a result, when it comes to spiritual experiences of prayer, the celebration of the Mass, and a person's personal relationship with the Lord, the questions become very specific and the desire for absolute certitude even more pronounced.

QUESTIONS ABOUT PRAYER

QUESTION: I say most of my prayers before going to bed, but sometimes leave a few out and fall asleep without saying them. Is this a sin?

ANSWER: Of course not. God sees your good intention, and he knows how easy it is for you to fall asleep, even when you are saying your prayers.

Father L. Miller, C.Ss.R.

QUESTION: My morning and night prayers have become a problem for me. They keep getting longer, and I say some of them over and over again, thinking maybe I have not prayed with enough attention. It is hard for me to concentrate, especially when I am tired. What can I do about this?

ANSWER: For one thing, you should follow a hard-and-fast rule in saying these prayers: Don't repeat them. Once you start repeating, you open up the door to endless worries. Even if it seems you were totally distracted when you said the prayer, don't repeat it. I advise you, also, to cut down on the number of prayers you are saying. You can't be comfortable if you are fretting about whether you will reach your set total of fifteen or eighteen separate prayers. Keep your morning and night prayers simple and short.

Father L. Miller, C.Ss.R.

QUESTION: Is all prayer lost if the individual is not in the state of grace?

ANSWER: Not at all. In such a case it is a necessary preparation for opening the heart and mind to God's grace. Saint Alphonsus used to say, "He who prays is saved, he who does not pray is lost."

Father L. Miller, C.Ss.R.

QUESTION: How long must our morning prayers and our night prayers last?

ANSWER: The Bible very strongly urges us to pray and to make prayer a regular part of our lives. To help us do this, the Church has always recommended prayer at the start of each day, at the end of the day, before and after mealtimes. By establishing a regular habit of praying at these times, we are sure of talking to God at least a few times daily. Each person is free to choose how much prayer he or she prefers to say at these times. Some, on arising, simply say, "Dear Lord, I give this new day to you." On retiring, they simply say, "Thank you, God, for everything. I put my life in your hands." There is no minimum duration of time that we have to cover. We are completely free in this. These prayer times are suggestions and recommendations, not obligations or orders.

Father Farnik, C.Ss.R.

QUESTION: Sometimes I feel so frustrated and angry because I can't pray right. I have to keep repeating my prayers over and over to say them in the right way. Sometimes this gets me very discouraged and depressed.

ANSWER: Remember that there is more than one way to talk. Even when a person cannot speak with his or her lips, this person can still speak through other signs—like shaking the head yes or no. The same thing is true about our talking to God in prayer. Prayer need not be put into word form. Prayer can be done through other signs. You can just sit in your chair with the palms of your hands turned upward and your arms comfortable on the armrests. No words are necessary. God is there. God sees you. God loves you. God knows your heart and your intentions and your sentiments, even though you don't formulate them into words. God accepts you as you are. Your open hands are a way of telling God that you love him, too; that you appreciate his love for you; that you are sorry for any and all wrongdoing; that you want to grow closer to him. That is genuine prayer, even though it is not in word form. Try to learn to pray that way. With practice, it will become for you a natural and comfortable way of praying.

Father Farnik, C.Ss.R.

QUESTION: I feel like I should pray about every half-hour. I feel guilty if I don't pray that often. I want to put God always first in my life.

ANSWER: There are few persons who pray as often as every half-hour. That includes priests and religious. But such frequent prayer is certainly a wonderful ideal. You could tell God that your smile would be a prayer of gratitude and of joy. Then smile every half-hour (or whenever you think of it) as your quick little prayer to God. That would be a beautiful prayer. No special words are necessary. Your smile could be your sign-language prayer.

Father Lowery, C.Ss.R.

QUESTION: For many years, our family has had the practice of saying a prayer as we begin a trip of over an hour or so. Recently we were driving our college-age daughter back to school. Two other students were in the car with us. As we started out, I was going to suggest our prayer. Then I wondered if our daughter would be embarrassed or if her friends would think us strange, so I just said a prayer to myself. In plain English, I did not have the courage to speak up. I am still worried about it. Was it a sin?

ANSWER: It is important for us to distinguish between what is an obligation for us as Catholics and what is up to our free choice. It is a wonderful idea to say a prayer before starting a trip. I've been doing it for years. But there is no strict obligation to do so. You committed no sin by omitting the prayer on your recent trip. If I were you, in the future I wouldn't worry about the reactions of others. It would be good for young people to know that some families start their trips with a prayer. It is nothing to be ashamed of. Even though they may not fully appreciate the practice now, they will probably appreciate it in the future when they have their own families.

Father Lowery, C.Ss.R.

QUESTION: Is there a strict obligation to pray at certain times, for example, morning and night, and before and after meals?

ANSWER: There is no general law of the Church commanding morning and night prayers, and prayers before and after meals. These times are suggested as being good times for most people to pray. To omit these prayers is not sinful. On a more general level, we can say that prayer is necessary for salvation. Certainly many of the great saints, Saint Alphonsus Liguori, for example, taught this doctrine. Many theologians have taught that a person is bound to pray "frequently" in the course of his or her life, but ordinarily it is not necessary to go into detail. It should be noted, however, that the obligation to attend Mass on Sundays (a serious law of the Church) clearly implies an obligation to pray at that time. The question of "strict obligation" tends to lead us into many legalistic distinctions. If prayer is a way of communicating with God, and if we are serious about our relationship with him, prayer will be a "natural" and frequent part of our lives.

Father Lowery, C.Ss.R.

QUESTION: Is it a mortal sin not to say your daily prayers? It's not that I forget them; I just don't take the time to say them.

ANSWER: There is no strict obligation to say specific daily prayers, such as morning and evening prayers, prayers before and after meals, and the like. It is not sinful, therefore, to omit such customary prayers. The great saints have taught that every person is bound to pray "frequently" in the course of his or her life, but not to go into detail. To neglect prayer entirely would be sinful.

Father Lowery, C.Ss.R.

QUESTION: I belong to a number of Catholic organizations that all have their own prescribed morning offerings, along with other regular prayers. A lot of these are repetitive, but no single devotion encompasses them all. Am I guilty of sin if I don't say all of these prayers every morning? Should I make up a composite of them to satisfy myself, or what?

ANSWER: First, none of these prayers binds in conscience. There is no sin if you omit them. Second, a good rule for vocal prayers is "the simpler, the better." It is far more important, as the gospel tells us, to pray a few prayers from the heart than to rattle on with a lot of prayers just to fulfill some "obligation." Your idea of making a simple composite makes sense to me. Give it a peaceful try.

Father Lowery, C.Ss.R.

QUESTION: Over the past few years I have acquired quite a list of people who have asked me to pray for them on a regular basis. It is to the point now where it now takes me almost fifteen minutes a day to name them all before I begin my prayers. Is it necessary to repeat all the names every time I go to pray, or is a general intention enough? I feel guilty when I don't say all their names and guilty when I do, in case I've left anyone out.

ANSWER: No, it is not necessary to repeat all the names every time you go to pray. According to a long Christian tradition—as indicated, for example, in the eucharistic liturgy—it is sufficient to have a general intention, such as "For all those who have asked my prayers" or "For all those for whom I have promised to pray." I hope you will be able to lay aside your guilty feelings. After all, the purpose of our prayers is not to inform the Lord about what is going on, but to show our loving dependence upon him for our own needs and the needs of others.

Father Lowery, C.Ss.R.

DISTRACTIONS IN PRAYER

QUESTION: Whenever I try to pray, I am plagued with a thousand distractions. How can I learn to control my mind better? It seems like the harder I try the worse it gets.

ANSWER: Maybe you are trying too hard. You've heard how some baseball hitters "press" when they're trying to come out of a slump. Their very effort to overcome their problem is making them tighten up more. They are so worried about the mechanics of their swing, stance, or grip that they can't hit the ball. That's why their coach might advise them to "stay loose in the batter's box." We could use the same advice in our approach to prayer. Do your best to pray well, but don't be too upset if your prayer is not "perfect." When a distraction comes, treat it as you would a fly buzzing around your head. Occasionally shoo it away, but don't spend all your time and concentration on it. The good Lord can read your heart. He loves you just as you are, distracted mind and all.

Father Kaler, C.Ss.R.

QUESTION: Sometimes strange thoughts go through my mind. I don't know where they come from. Last Sunday at church I caught myself thinking, *Darn it, I want to get up after Mass and go out like others do instead of staying here to pray.* Was that a sin of disrespect?

ANSWER: No, it was not a sin to have that thought. All of us have wayward thoughts at times. These are just part of our human condition, things that happen to us when we feel irritated or out of sorts. We don't really mean them. Our Lord knows that. He knows we are trying to love him. So, the less you make of matters like this, the better. I hope you can be at peace about this.

Father Kaler, C.Ss.R.

QUESTION: Often when I say my prayers, I can't keep my mind on them, and discover I'm finishing a prayer without having thought of it as I said it. Then I go back and say it all over again. Am I doing the right thing?

ANSWER: I really don't think this is advisable, because when a scrupulous person starts this repetition route, it is like falling into a sticky spider web; you turn and twist, and there doesn't seem to be any way out. Distractions are almost as natural as breathing; even the saints couldn't pray without them. So make a good intention, say your prayer, and even if your mind wandered far, don't repeat it.

Father L. Miller, C.Ss.R.

THE CELEBRATION OF THE MASS

QUESTION: I am at the point where I actually dread attending Mass. I feel that each word must be said with the utmost devotion, so naturally I fall behind in the prayers and readings. By the time Mass ends, I am tense and nervous from trying to catch up. I know God can't be too pleased with this sort of performance, but I just can't seem to do otherwise.

ANSWER: God is always pleased when he sees our good intention, and this is clear in your case. But remember that God is kind and merciful and knows our human frailty. He knows your difficulty in following all the prayers, and I feel sure he will be well pleased if you concentrate just on every other prayer, or even every third prayer. Prayer, even the Mass prayer, is not supposed to be a strait-jacket.

Father L. Miller, C.Ss.R.

QUESTION: If I am not paying attention during some part of Sunday Mass, do I have to make it up later? For example, if I daydream during the reading of the gospel, do I have to read that gospel later? And if I don't do that, have I failed in my obligation? Have I sinned?

ANSWER: No, on all counts. God sees your good intention in attending Mass. He understands how easy it is to be distracted during even the holiest of actions. I recommend that you do not repeat any of the Scripture readings or prayers of the Mass. Otherwise this could get completely out of hand.

Father Kaler, C.Ss.R.

QUESTION: Are major distractions that come during Mass serious sins? I mean sometimes I realize after the consecration that my mind was a million miles away, or I was thinking of something completely trivial like a TV show I had seen the night before. When that happens, did I miss Mass, even though I was physically present?

ANSWER: No, you didn't miss Mass, and you've committed no sin. There are two kinds of distractions: deliberate and not deliberate. You've been the victim of not deliberate distractions. Think of them as something like a sneeze or a cough. You hope you don't have to sneeze or cough at Mass or at any public gathering (such as a concert), but it might happen anyway. In a similar fashion, you may hope that distractions don't interfere with your prayers and attention at Mass but they might come anyway, even during the most sacred parts. The Lord understands. Tell him you're sorry and you hope to do better next time.

Father Kaler, C.Ss.R.

QUESTION: Recently after something happened that upset me very much, I attended daily Mass and received holy Communion. I could not keep my mind on what I was doing and wondered if that was a serious sin.

ANSWER: Not at all. This happens to everybody at one time or another. Circumstances can send a flood of distractions into our minds, and they keep buzzing like bees in a beehive, even at the time of prayer. God understands how we are made, and what he looks to especially is our good intention and our honest effort. Try to be recollected, but gently, without force, and leave the rest to God.

Father L. Miller, C.Ss.R.

QUESTION: I had a regular confessor for many years. Four years ago he died at the age of eighty-two. Since then I have been making my own decisions to the best of my ability and taking into consideration his past advice. I am at an impasse concerning his advice to me that one should never go on vacation if one couldn't get to Mass on a Sunday because of the vacation. I didn't have the courage to ask him if it was actually a mortal sin to miss Mass while traveling. I have been afraid to travel at all when Sundays would be involved. Please advise me if it is a sin to miss Mass on Sunday when traveling. Of course, I would attend if at all possible.

ANSWER: For centuries the Church has had an explicit law obliging Catholics to participate at Mass on Sundays. The obligation is certainly considered a serious one. To deliberately miss Mass without a sufficient reason is considered a serious (not light) transgression of the law of the Church. At the same time, the law of the Church, in this case as in others, is not unreasonable. Proportionate reasons excuse a person from participating at Sunday Mass. There is no doubt that taking a well-earned vacation is sufficient reason for missing Mass if necessary. Once on a trip to the Far East I missed not only Mass but also the whole of Sunday when I crossed the International Date Line! Your affirmation that you would attend Mass if at all possible is a clear indication to me that you have no problem and should not hesitate to take a vacation trip when possible.

Father Lowery, C.Ss.R.

QUESTION: I have a neighbor lady who is elderly and has to travel by taxi to go anywhere. I am distressed because she is not going to Sunday Mass. I have at times invited her to go with me. She told me that her confessor said she is not obliged to go because she is old and physically challenged. I know she watches the TV Mass early Sunday morning. But I think in her heart she worries about this obligation. I would like your advice because I would like to help her.

ANSWER: It is good to be concerned about your neighbor, especially since she is elderly and physically challenged. But, as far as the Sunday obligation is concerned, she should follow her confessor's advice. Should she express any worry about it to you, you can reassure her that she is acting in a way that is pleasing to God. If occasionally you want to invite her to go to Mass with you—if she feels up to it—that would be all right; but make sure she doesn't think it's an obligation.

To sum up, following her confessor's advice is the right thing to do. It's nice that she watches the Mass for shut-ins on TV, and you can encourage her in that. But if she misses it for any reason, she needn't worry about that, either.

Father Kaler, C.Ss.R.

Chapter Eight

Thoughts That Cannot Be Shaken

Not a day goes by that I do not find myself daydreaming, my mind wandering to some unconnected thought or action having nothing to do with the moment at hand. I might be sitting at a meeting. I might be watching television. I might be saying my prayers or attending Mass. Out of nowhere, I find myself distracted by something else and I almost have to force myself to concentrate on the present moment. I don't believe this is unusual. In fact, I am pretty sure this is a normal occurrence for all people.

On still other occasions, I find myself thinking about something that surprises me. More often than not, it is an opinion that I would never think of expressing, or sometimes a judgment, seemingly made on the spur of the moment. When thoughts such as these occur, I am again pretty sure that I am not the only person in the universe who experiences such occurrences. Even though they happen, I do not consider myself to be responsible for them. I just think they are a natural part of being human, and I try not to think anymore about it.

On still other occasions, I find myself thinking thoughts that seem weird, or sometimes sexual, and, at times, even thoughts that might seem violent. Again, such thoughts surprise me. They surprise me, not because I don't consider myself capable of the weird, the sexual, or the violent (although I do not normally choose such expressions), but rather because they seem to come to me unplanned for. I do not freely choose to be distracted by such thoughts, and I certainly do not choose the moment that they happen, but they are, nevertheless, part of my reality. Again, I believe they are a natural part of being human, and I try not to give them anymore attention than they deserve.

The power of the mind is awesome. The mind, our ability to think, to plan, and then to put into action our choices and decisions, is one of the greatest gifts that our Creator has given us. However, it is also good to remember that not everything the mind spends time on is under our control. Such a blessed and powerful capacity oftentimes seems to have "a mind of its own."

I am not talking about demonic possession. I am not talking about psychological illness. What I am referring to is the normal, the everyday, and the natural. However, for the scrupulous person, what is normal, everyday, and even natural is not always understood as such.

When the *SA* archives are examined, a persistent question becomes immediately obvious. This question—actually, it's a type of question—complains about distractions in prayer or in work, and then assumes that such an everyday occurrence is somehow sinful. Such questions portray simple distractions, which are everyday normal occurrences of life, in a manner that assigns a seriousness and sinfulness to such thoughts that is simply unwarranted. There is no way a human person can be completely 100 percent focused without some form of distraction in life. It seems to be how God created us. Distractions are normal and are simply not sinful, no matter how surprising they may be, even when such distractions take place at Mass or when a person is praying his or her prayers.

Still other letters from the archives reveal questions dealing with unwanted thoughts (as I myself just acknowledged) of a weird, sexual, or violent nature. The questions insist, and rightly so, that these thoughts just seem to appear, and often with some frequency. Again, there is an assumption that, since such thoughts cause some embarrassment or because they deal with sexuality or violence, they then must be sinful.

When I have been asked a question that concerns an unwanted thought, I try to assure the person immediately that no sin has occurred because the thought has not been freely chosen. Since free choice is necessary for sin, there can be no sin when something appears uninvited and unwanted. However, with this answer, I am often confronted with a second, follow-up question: "But Father, I freely chose to dwell on the thought, and so therefore I must have sinned."

"No, you did not sin," I tell them. "What you did was to come to a conscious awareness of the thought. In other words, you gave the thought some attention; otherwise you would not have even known that you had the thought in the first place." I try to assure the questioner that mere awareness of a thought is not an indication that he or she has chosen to sin; there can be no sin involved in the involuntary awareness of something: "Don't confuse something that is distasteful, embarrassing, or associated with a strong feeling, as something that therefore must be sinful."

There is, however, another type of question that, when asked, clearly indicates that the person who asks the question is in need of some professional help. What I have in mind here are those questions that detail a thought to which the person assigns a power and a responsibility which is not the usual interpretation of that thought. For example, there are people who believe when they think of a natural disaster, such as a tornado, and a tornado occurs, that somehow—voluntarily or involuntarily—they caused it and are responsible for the disaster because they were *thinking* about a tornado. More often than not, the thought doesn't even have to be as dramatic as a tornado; they might think something like, *I wish that Mary has a bad day,* and because I wished it Mary will have a bad day and I will have seriously sinned.

Human beings do not have the power to translate random thoughts into this type of response. No human person can be the cause of such a reaction simply by thinking about it. And if they think they can, they need professional help. Because—even though

I am sympathetic—we're now talking about something more than scrupulosity. I can only imagine the pain and the agony such a person must suffer as they assume to themselves, and believe as very real, that they are responsible for all that is going on around them. It is a terrible cross to bear.

IMPURE THOUGHTS

QUESTION: I love my husband and would never be unfaithful to him, but I am constantly troubled with bad thoughts and desires. I do not want to have them, but sometimes I am not sure whether I consent to them or not.

ANSWER: So-called bad thoughts and desires are common human experiences. Like some house visitors, they often come unbidden and stay as long as they please. In themselves they are not sinful. The fact that you love your husband, intend to be faithful to him, and do not want the alien thoughts and desires indicates to me that these are temptations, not sins. Therefore, there is no need to confess them.

Father Kaler, C.Ss.R.

QUESTION: I look at statues and get bad and impure thoughts. Is this a big sin?

ANSWER: You should not consider yourself guilty of sin if, while gazing at the crucifix or the statue of the Little Flower, Saint Joseph, or your favorite saint, your mind runs wild with sexual images. You are not committing a sin. And you do not have to tell it in confession. In fact, it would be better if you did not tell it in confession, since it is all swallowed up in doubt and uncertainty. You are only feeding your scruples when you keep bringing up these things in confession. By constantly feeding them you make them so fat and heavy that it becomes almost impossible to shake them off.

Father L. Miller, C.Ss.R.

QUESTION: I am plagued with immodest and impure thoughts and feelings, sometimes even in regard to Jesus. This makes it hard for me to go to confession. Is it really necessary for me to explain these thoughts and feelings, or could they be confessed just in a general way?

ANSWER: You should not confess these things at all. They are not sins. You do not truly desire and want these thoughts and sensations. You do not sin when they occur. They are mosquitoes in the mind, pests that make a terrible nuisance of themselves. But they are certainly not sins. You should disregard them. They are not a matter for confession.

Father Farnik, C.Ss.R.

QUESTION: When I look at the crucifix or think about Jesus I often get impure thoughts in my mind about Christ. I seem more likely to be this way when I am upset or afraid. These thoughts come at the most unlikely times and I don't want them. Sometimes it seems that the more these thoughts upset me and the more I try to push them out of my mind, the more of them I have.

ANSWER: You are not the only scrupulous person who suffers from these obsessive thoughts. It is a rather common malady. There seems to be a certain perversity in the imagination of a scrupulous person that makes that person's thoughts return again and again to what he fears and dreads. Impure thoughts about Jesus or about saints or about priests or religious or about statues or the crucifix, God knows about this. God sees what is happening, and he sees how this troubles you. God is not shocked or scandalized or offended by this. I suggest that your best approach is to talk about these thoughts to God himself. Do it in your own words. For instance, "Dear Lord, you see right into my heart and into my mind and into my imagination. You know how obsessed I get with these terrible thoughts, how they keep coming back, and how guilty and unworthy they make me feel. But I don't know how to make them go away and stay away. I have a crazy, mixed-up imagination. Lord, if this is a suffering and a cross that I must bear, I accept it and I carry this burden in imitation of Jesus."

Or maybe in your prayers a bit of humor or poking fun at yourself will help. "Lord, those screwed up thoughts are back plaguing me once more. Here is your weirdo child talking to you again. You know I don't want to consent to anything sinful. But it is so impossible to be sure what I give any consent to and what I don't. So I put my weirdo self in your hands, Lord." If you deal with these thoughts as though they were too terrible to tell God about, then they will continue to plague you indefinitely. But if you can learn to pray about them to God and talk honestly to God about them, then you will learn to see them in perspective. They are not horrendous at all. These seeming mountains will come to be seen as the molehills they really are.

Father Lowery, C.Ss.R.

QUESTION: I am troubled with bad thoughts and desires. I am afraid to bathe or brush against my breast for fear I will feel sexual pleasure. I have harmful and envious thoughts about others. I am afraid to watch TV because of the bedroom scenes. I'm even afraid I'm abusing my health by getting so upset about these things and that maybe that is a sin also. My common sense tells me these are either no sin at all or, at most, venial sins, but I'm never sure so I stay away from holy Communion. When I see so many people receiving Communion, I want so badly to go, but I can't because I feel so unworthy.

ANSWER: I have quoted at some length from your letter because it is so typical of the scrupulous conscience. One moral theologian even defines a scrupulous conscience as "one that sees sin where there is none or sees mortal sin where there is at most venial sin." I know that you are suffering terribly. I would like to encourage you in two ways: (1) Listen to your common sense. It is a gift of God, and he wants you to use it, despite your fears and doubts. Say *no* to these groundless fears and doubts. (2) Receive holy Communion whenever you participate in the Mass. Say *no* to your false fears and worries and approach the Lord's table. No one could ever be really worthy to receive the Lord. The point is that he wants you there.

Father Lowery, C.Ss.R.

QUESTION: If I have an impure thought and just leave it there, is that automatically a mortal sin?

ANSWER: There is no such thing as an "automatic" mortal sin. Sin of its very nature involves sufficient reflection and full consent of the will. The simple fact that an impure thought comes to your mind does NOT mean that you have committed a sin.

Father Kaler, C.Ss.R.

QUESTION: I frequently find myself tempted to commit sins against purity. I have to admit that at such times I feel a strong, a very strong, attraction for what is being presented. Since I'm so strongly pulled in that direction, does this mean there is something wrong with me or that I've already sinned?

ANSWER: The mere presence of a temptation, no matter how intense or long lasting, doesn't mean that a person has sinned. A temptation would not be a temptation if it did not tempt, that is, if it did not offer something that appeared attractive. The fact that you experienced its pulling power doesn't mean that you gave in to the temptation or that there's something wrong with you. There's a story about Saint Catherine of Siena, a great mystic and wonderful saint. One day she experienced a most severe temptation that lasted for hours. She prayed and prayed, but nothing seemed to help. It was agony for her, since she felt that she was on the brink of offending the God she loved so much. Finally the temptation left and the Lord appeared to her in a vision. "Oh, Lord," the saint complained, "where were you when I needed you? Why didn't you answer my prayers?" The

Lord responded, "Catherine, did you sin?" "No, Lord, but I came so close." "You didn't sin, Catherine, because I was in your heart the whole time." Saint Paul has a similar story. He also complained to the Lord when he was tempted. Read what the Lord answered him in 2 Corinthians 12:7–10. Finally, the best advice I can give: Try to love the Lord as much as Catherine and Paul did, and you'll have nothing to worry about.

Father Kaler, C.Ss.R.

QUESTION: I had some thoughts concerning the possibility of being raped. I would hope, if the situation would occur, that the rapist would use protection to protect me from HIV, pregnancy, and whatever. Are my thoughts and feelings mortal sins?

ANSWER: Your thoughts and feelings are not mortal sins, they are simply imaginings about a potentially serious problem. My reaction is, "Why worry about such things? Life has enough real problems of its own without becoming concerned with 'what if' scenarios." The amount of emotional energy that is spent on people, events, and experiences beyond our control is unproductive, at best. Live in the present moment now, in love. That is where you will discover God, and in the process of discovering the presence of God, you will discover the absence of fear, anxiety, and guilt. God bless.

Father Santa, C.Ss.R.

QUESTION: The most horrible, impure thoughts come to my mind over and over again, especially at Communion time. I have horrendous thoughts about Jesus. If I can't get to confession first, I stay in my pew and do not go to Communion because of these horrible thoughts. What should I do?

ANSWER: Regardless of your thoughts, you should go to Communion. I can say this with absolute certainty, because when fear goes out of control, it becomes a disease. That is what scrupulosity is: uncontrolled fear of having done wrong. You know that you suffer from this disease. You also know that your fear allows these thoughts to obsess you. A vicious cycle then sets in and you find yourself depriving yourself of holy Communion—the very gift that the Lord desires for you the most. For a person suffering as you are suffering, the best advice is to try and find the strength to force yourself out of your pew, to walk down the aisle, and to receive Communion. This is the strongest statement that you can make to your fear. "I am not guilty, and I will not be punished!" May God bless you.

Father Santa, C.Ss.R.

QUESTION: Am I right about this? A bad thought is mortally sinful only in the following cases: (1) You deliberately dwell on an impure thought in order to have forbidden sexual feelings; (2) you really plan to carry out the evil you are thinking about [for example, you deliberately think of stealing your neighbor's car and really hope or plan to do just that]; (3) somebody else commits a serious sin. In your mind you think about what he or she has done and you really and truly agree with it. Any other "reasons" for bad thoughts are not mortally sinful. For example, you might have a thought in your head practically all day long—such as, *I'm going to rob a bank...I'm going to rob a bank.* But as long as you don't desire or plan to do the evil, you have committed no sin. Do you agree with my explanation?

ANSWER: Yes, I think your explanation is quite correct. If you, as a scrupulous person, can live by your own explanation, you should be able to spare yourself a lot of torture over bad thoughts.

Father Lowery, C.Ss.R.

DREAMS

QUESTION: I have been told that one is not responsible for what happens in one's dreams. Does this apply to impure dreams? I experience them occasionally and it worries me.

ANSWER: There is no need to worry at all about what happens when you are asleep. You have to be *awake* and *conscious of what you are doing* for there to be any sin connected with bad thoughts or actions.

Father L. Miller, C.Ss.R.

QUESTION: I know we are morally responsible for impure thoughts that we hold in our minds, but are we also guilty for what goes on during sleep or in that twilight state of consciousness just prior to waking? I don't have too much trouble with waking thoughts, but I do have recurring battles with dreams and twilight fantasies and don't know if I should confess these or not.

ANSWER: You cannot be morally responsible for dreams or semi-conscious fantasies. These cannot be sins. This is clear if you recall the classic "conditions for mortal sin": grave matter, sufficient reflection, and full consent of the will. Sufficient reflection implies that a person is clearly aware of the seriousness of the action he or she is contemplating or the choice he or she is making. Full consent of the will means that a person freely chooses to do what he or she knows is seriously evil, even though he or she could stop from doing it. Sleep or half sleep renders such reflection and freedom impossible. Therefore, dreams and twilight fantasies cannot be sins and should not be confessed.

Father Lowery, C.Ss.R.

QUESTION: I have been having trouble with dreams in which I commit sins against the sixth and ninth commandments. I sincerely wish I didn't have these dreams. I try to get them out of my mind when I am fully awake. But then I'm afraid of going to Communion without going to confession. Since they aren't willful, should I keep on going to Communion without confession and ask God to help me?

ANSWER: It is not possible for a person to commit a sin while asleep. (I repeat in capital letters: IT IS NOT POSSIBLE!) We have no direct control over dreams, and therefore we have no moral responsibility for them. No matter what you dream, no matter how vivid your dreams are, no matter how frequently the same topics return, there is no question of sin! Therefore, there is no need to confess your "evil dreams," and there is no reason to abstain from Communion because of them.

Father Lowery, C.Ss.R.

QUESTION: I have a problem that is making my spiritual life miserable. I make a good confession, go to bed eagerly looking forward to holy Communion the next morning, and that night I have an impure dream. This has happened so often, I'm afraid to go to sleep. Sometimes I even take sleeping pills so I won't dream, but still I do. I know we are not responsible for dreams, but these dreams are so impure that when I awaken I feel unclean and sinful. I feel I could have controlled them but didn't want to do so because I really wanted them. I seldom receive holy Communion because of these terrible dreams. I would rather die than make a sacrilegious Communion. What should I do?

ANSWER: I am saddened that you allow this kind of problem to destroy your peace of mind. Morally speaking, dreams don't count! You have no direct control over your dreams. Dreams cannot be sinful. Sin always demands a free and deliberate choice. No such choice exists in regard to dreams. You say that you feel you could have controlled these dreams, but that is a false perception on your part. You also say that when you awaken you feel unclean and sinful. But sin does not consist in having such feelings. To me it is very sad that you do not receive holy Communion because of dreams over which you have no moral control. I strongly encourage you to put your trust in the Lord, to act against your fears of sin, and to receive holy Communion on a regular basis, dreams or no dreams.

Father Lowery, C.Ss.R.

QUESTION: I've had long years of scrupulosity and I don't want to start up again. I am worried about believing in dreams. When I was a child we were told that believing in dreams was against the first commandment. Now psychologists talk a lot about dreams. My dreams are not sad or tragic. Once I even dreamt I was in heaven. If I could have the satisfaction that it's OK to think about my dreams, it would make my waking hours happier.

ANSWER: You use two different terms about your dreams: "believing in them" and "thinking about them." There is certainly nothing wrong in thinking about your dreams or even trying to analyze them. But some people get themselves in trouble by "believing" in dreams. That is, they take their dreams as absolute truth or as omens for the future. Dreams are fascinating. If you enjoy thinking about your pleasant dreams, no problem! But do not take them too seriously.

Father Lowery, C.Ss.R.

QUESTION: When I awoke one morning I remembered having a dream. Later on it seemed so real that I don't know if I was awake or asleep. If I were awake, it would have been a sin. This bothers me, and I don't know if it should be told in confession.

ANSWER: You aren't sure you were awake, and therefore you should dismiss this whole matter from your mind. There was no sin, and you should not mention it in confession.

Father L. Miller, C.Ss.R.

THOUGHTS OF ANGER AND/OR VIOLENCE

QUESTION: At times when trying to fall asleep, either when I first go to bed or after I awaken, thoughts of cursing and swearing flash through my mind. I do not use this type of language and would be happy if these thoughts never came. But I'm not sure whether I should confess them or not.

ANSWER: No, you should not confess them. It is obvious that it is not your intention to use such language. But this cannot stop the subconscious mind from dredging up some thoughts from time to time. Stay calm and try to turn your thoughts into another channel. There is no sin.

Father L. Miller, C.Ss.R.

QUESTION: I have frequent thoughts and desires to curse people and wish them to die—like the pope, my bishop, my pastor, Jesus and the Blessed Mother, my deceased husband and my parents, and so forth. I really don't want this to happen, but I am afraid if I don't confess these thoughts and desires, I will be making a bad confession.

ANSWER: You will not be making a bad confession. These thoughts and desires are nothing but strange little quirks of your imagination. Everybody's imagination puts together some strange things in dreams during sleep. Some people's imaginations just seem to work overtime and keep putting together some strange things even while these persons are awake. That is OK. There is nothing wrong in that. These thoughts and desires are not sins. Forget about them. Don't confess them. Your confessions will be perfectly correct and good and in order without confessing such things at all.

Father Farnik, C.Ss.R.

QUESTION: I have problems with all kinds of hostile, violent, and angry thoughts that keep me from receiving Communion more than once or twice after I have gone to confession. Please help if you can.

ANSWER: Obviously, you realize that God would like all his sons and daughters to live in harmony and peace and not harbor hostile and angry thoughts toward one another. In the ideal world, as God would like it to become—everyone would love everyone else in thought, word, and deed. But we don't seem to have such a world. Sometimes we are treated unfairly in some way by others. We see our neighborhoods going downhill, the streets not as safe as they used to be, and crimes and burglaries increasing. Naturally, we feel afraid, we get angry, and we feel hostile when we see how unfair this is to good people and to old people. Also, older persons do not have the patience they had when they were young adults. Now they get very irritated with the neighborhood children who skate on their sidewalk, run over their lawn, play the radios extremely loud, and so on. Your thoughts and feelings of anger, hostility, and violence are understandable in this world in which we have to live. These thoughts and feelings are not of a serious nature and do not exclude you from holy Communion. You may continue to receive our Lord in Communion in spite of such feelings and thoughts.

But I recommend that you think about the gentleness of Jesus when he comes to you in Communion. As Jesus hung on the cross in pain, he prayed for forgiveness for his executioners. Ask our Savior to give you a greater share in his gentleness, mercy, and forgiveness. Offer your own sufferings and troubles to our Lord and ask him to join them together with his own offering and gift to the Father. This can be a big help. Don't think you should refrain from going to Communion. Remember that Communion is not for the perfect—it is for the imperfect who want to grow more like Jesus and who realize they need to grow more like Jesus. Each day try to say the prayer that Jesus said from his cross: "Father, forgive them; for they know not what they do."

Father Lowery, C.Ss.R.

QUESTION: For the past five years I have lived daily with the fear that I walked in my sleep one night and killed a man. My psychiatrist tells me to keep pushing this thought out of my mind, as it is an obsession. But this is very difficult to do. Some days are pure torture for me.

ANSWER: It would seem that this indeed is a deep-seated obsession you have, and in such a case professional advice from a psychiatrist may be necessary. I am glad you have sought it. On the spiritual side, try to strengthen your confidence in God by frequently saying in your heart, "My Father in heaven, I trust in your mercy."

Father L. Miller, C.Ss.R.

QUESTION: Lightning and thunder almost drive me out of my mind. I saw in a magazine somewhere that these eruptions of nature are signs of God's anger, that when someone is leading a wicked life he hurls down upon the person's head a bolt of thunder or electrocutes him or her with a streak of lightning. I must admit that I am not a particularly good person, though I never killed anybody or robbed a bank. That's why I'm so afraid. To my shame, I even crawl under the bed when the lightning and thunder are more than ordinarily fierce. Tell me, is what I read about God true? Is he pursuing me with thunderbolts? And can you tell me how I can overcome my fear?

ANSWER: It is quite possible for God to use thunder and lightning to show people his power. But he is not out to "get you" in this way. There are 300 million people in the United States, and the yearly average of 66 people who die in this way were standing in the middle of an open field or under a tree or on top of a tall building when the storm came. They were a target for the lightning. So, come out from under your bed and stand erect. You have nothing to fear from the sky as long as you use the precautions suggested by the experts. God has other plans for you. Don't worry any longer.

Father L. Miller, C.Ss.R.

QUESTION: I experience frequent episodes of terrible thoughts: insults to God, the saints, doubts of faith, and so forth. They are very brief, but fill me with feelings of intense guilt and depression because I can't seem to conquer them. My rational mind tells me I am a true believer, but these thoughts worry me. What can I do?

ANSWER: Such thoughts are not unusual in some states of scrupulousness. Perhaps it will help if you regard them as the rust on the outside of a water pipe that is carrying pure, sweet water. The rust outside doesn't in any way touch the water inside. You don't want these thoughts, and there is no sin in the mere fact that they come to you.

Father L. Miller, C.Ss.R.

QUESTION: I have feelings that people are going to die, or that I want them to die, sometimes for no reason at all, and at other times out of resentment or anger for something they did to me. One priest told me I should see a psychiatrist. Am I guilty of mortal sin if I refuse to see a psychiatrist about this? I have seen a psychiatrist twice before and he did not help me. I am in a dilemma and need your advice.

ANSWER: I think you are making a reasonable judgment, based on your past experience, that a doctor will not bring you any benefit and relief from this obsession with death. When these thoughts come to you, tell yourself, *Of course, he or she is going to die. Every person is going to die. Death is the doorway that every person must stoop down and go through in order to enter into eternal life with God. Jesus has gone through that doorway already, and the Father in heaven has raised him back to life.* This belief in our future resurrection is the basic belief of all Christians. That's why Saint Paul could write in a sort of mocking way, "Where, O death, is your victory? / Where O death, is your sting?" (1 Corinthians 15:55).

Father Lowery, C.Ss.R.

SPONTANEOUS AND/OR OBSESSIVE THOUGHTS

QUESTION: My question is, I have many spontaneous thoughts that go through my mind when I see someone. Like, upon seeing a neighbor who has hurt me in the past, I'll think, *Oh, there she is. I hope she's envious of me,* and so on. Or, I'll just have a resentful feeling come over me. I apologize a lot for these things. I don't want a critical or judgmental or resentful attitude, but it's like…spontaneous; it just pops into my mind. I would like to know if these spontaneous thoughts and feelings are sinful. When do they become sinful?

ANSWER: You used the word *spontaneous* three times in your letter, which is the tip-off to this entire matter. The most common meaning of spontaneous is "arising from a momentary impulse." These impulses are going to come to the average person whether or not he or she likes it! There is no way to avoid all such momentary impulses. But how can they be sinful? Sin, by any definition, involves a firm act of the will, a deliberate choice of what you know to be evil or immoral. The idea of sin is the direct opposite of a momentary impulse. You will find help, I believe, in simply accepting the fact that some of these impulses are going to occur and reoccur. Accept! Don't fight or panic! When you become aware of them, gently turn your mind and will away from them. They are a fact of human life, but there is no way they can be sinful. Be at peace.

Father Lowery, C.Ss.R.

QUESTION: I'm terribly troubled by evil thoughts that keep coming into my mind. Sometimes they are so immoral or so sacrilegious that I'm shocked I would have such thoughts! Oftentimes they come at the most sacred of times, like during Mass or just before holy Communion. How can a person be sure that consent to these evil thoughts was not given?

ANSWER: It's the nature of obsessive thoughts to come unbidden into your mind (so you're not at fault there). They are also very stubborn, very difficult to dislodge (so you're not at fault that they remain in your mind). So, they persist even though your common sense, your goodwill, and everything says you would like nothing better than to get rid of them. You ask, "How can one be positive that consent to these evil thoughts was not given?" It is impossible to consent to these thoughts when you don't want them (and you don't, that's why they are so upsetting). It's just a fear you have because these thoughts are so bad, or so sacrilegious. So, say to yourself, *These are those strange, obsessive thoughts. I don't want them, but they probably won't go away. But I have better things to do than to worry about them. The less I make of them the better.* And, of course, continue to go to holy Communion. There's no sin there.

Father Kaler, C.Ss.R.

QUESTION: Though I sometimes have trouble deciding the morality of a given act, my main problem is obsessive thinking of various specific ideas or the general idea of mentally sinning. If my obsessive thoughts should be freely approved, they would be mortal sins. Also, I seem to have a need for absolute certainty about religious truth. What suggestions do you have in this matter?

ANSWER: In reference to obsessive thinking and free will, my answer can be short and to the point. By their very nature, obsessive thoughts are not freely chosen. People do not freely choose to become obsessed. Therefore, there is no way that you can be guilty of sin when you are talking about obsessive thoughts, no matter how grievous they may be and no matter how bad they may make you feel. You did not freely choose them, and for something to be a sin there has to be an element of free choice.

Regarding your question about your need for absolute certitude in reference to religious truth, there is no such thing as absolute certitude. That is where faith comes into play. Even the most central doctrines of the Church (which I believe and firmly hold, so I am not questioning them) cannot, in fact, be proven with absolute certitude.

A person of faith will argue that they are absolute, but a person with no faith will argue that they are not. That is the way faith is. May God bless you.

Father Santa, C.Ss.R.

THOUGHTS AS POWER

QUESTION: I have trouble with wishing evil on people. When I was a girl I wished my neighbor would get sick, and he did. I prayed hard for him and he got better. One day I got upset at someone and I wished her to have cancer. Now she has cancer and I feel it is my fault. I pray for her a lot. Sometimes I wish that bad accidents would happen and that people would get hurt. I really don't want these terrible things to happen, but these thoughts keep coming anyway. Am I committing sin in having all these evil thoughts?

ANSWER: No, you are not sinning by having these thoughts. They are nothing but strange little quirks of your imagination. Everyone's imagination puts together some strange things in dreams during sleep. But it seems that some people's imaginations work overtime and keep putting together strange things, even while these people are awake. This is what is happening in your case. These disturbing thoughts and wishes come unbidden into your mind. You don't want them. And, of course, your thoughts are not the cause of someone's getting sick or being hurt. Try to ignore these "strange things." The less you pay attention to them, the better. They are not sins.

Father Kaler, C.Ss.R.

QUESTION: Could anyone do bodily harm of any kind to someone else by thought or desire, and would this be a grievous sin? Would God listen to such prayers that people might be hurt?

ANSWER: We have all heard stories about voodoo practices and putting a curse on someone, and the Bible tells us that "the devil goes about like a roaring lion, seeking someone to devour." I don't see how it can be denied that there are evil influences abroad in the world. But they aren't set in motion by the spiteful thoughts that we all have now and then, when we find ourselves wishing that so-and-so would "get what's coming to him." God isn't about to loose a thunderbolt on someone just because, in a moment of fretfulness, we find ourselves wishing that that person would get knocked down. Don't get all tensed up about these thoughts. Calmly try to replace them with good and positive thoughts.

Father L. Miller, C.Ss.R.

LOSING FAITH

QUESTION: What am I going to do? I have lost the faith. In a moment of despair I said, "I don't believe in God." So that means I can't be a Catholic anymore, and I can't receive Communion. I'm so troubled. What am I going to do?

ANSWER: I don't think for a moment that you have lost the faith, even despite your saying, "I don't believe in God." This was simply a cry of agony in your darkness, and the Lord, who is merciful to our human frailty, knows that you didn't really mean it in the deepest part of your soul. Make a little act of sorrow and, by all means, receive holy Communion the next chance you have. You need the consoling presence of Christ.

Father L. Miller, C.Ss.R.

QUESTION: I am troubled with all sorts of doubts of faith. I find these thoughts very frightening and I don't know what to do with them. I say some desperate prayers, but they don't seem to help because then I get doubts about them. Have I lost my faith? Have I committed many terrible sins? Please help me.

ANSWER: Let me say right away that it's not a sin to have these worries and doubts. They seem like doubts of faith, but they really aren't true doubts. I have seen this kind of thing happen to very good, holy people. In fact, some of the saints tell how they went through terrible periods of darkness during which everything they believed in and had worked for seemed to be gone. Saint Thérèse of Lisieux said several times that her faith seemed to have vanished, that her prayers seemed to be going nowhere, and she felt that she was lost. Other saints have expressed the same sentiments. You are not alone in what you are experiencing. Saint Alphonsus recommends that a person who is hounded by such "doubts" should not try to argue with them in the heat of battle, should not have a type of debate right there, giving reasons why such a doctrine is believed, but rather should "run away"—that is, make a brief act of faith and try to move on to something else, get involved in some distracting activity. The temptation or "doubt" might persist (it most likely will), but it isn't necessary to keep repeating acts of faith. Don't believe these dark feelings. The devil is the father of lies. He is trying to make you think you are lost when you are not. By making you upset and agitated, he keeps you from your prayers and other good deeds.

To sum up, when a doubt arises about anything just say a short prayer, such as "My Lord, I believe in you, I hope in you, I love you." Once you have said a little prayer, you can ignore the temptation (you don't have to keep repeating prayers), even if the temptation or "doubt" keeps roaring in your head. Remember that the dear Lord can read your heart and knows that you do not want to offend him, but rather to love him with your whole heart.

Father Kaler, C.Ss.R.

QUESTION: I am troubled by all sorts of doubts of faith. I find these thoughts to be very frightening and I don't know what to do with them. Have I lost my faith? Have I committed a sin of despair?

ANSWER: It is not a sin to have doubts of faith. I don't believe there is a person who ever lived who has not experienced a doubt of faith. In fact, I would go so far as to say that it is almost necessary to have doubts in faith in order to become a faith-filled person. Let me explain. When you have a doubt, the only way to assure yourself of the doubt is to study, reflect, and pray. When you do these things, you enter into a process of "claiming as your own" that which you doubted. You now believe, not because you are supposed to believe, and/or not because someone told you to believe, but rather because you have come to your own sense of faith and belief. This kind of process is needed for an adult faith. It is not something that should be feared, but rather something that should be seen as a necessary step in growing in faith.

Father Santa, C.Ss.R.

CONCLUDING ADVICE

QUESTION: How can a person be absolutely certain that he has resisted sufficiently all impure, obscene, or blasphemous thoughts or desires that have come to him? This seems almost impossible to me. But without this certainty, how can peace of mind be achieved?

ANSWER: You have expressed very well the dilemma that is at the heart of much scrupulosity. Of course, it's important to know how one stands before the Lord. At the same time, it's very difficult to measure what one's resistance level was when under stress, not to mention other conditions that might have been present. There is so much ambiguity here that it all seems hopeless, doesn't it? But take heart! There is a way out of this dilemma. You might not believe it at first because it sounds like a paradox, but it's the truth. You don't need absolute certainty in this matter! All you need is a doubt. That's right, a doubt! The doubt can be about the origin of the thoughts or feelings (Did I bring them on?), about the gravity of the matter (Is this really a serious matter?), about the level of attention at the time (Did I realize what was going on?), about the promptness and vigor of the resistance (Did I resist fast enough and strong enough?), or any other aspect of the whole situation. If there is any kind of doubt, then you have nothing to worry about. Scholars, saints, and confessors have been saying this for ages. But one SA member put it best of all: "The key concept is simple—namely, to resolve all doubts in your own favor." That hits the nail on the head. It is the best advice that can be given to the scrupulous!

Father Kaler, C.Ss.R.

QUESTION: I read a quotation that is ascribed to the late Father Daniel Lord, SJ: "If there is a doubt, there is no doubt." What did he mean?

ANSWER: I am not familiar with the context of this saying, but it is certainly true as applied to scrupulous people. If you think you might have committed a serious sin, if there is doubt in your mind, then you did *not* commit a serious sin. If you *had* sinned, you would know surely, *without any doubt*. This is a safe principle to follow. May God bless you!

Father Santa, C.Ss.R.

QUESTION: I have all sorts of doubt and fears about sin. I don't know whether or not I should confess something or whether I was specific enough. What if I am wrong, what can I do? Should I depend on the mercy of God and try and convince myself that God has understood?

ANSWER: By all means, depend totally on the mercy and the forgiveness of God. When all is said and done, the only thing we have is our faith in the mercy and forgiveness of God. The second thing you should do is remind yourself of the two rules we have often repeated in this newsletter:

1. Doubtful sin does not have to be confessed. You do not even have to give a doubtful sin a second look. You can forget about it completely.
2. Doubtfully confessed sins do not have to be confessed. If you remember having told in confession certain possible sins in any way, then you can forget about them. You don't have to

ask: Did I give enough detail? Did I explain it well enough? Did the priest really understand what I was talking about?

Please remember to place yourself in God's mercy, that is, try and permit yourself to experience the loving embrace of your God in heaven. After all, you are most precious to God. May God bless you!

Father Santa, C.Ss.R.

Chapter Nine

All About Sex

A few years ago I was privileged to be invited to direct a series of retreats for religious men and women. The religious brothers and religious sisters who attended the retreat were all active in their community, and very well-respected ministers. About halfway through the ten-day retreat experience, a young religious brother, informed about my ministry with the scrupulous, came to me and shared with me his poignant story about sexuality and scrupulosity. It is a story I found to be very helpful in understanding what can sometimes happen to good-hearted people who are struggling with scrupulosity, and who desire nothing more than to serve the Lord. I am grateful to him for his permission to use his story in the pages of this book.

The young brother, about twenty-five years old at the time, committed an act of masturbation. It was his intention to confess the act and to seek the absolution that he desired. However, it was not possible for him to go to confession at his place of residence (there were priests in his community, but he was too embarrassed to confess them—a completely understandable reaction). His desire to celebrate the sacrament of reconciliation was further complicated by the fact that he did not have access to an automobile and did not have the necessary time to make an appointment with a confessor.

As is the tradition in many religious houses, the Eucharist was celebrated daily, and all members of the community were required to be in attendance. He attended the Mass, but when the time came to receive holy Communion he felt trapped. To go to Communion in the perceived state of serious sin was a sacrilege; to not go to Communion was to reveal to the gathered community that he was in serious sin (there could be no other reason)—a very uncomfortable choice.

So the brother decided to go to Communion, but not consume the Blessed Sacrament. On his return to his pew he removed the host from his mouth, and reverently wrapped the host in a handkerchief. At the end of Mass, he went to his room and put the host in the drawer of his desk. In this way, he surmised, he was not committing a sacrilege and he was not revealing the state of his soul.

All the events and the circumstances of that first day were repeated, with the exception of the act of masturbation, for a period of eight consecutive days. It was impossible for him to secure a car and go to a church in order to celebrate the sacrament of reconciliation; it was impossible for him not to attend the community Mass; and it was impossible to not go to Communion without revealing the state of his soul.

His anxiety increased during this entire time. What would happen to him if someone discovered the hosts in his room? What would happen if he suddenly got seriously ill and died? What would happen if he were somehow discovered? What could he do? How could he stop this train to disaster?

Finally, on the ninth day, a missionary priest whom he trusted and admired returned home from a parish mission. The young brother immediately went to the priest and confessed not only his sin of masturbation but also all the other choices and decisions that were now related to this single act.

The brother was blessed that he confessed to a priest who understood the scrupulous condition and who was understanding and gentle. The priest informed him that from now on the brother was to go only to him for the celebration of the sacrament (establishing a relationship as the brother's regular confessor) and that when he was not home, regardless of what condition he found himself in, to go to Mass and to receive and *consume* the Blessed Sacrament. And finally, for his penance, he was to return to his room and immediately consume the eight hosts that he had stored in his desk drawer. There was no chastisement, only patient understanding and helpful direction. As the young brother left the room where the confession was celebrated, the priest said to him, "Now, go in peace, and believe in the Lord's love for you."

Not all scrupulous people who struggle with sins of sexuality are so blessed as this young brother was.

I receive many letters from people asking me particular questions about sexuality. I seldom answer them, not because I do not care or because I am not moved by their questions, but rather because I respect them and desire the best for them. Our story vividly illustrates my reasoning.

What made the memory of sexuality and scrupulosity a positive memory and not a negative memory for our young brother was his relationship with the confessor. It was the presence of the confessor, who was able to listen to him, and to listen not just for the sin, but also for the nuance, the feeling, and the interpretation of the act, that made the experience a positive experience and a blessed memory. All confession of sin profits from such a personal exchange; for sexual sins and concerns, it is essential.

In the questions that follow you will find a faithful reporting of the answers from five directors of Scrupulous Anonymous, with very few from me. This is because I have made it a policy not to regularly answer questions about sexuality in the pages of the *SA* newsletter. I have adopted this position, which has caused some consternation from the members of SA who are not in agreement with me, for a reason that is summed up in the following question and answer that I did address.

QUESTION: If I haven't confessed all of the sins that I have committed against impurity throughout my life are they nevertheless forgiven? I realize that it is difficult to know what has been covered and what has not. I hope to hear from you soon because I may not receive Communion until I do.

ANSWER: I mean this question, which will serve as the introduction to my answer to you, with all due respect to you and to all of the other members of our group. "Why are we always concerned about the sexual sins that we may have forgotten to confess? Why are our sexual sins more of a concern for us than any of the other sins that we might have not confessed as accurately as possible?"

I am afraid if I tried to answer the question that I posed to you it would take pages and pages of this newsletter and I would still not be able to answer it in a way that would satisfy all of our readers. But it is an important question to try and answer for ourselves. It is important to try and come to some understanding of why we might be so concerned about our perception that we might have some kind of unconfessed or imperfectly confessed sexual sins. Do we believe that God will deal more harshly with us because of our sins against the sixth commandment and not as harshly with us concerning the other nine commandments?

One possible answer is that we feel more responsible for our sexual sins because of the nature and the intimacy of the thoughts, words, actions, and desires associated with sexuality. Sexual expression always produces some deep feeling or emotion, the strongest, which seems to often be guilt, and as a result the memory is with us for a long time. Perhaps it might be helpful to bring before the Lord in our prayer, not the memory of our sexual sins, but rather the feeling of guilt that we often have as a residual memory and ask for his healing power and help in this regard. God bless you.

Father Santa, C.Ss.R.

QUESTION: My wife and I are both in our seventies and have been happily married for fifty years. Our sex life has always been important to us. Now, however, it seems that the sexual expression we once used no longer works for us. I am very uncomfortable with trying something new. I always worry that it will be sinful and that we will not complete the marriage act in the way that God intended. Could you please tell me what is acceptable and what is not acceptable?

ANSWER: Thank you for your letter and for the trust that you express in me by sharing your care and concerns. What I am about to say might seem to be a "cop-out," but it is the best answer that I can give you. It would not be either helpful or appropriate to answer your letter by mail or in this column. Your question deserves honesty and a real openness to God's will. To arrive at the answer you seek, a real time of listening is necessary. To accomplish what you need suggests a face-to-face dialogue. Sexuality, and questions dealing with it, is filled with nuance, and there are many questions I will need to ask you in order to provide you with an answer. As we talk, there will undoubtedly be other things you may want to tell me that are very important for us to understand the question we are discussing. We may even discover, as the dialogue continues, that sexuality is not the primary issue and that there are other issues that are even more important.

For all of these reasons, I suggest you seek an appointment with a priest or with someone else whom you trust, closer to home. You might find such a person at a local retreat center or possibly at Catholic Social Services. My experience is that people in these helping ministries will be more than happy to steer you in the right direction. You might also be surprised to discover that your local pastor might also prove to be a valuable resource. In conclusion, let me state that I know it took courage for you to write to me. Let me also state that I am aware that my letter of response might not be what you had in mind. However, I do believe that it is an honest answer and it is an answer that will serve you best in the long run. God bless!

Father Santa, C.Ss.R.

In a sense it would be easy to answer questions about sexuality. The Church has a strong tradition of moral teaching about sexuality, and it would be a simple matter to faithfully report the teaching. Admittedly, there are some voices in the Church who propose that this is always the correct response and who would urge this response to any question I may be asked. However, I am troubled by this approach because I do not think it is helpful in the long run.

I understand sexuality as always being relational. By relational, I understand sexuality to be a form of communication with self, with another, and with society at large. All sexual acts, even the most intimate and the most seemingly private, "speak" about who we are, what we believe, and what we hold as sacred and as special. For this reason I believe that all discussions about sexuality, including even the simplest question and answer, should always include the components of listening, respect, and, above all, an attitude of patience and understanding. That is why I insist on a face-to-face meeting with a regular confessor and why I am hesitant to answer any questions in the *SA* newsletter or through personal correspondence.

SEXUAL CONCERNS

QUESTION: My husband died twenty-five years ago very suddenly, and without having the opportunity to receive the last sacraments. Not long before that, we had committed sin together. If I caused him to go to hell, is there any chance for me to save my soul?

ANSWER: There is unlimited chance for you to save your soul, bounded only by the infinite mercy of God. And you can certainly have good hope also that this same mercy reached out to your husband so that he had sorrow in his heart for his sins before he died. It is important for a scrupulous person not to keep looking backward in life. What is past is past; the significant thing is that here and now we can always make a new beginning; we can start over with God's grace, like the morning sun shining before us. Don't look back. Look ahead!

Father L. Miller, C.Ss.R.

QUESTION: I have a great deal of perplexity in regard to "words" that are parts of the body. I despise impurity, yet I frequently bring these words to mind. I certainly don't enjoy them, but many times I think, *Should I think the word?* and I do. I feel this is sufficient reflection and full consent of the will, making for mortal sin. Due to my uncertainty, I have been to holy Communion only about seven times in the last thirty years.

ANSWER: It truly saddens me that you have been so tortured by this compulsive behavior and that you have stayed away from Communion for no good reason. The parts of the body are not impure; they are the creation of God. Nor can any words make them impure. Nor is your bringing to mind these so-called impure words a matter of mortal sin. I can only encourage you to try to find a regular confessor, explain this entire matter to him, and do as he advises. I hope that you will at least be able to deal with this problem in a more constructive way; and, above all, I hope you will soon be present at the Lord's table where you belong.

Father Lowery, C.Ss.R.

QUESTION: The book, *Helps for the Scrupulous*, by Russell M. Abata, says that as a human being you are a sexual person. You are either a male or a female and, if you are normal, you will often have sexual feelings toward others. Could you explain in the *SA* newsletter how sexual feelings affected Jesus? He was human in this way, too, wasn't he? If so, how did he handle these feelings and were others sexually attracted to him? Do you ever think that he may have felt attracted to Mary Magdalene and would have liked to have married her and have a family, if he hadn't also been God with another purpose in mind? I hope it isn't wrong for me to have these thoughts and to ask these questions.

ANSWER: It isn't unusual (or wrong) for good, sincere people to have questions about Jesus' humanity. It means that his human nature is being taken seriously, that Jesus was truly human, not just pretending to be one of us. It means realizing that Jesus possessed a full human nature, that is, he had a human body, a human soul, a human will, a human intellect, a human imagination, human emotions and feelings, and a human subconscious. Of course, at the same time Jesus also possessed the fullness of the divine nature, that is, he was truly God. In a word, we believe that he was both human and divine.

But with regard to his humanity, does this mean that Jesus might have had sexual feelings, that he might have been attracted to Mary Magdalene, that he might have liked to marry her if he hadn't had another purpose to fulfill? We start with these truths: In God's plan human sexuality is a good. A person's maleness or femaleness is good. Marriage is good. The dual purpose of the marriage act is good: (1) the begetting of children [the continuation of the human race], and (2) the act of self-giving love of the spouses for each other. Jesus would have had the highest respect for and appreciation of the goodness of human sexuality in all its aspects. What about his own feelings as a male? Did he feel attracted to the opposite sex? A comparison might help. Picture a husband who is deeply in love with his wife. He loves everything about her. He loves her so much he considers himself the luckiest man in the world. In fact, he views the whole world from this happy perspective. Let's say another woman enters the picture. She is beautiful and very attractive. How will he act? He will instinctively be attracted to her. At the same moment, he will be seeing her within his own unique worldview, that is, the great love he has for his wife. Does he have to deny that the other woman is attractive? No. Does he have to feel guilty that he experienced the attractive qualities of this woman? No. But does he think, *If I weren't married, I would like to marry her?* No, because it doesn't get that far. Because of his great love for his wife, because she is his world, the presence of another attractive woman isn't even a temptation for him. Her beauty and attractiveness only serve to remind him how blessed he is to have his own beloved wife as his wife.

Every comparison limps, but something like the above scenario could help us understand Jesus' worldview. Scripture tells us that Jesus was completely given over to doing the will of his Father (which was our salvation), that it was his meat and drink, that he would freely carry out his Father's will, even if it meant suffering and dying, which it did. Would Jesus have experienced instinctive attractions toward certain individuals (such as Mary Magdalene)? Yes. Would this have been sexual? Only in the broadest meaning of the word, that is, a male was responding to a female. But in Jesus' total worldview (which was his Father's), genital sexuality was to be used only within the confines of marriage. And since his Father's will did not include marriage for himself, a particular question along those lines would not have even come up. Our Lord's human mind and will, his imagination and feelings, and even his subconscious, were never out of line. Their various relationships were all perfectly ordered to every other part of his humanity. This doesn't make Jesus a cold, unfeeling automaton. Quite the contrary. His emotions would have been all they were meant to be, free and strong, but always subject to his mind and will.

Perhaps we cannot understand how emotions can be that way, since we have trouble controlling ours. But sin has entered our lives. Original sin has darkened our minds and weakened our wills, and our own personal sins have abetted this. But sin never entered Jesus' life, so his emotions would have been in perfect harmony with his worldview, that is, with the will of his Father.

Father Kaler, C.Ss.R.

SEXUAL CURIOSITY

QUESTION: At times when I read the paper or watch television, an item or a picture will appear that has to do with sex, like a rape story or scantily dressed chorus girls. I try to stop reading or to look away. But often I find myself taking a second look, as it were, a kind of peek, a furtive glance out of the corner of my eye. I do this perhaps three or four times before I stop completely. Then I start to worry. Did I commit a sin? Should I run over to confession? What should I do in the future? Stop reading the paper? Stop watching television?

ANSWER: None of these things. When you see something not very nice in the paper or on television, look away for a moment. If your eyes grab a second glance momentarily, don't consider yourself guilty of a mortal sin. Not at all.

Father L. Miller, C.Ss.R.

QUESTION: I have a very peculiar and humiliating problem. When I was about fourteen years old, I went to my friend's house and he was taking a shower. I went into the bathroom to visit him and we talked. When he got out of the shower, towel drying himself, I touched one of his private parts—not from an impure motive, but rather a motive of teasing. Did I commit a sin by this action?

ANSWER: The quick and easy answer to this question is a resounding NO. You did not commit any sinful action in anything you did. In fact, what you did do was simply be present to a friend, in this case a friend who was nude, and you engaged in some horseplay. My guess would be that what makes this instance a painful and a humiliating memory for you has nothing to do with your horseplay, but rather has a lot to do with the fact that your friend was nude. If the same set of actions took place and your friend was not naked, would you have had the same response? Many times people are uncomfortable with nudity and often associate nudity with sexuality, and sexuality with sin. With this starting point, your interpretation of the experience was that, since your friend was nude, the experience was sexual—and, hence, the experience was "sinful." However, nudity and sexuality are not necessarily the same thing. While it is true that many forms of sexual expression demand nudity; it is also true that there are particular times in our lives when we are very sexual and we are not nude. It is also true that sexuality is sometimes sinful, but not all sexual activity is sinful.

In your experience, there are present many different ingredients of what is sometimes associated with sexuality, but these were not, in fact, associated by you in a sexual way. As a result, you are not guilty of sin. God bless, and be at peace.

Father Santa, C.Ss.R.

MARRIAGE

QUESTION: I have been widowed almost two years. But lately, I feel the urge to be with my husband sexually. I think I truly take pleasure in these feelings. I am worried about this. Is it a sin?

ANSWER: It seems to me that too often in the past we Christians have approached the reality of our human sexuality in too negative a way. We tended more to stress the dangers of sin than to foster the goodness and positive aspects of this gift of God. A husband and wife usually experience sex as a way of sharing themselves and revealing the love, tenderness, devotion, and trust they have for each other. Sexual union involves their bodies, their emotions and feelings, their minds and wills, and their very souls. The many years of married life together form deep and enduring habits of sexual feelings and experiences. When death comes to one of the partners, it is wholly natural, and to be expected, that the body, mind, and emotions of the other spouse still retain these memories and experiences and feelings and desires.

Since God himself made human beings in this way, surely these memories and feelings must still be good, even after the death of one's spouse. God made us in such a way that we cannot jump out of our skins. We cannot cut ourselves off from our past history and from all that has been a vital part of our lives. So my judgment is that these feelings and memories that remain are good, not bad. Give thanks to the Lord for the marriage you enjoyed and for the love you and your husband shared together for so many years.

Father Farnik, C.Ss.R.

QUESTION: I worry about my past sins. I confessed these sins many years ago, but I wonder if those confessions were really good. Here's where my problem lies: I can't feel sorry that things turned out the way they did. For example, because of much abuse, my first marriage ended in divorce. I then met a wonderful, gentle man and married him outside the Church. Eventually my first husband died, and the Church blessed the second marriage. Now my beloved second husband has died and I miss him terribly. No matter how I try, I can't feel sorry about those years with him, even those years when I wasn't able to receive the sacraments. What should I do? Should I continue receiving Communion?

ANSWER: Yes, continue receiving Communion. Life can be very complicated and confusing at times. Good and evil can be all mixed up. Often it's difficult to analyze our feelings. They can be all over the place. We can be happy about certain aspects of a situation and unhappy about other aspects. My advice to you is: Don't waste your time trying to figure out your feelings about this whole matter. It's not necessary. It's all right to assume that your past confessions were good. You are trying to lead a good life. The Lord knows that, because he can read your heart. He has been with you throughout your life. Put your worries aside, and be thankful for the many blessings God has given you.

Father Kaler, C.Ss.R.

HOMOSEXUALITY

QUESTION: Could you say something helpful for those who are homosexually oriented? I know they are expected to refrain from genital sex, as are all unmarried people, but coping with mental tension is the hard part.

ANSWER: I think the words of the American bishops, in their pastoral letter of a few years ago, are helpful to the homosexual person and enlightening to other Christians. The bishops point out that some men and women have a homosexual orientation "through no fault of their own." While acknowledging that such persons carry a special cross because they cannot ordinarily look forward to a fulfilling marriage and family life, the bishops encourage these persons to play an active role in the Church community, develop a life of prayer, and concentrate on the virtue of charity in their lives.

Father Lowery, C.Ss.R.

QUESTION: I am a homosexual. Although I do not have, and never have had, a sex partner, I can't help the fact that I'm attracted to men and not women. I cannot believe that God will banish me to hell because of this. What is the Church's teaching on homosexuality?

ANSWER: The American bishops explain the Church's teaching in this way: "Some persons find themselves through no fault of their own to have a homosexual orientation. Homosexuals, like everyone else, should not suffer from prejudice against their basic human rights. They have a right to respect, friendship, and justice. They should have an active role in the Church community. Homosexual activity, however, as distinguished from homosexual orientation, is morally wrong. Like heterosexual persons, homosexuals are called to give witness to chastity, avoiding, with God's grace, behavior that is wrong for them, just as nonmarital sexual relationships are wrong for heterosexuals. Nevertheless, because heterosexuals can usually look forward to marriage, and homosexuals, while their orientation continues, might not, the Christian community should provide them with a special degree of understanding and care" (*To Live in Christ Jesus*, 976).

Father Kaler, C.Ss.R.

MODESTY

QUESTION: I have a bunch of questions about modesty. Is it wrong to buy clothes that make me look attractive? Is it wrong to wear polyester and rayon materials that sort of cling and are thin enough so that undergarments can be seen in a hazy way? Is it wrong to use a padded bra to look more feminine? Is it wrong to wear shorts or snug jeans when cutting the grass or working in the garden, even if one of my neighbors is a bachelor? Would I be responsible if I was a source of temptation to him?

ANSWER: Dressing in a modest way depends very much on the current times and customs. For instance, early in this century, even bathing suits kept almost the entire body covered. At that time, every bathing suit sold today would have been a scandal, a sensation, and a temptation. Because customs gradually change, and because customs differ from place to place, it is impossible to lay down hard-and-fast rules about what is modest and what is not modest. You have to use common sense. Also, you have to accept yourself and your body as gifts from God, as good and wholesome. Your body is not shameful and evil, and no part of your body is shameful or evil. It's all standard equipment and a gift from God and created by God and intended by God. So accept yourself as a bodily being, a wonderful creation of God. Use common sense in your way of dressing. Dress appropriately for the beach, appropriately for church, appropriately for working outdoors. Follow the current practices of other ordinary, decent people. That's all that God asks you to do.

Father Lowery, C.Ss.R.

QUESTION: I am concerned about modesty. I went twelve years to a Catholic school, and our nuns talked much about modesty. I am now forty-nine. We were always reminded what was allowable—no strapless dresses, no two-piece bathing suits, no short shorts, and so on. This has been a problem to me my entire life. I have always worried if my clothes were too tight or if I wore shorts in the garden that someone would see me. Of course, my husband thinks I am being ridiculous.

ANSWER: Modesty is not an absolute virtue but a relative one. I am firmly convinced that an adult Christian woman can determine what is modest and what is not. I do not think you need a long list of rules. I have often suggested that a scrupulous person accept the advice of others on matters about which they are troubled. I suggest that in regard to modesty of dress you let your husband be your guide. He has your good at heart, knows your hang-ups, and should be a safe guide for you.

Father Lowery, C.Ss.R.

SEXUAL THOUGHTS AND FEELINGS

QUESTION: In Father Abata's book, *Helps for the Scrupulous,* there is a chapter on sexual feelings. I am single. Father Abata says that to suppress or ignore such feelings is only asking for trouble. Well, I get into trouble when I deal with them openly. It just brings on thoughts about sex, and before I know it, a thought comes that only makes matters worse, and I think that I am committing a mortal sin. So I am going to do battle against all sexual thoughts and feelings until I hear your verdict.

ANSWER: A scrupulous person tends to think that every thought or feeling of a sexual nature is sinful. This is simply not true, and this is the point Father Abata is trying to stress in his book. Very often a person who has resolved "to do battle against all sexual thoughts and feelings" runs into a lot of difficulty. It is much better to be relaxed about the normal, natural sexual thoughts and feelings that tend to arise. We must always remember that sin is in the will and is a fully deliberate choice of evil. I would say that your basic understanding of sin in this matter is off course. It would be helpful if you could approach all sexual matters in this context.

Father Lowery, C.Ss.R.

QUESTION: Are all thoughts about sexual matter sins? Suppose a person feels an attraction for a particular sexual thought, would that be a sin?

ANSWER: The phrase "all thoughts about sexual matter" covers a lot of ground. Some people would say that every thought is "sexual" in a sense, because everyone is either a male or a female, which would influence the thought patterns of that individual. But that's not what is being asked about here. What about those more explicit sexual thoughts that sometimes flash through a person's mind? The normal good person doesn't pay much attention to them. It usually doesn't come to a crunch, that is, to decision time. Even if he or she might feel a momentary instinctive attraction for some of these thoughts or feelings, they are quickly brushed aside. In fact, they wouldn't stand a chance against the person's strong value system, his or her honest stance before God. So these passing thoughts or feelings are simply that: passing thoughts or feelings. At best they are weak temptations that didn't get a second glance. They are not sins.

Another point: Married people have the right to have sexual thoughts about their spouse, even very explicit ones. It's all part of God's plan of procreation, their partnership with God of bringing new life into this world. What about those people (who are not married) who deliberately conjure up thoughts about sexual matters by reading obscene literature or by watching pornographic shows? If they are not mentally deranged, if they know what they are doing, if they know it offends God—that's a different matter. The three conditions for mortal sin would most likely be present:

(1) serious matter, (2) sufficient reflection, and (3) full consent of the will.

(P.S. for our SA members: This question and answer was not put here to cause any difficulties. If you have worries in this area, please talk them over with your confessor. If he doesn't know already, be sure to tell him you have scrupulous tendencies.)

Father Kaler, C.Ss.R.

QUESTION: I am deeply troubled by sexual thoughts. There are times when I am tempted to masturbate in order to reduce the tension that I feel. I usually resist this temptation because I know it is a mortal sin. What I do is try and distract myself with something else. Sometimes I just pretend that I am not bothered, and I hope my feelings just go away. I don't think any of this is really helping. Do you have any suggestions that you could give me that will solve my problem?

ANSWER: As many times as I answer a question about sexuality or write a reflection on the subject, I am invariably asked another question or prompted to provide a further clarification. Unfortunately, most questions about sexuality, answered in the forum of a question-and-answer column, by their very nature need to be very general and not at all specific. All people, by the fact of their humanity, are sexual. Sexuality is also very personal. Each individual person has particular sights, sounds, smells, events, and experiences that are sexual for them but may not be at all sexual for someone else. A primary reason for this is the fact that sexuality, and by extension, sexual expression, is subjective and open to interpretation. In addition to finding its expression in many different forms, sexual expression is also a very powerful drive within the human person.

It seems that sexuality demands attention and cannot be ignored or repressed for any length of time; it demands to be listened to! If we close off one avenue, another path will be discovered. The key to finding peace with your sexuality lies not in trying to suppress it, but rather in learning how to dialogue with it. Try to come to an understanding of why you feel sexual. What is it that happens to you when you feel you are the most sexual? How do you feel when you have urges and desires? When are the periods in your life that you feel the least amount of sexual energy or desire? Are there any other questions that you feel you need to discover an honest answer for? Sometimes scrupulous people feel they are committing a serious sin when they think about sex. As a result, they are not able to enter into a dialogue or an understanding of who they are as sexual persons.

If you find yourself in this category, I can only strongly recommend that you find a confessor or a counselor who will help you in this process. I know it is frustrating and difficult to find someone to help you, but I also know that it is worth the effort. By coming to an honest answer and appraisal of yourself as a sexual person, you will then be able to understand your sexual needs, desires, and expressions. When you begin to understand who you are and what you need, you will then be able to recognize the signs of what you are feeling and pay attention to your needs before you find yourself in a situation or in an experience that you would prefer not to be in. In the long run, this might be far more helpful than trying to determine what is sinful and to what degree; not because this is not important, but rather because such a response will not lead to a healthy and grace-filled solution. May God bless you!

Father Santa, C.Ss.R.

QUESTION: I am seventy-one years old, a widow for the past six years. I sometimes experience strong sexual feelings and thoughts when I recall my happy and intimate years with my husband. These feelings and thoughts almost overwhelm me at times. Are they mortal sins?

ANSWER: I am sure they are not mortal sins; they are perfectly natural. Instead of worrying about them, I suggest that when you are aware of them you take a moment to thank God for your loving husband and for all the love you shared and expressed to each other.

If you do that, you will soon find that these feelings and thoughts are not occasions of sin, but rather occasions of gratitude and love.

Father Lowery, C.Ss.R.

QUESTION: When you read in the newspaper about immoral happenings, and have sexual feelings, is that a mortal sin?

ANSWER: Sexual feelings in and of themselves are not mortal sins. They are only sinful when they are knowingly and willingly fostered. Scrupulous persons should pay as little attention as possible to sexual feelings that arise from reading a newspaper story.

Father Lowery, C.Ss.R.

QUESTION: I suffer a lot from anxiety, anguish, fear, and panic when I am not able to deal with thoughts, feelings, and fantasy. I dread their very coming into my mind, lest they cause sexual feelings. I fear that I will not be able to control these, but oftentimes there are no sexual reactions at all. Regardless, I still think I am gravely guilty, I try to fight them, then panic, suffer from fatigue and loss of energy, and become depressed. I run off to confession, but in a short time I am back to square one again, and it becomes a vicious circle. I can never be sure whether these are grave matters, but it is so hard to explain what I mean by "these." Are they feelings of anxiety about being guilty, a kind of emotional response, or a kind of shock or panic when the very thought, image, or fantasy hits my mind; or are they voluntary acceptances? Once the problem is objective, I am not bothered. But once it is subjective, I look into my own conscience and analyze all aspects of the matter. What can I do?

ANSWER: The sense of pain and real suffering is very much present in your letter. Your description of the process that engages you provides an insight and an introduction to the depth of feeling and emotion truly present in the scrupulous mind. My heart goes out to you, and I pray that you enjoy some peace. My answer may well seem cold and heartless, especially in comparison to your question.

However, my answer may help you find the peace you seek. It seems your main concern is that these thoughts, feelings, and anxieties that you describe may lead to sexual feelings. For some reason, you make the assumption that sexual feelings, when they occur, must be sinful, and therefore avoided. You pour all your energy into trying to avoid such thoughts and feelings, in the hope that you may then avoid the sexual feeling they create. You feel hopeless because the attempt does not work. The reason your attempt to deny sexual feelings does not work is that you are a sexual person.

God made us to be sexual people, and we cannot not be sexual. In addition, sexuality is a particular "energy" within us. For some mysterious reason, all the emotional energy you are using to deny your sexual feelings, and to avoid them, in fact feeds the "sexual energy" that is within you. Which is why, as you reported, you return to "square one" again and again. By fighting the possibility of having a sexual feeling, you are in fact encouraging and enabling the sexual feeling. Now, is this sinful? No, sexual feelings are not, in themselves, sinful. Is this frustrating and exhausting? Yes. By your own testimony, you witness to this truth. What can be done? With the continuing grace of God, and with the help of a confessor or counselor, you need to come to an understanding of who you are as a person. You need to learn the normal reaction of the body—including the normal reaction of your body as a sexual person. This includes coming to the realization, and hopefully enjoying the peace of mind this realization brings, that sexual thoughts and feelings are part of who we are. Our Creator made us this way. To avoid, or expend efforts in an attempt to avoid, any sexual thought or feeling accomplishes nothing. May God continue to bless you!

Father Santa, C.Ss.R.

SEX AND TELEVISION

QUESTION: My biggest dilemma is how to handle scenes on TV that are immodest and immoral. My youngest son living at home is twenty years old. Even a momentary flash of something on the newscast makes me wonder if I should jump up and turn it off and risk feeling foolish. Different priests have given me advice: Ignore it….Use the issue as a means to instruct younger children….Check the TV guide beforehand….I have also been told my children are old enough and I cannot control what they watch. I hope you can help me with this matter.

ANSWER: You have already received very good advice. All the points you mention are helpful. Certainly a "momentary flash" of any kind should be completely ignored. I agree that your children are beyond the formative years and will probably decide on their own what they are going to watch. For yourself, be calm. Do not make too big a deal out of small things. Yet, when it becomes evident that a show is immoral (and I would emphasize that "immoral" refers not only to sexual matters but also to pagan philosophies of life and violence), we should simply turn it off, choose another channel, or do something else. When younger children are still at home, TV provides a good springboard to discuss moral standards, Christian approaches to life, and what we, as individuals, believe in.

Father Lowery, C.Ss.R.

QUESTION: At times, when watching television shows that include romantic scenes, I am aware of sexual sensations. I am uncertain just when these physical sensations become sinful. I try to avoid shows that are blatantly sexual, but sometimes a usually good show will have an episode that bothers me, but not the rest of the family, so I feel trapped into watching it, and then feel I have sinned.

ANSWER: Since the shows you are talking about are basically good shows, and since they don't bother the other members of your family, I think you should simply forget about any passing sexual sensations that you may experience. Such sensations are not of themselves sinful. The less attention you pay to them, the better off you'll be.

Father Lowery, C.Ss.R.

MASTURBATION

QUESTION: I am too embarrassed to talk to my priest about this. I am a teenage girl and I would like to know why masturbation is wrong. I am very scrupulous, and after I commit a sin I feel I must confess it immediately. I feel guilty and sad because I've done wrong. But I'm so scared of God punishing me that I need to confess right away or I punish myself with guilt. Please help me.

ANSWER: The first point of advice I want to give you is that you find yourself a confessor with whom you feel comfortable. Go to confession to him on a regular basis. At the outset, it will be important to explain to him the problems and difficulties you have been experiencing, your fears and guilt feelings. Please do not let embarrassment hinder you from doing this. Masturbation is a common problem, especially for young people, and you will find that the confessor will be understanding and helpful.

Also, I want to say just a few words in response to your question. (A complete response would take much more space than is available here.) Catholic teaching on masturbation was presented in a document from the Vatican Congregation for Catholic Education, entitled *Educational Guidance in Human Love: Guidelines of Sex Education* (1983). The document emphasizes that masturbation is "a particularly complex and delicate problem." The teaching of the Church is that, objectively, masturbation is a serious moral disorder "principally because it is the use of the sexual faculty in a way which essentially contradicts its finality, not being at the service of love and life according to the design of God." At the same time, the Church recognizes that many personal and subjective influences can underlie this habit and advises that we be "cautious in evaluating the subjective responsibility of the person." Most important, the person struggling with this problem should try to keep growing toward self-giving love, to be open and interested in others, be involved in works of justice and charity, and have recourse to prayer and the sacraments. Crippling discouragement and guilt are fierce enemies in this particular struggle. That is why I recommend a regular confessor with whom you can communicate and from whom you can obtain positive guidelines.

Father Lowery, C.Ss.R.

QUESTION: I am a single person who for many years has been plagued with the habit of masturbation. Even with my best efforts, prayers, and spiritual counseling, I have been unable to overcome it. It always makes me feel tremendously guilty and worthless. I feel like a hypocrite going to confession. This is the main thing that keeps me from receiving the Eucharist. Is there any way of knowing if this is a mortal sin in my case?

ANSWER: I can only recommend to you what I have recommended to others so often in these pages: Get yourself a regular confessor. If you explain to him the problem you have and what you have tried to do about it, he will be able to discern with you the state of your soul regarding sin and what approach you should take in receiving the Eucharist. At first glance, this advice may not seem very helpful to you. But, practically speaking, it is the best advice I can give you.

Father Lowery, C.Ss.R.

QUESTION: I have never been able to get a clear-cut answer as to whether masturbation is a mortal sin. If a person avoids as much as possible the occasions that lead to this, isn't a necessary requirement of mortal sin lacking?

ANSWER: I don't think this question can be answered with a simple yes or no. So much depends on the individual case and the particular circumstances. Masturbation can be serious, but often is not because of lack of full deliberation or consent.

Father Kaler, C.Ss.R.

QUESTION: I know this is a delicate matter, but why does the Catholic Church condemn masturbation so severely? It seems like just about everyone else sees nothing wrong with it. It's hard to keep to the Church's teaching when the rest of society says it's all right.

ANSWER: When the Catholic Church condemns the practice of masturbation, it's merely stating traditional teaching—teaching that goes back many centuries. The Church is speaking objectively, that is, it is saying that this action, by its nature, goes contrary to the God-given purpose of human sexuality. The sexual organs of one person are clearly designed to be used in conjunction with the sexual organs of the opposite sex. Use of this organ alone, then, indicates a turning in toward self, rather than toward the other. There is a basic self-centeredness involved. This occurs in place of an action that is supposed to be totally self-giving, so self-giving that it has the potential of becoming life-giving, of becoming a cooperative venture with God and a spouse in the bringing forth of a living human being.

The fact that the Church speaks objectively in this way does not mean that there is a lack of compassion or understanding in the concrete situation. Confessors and moral theologians are aware that oftentimes there are several reasons why a person might be acting in this way and yet not be committing serious sins. As you know, there are three requirements for a mortal sin: (1) serious matter, (2) sufficient reflection, and (3) full consent of the will. Some people, indeed, are not aware that there is serious matter here. Usually they are not at fault for their lack of awareness. Poor instruction, prevailing ideas of their surroundings, and so on, prevented them from acquiring a well-formed conscience in this matter. Many people began this practice while very young and have it so ingrained in their life that they instinctively do this whenever they become pressured. In that case they would surely be lacking in sufficient reflection or full freedom. Changing a habit is very difficult, especially if the habit is long-standing and tied in with one's feelings. That's why I recommend that you try to find a confessor you can consult with. The right confessor can be a great blessing from the Lord. He can help you not only in this matter but also with the whole area of scrupulosity. Meanwhile I will keep you in my prayers.

Father Kaler, C.Ss.R.

ABORTION

QUESTION: I am seventy-six years old. When I was only nineteen I was already married and had one child and discovered I was pregnant again. My husband had become very ill. My parents were in Europe, but my uncle arranged for me to have an abortion. I didn't even know what abortion was. After I knew what abortion was, I confessed my sin and repented, but even now I feel so guilty and depressed. I can hardly stand it.

ANSWER: I want to encourage you to place your trust in the Lord. Your sin is forgiven. He loves you very much. Try to let go of the past. I also want to encourage you to talk about this matter with someone whom you trust. It may be that you have never really had the opportunity to unburden yourself of all your feelings and fears. It would be helpful, I believe, if you could talk it out with a friend or counselor.

Father Lowery, C.Ss.R.

Chapter Ten

Three Very Important Considerations

Every question is important. There is no such thing as a question that has no value. If the question has been formed within a person's consciousness, and is consuming the energy of worry, anxiety, and fear, it requires an answer. However, that being the case, it is also true that at the moment when the question is consuming energy, it is probably not the best time to try and educate yourself or try and reflect on the "bigger picture."

In my experience there are at least three very important considerations that can be subjects of great concern for a scrupulous person, and, as such, require special effort. The task of trying to learn about the subject, trying to understand what may well be going on, and the opportunity to perhaps acquire a different point of view, is well worth the time that may be required.

The three considerations include the perennial fear that is routinely identified as the sin against the Holy Spirit; understanding the dynamic of impulse and compulsion; and clarifying the decision-making process that is required for responsible citizenship. In one form or another each of these considerations appear again and again in the questions that are frequently asked.

THE SIN AGAINST THE HOLY SPIRIT

One of the single most persistent questions that I am asked, almost on a monthly basis, is a question about the sin against the Holy Spirit. It is a question that has its roots in the following biblical reference: "Therefore I tell you, people will be forgiven for every sin and blasphemy, but blasphemy against the Spirit will not be forgiven" (Matthew 12:31).

The fertile ground that gives rise to the fear, anxiety, and sense of eternal doom associated with the sin against the Holy Spirit is easily identified. When a person is very tired, worn out, and discouraged with all of the other possible manifestations that may accompany the scrupulous condition, there is yet one more ultimate doubt and anxiety that may occur. It is at the moment of the greatest vulnerability when some people begin to think they have committed the ultimate sin, the sin against the Holy Spirit.

What happens is that the person becomes so overwhelmed with the constant doubts, the anxieties, and the supposed never-ending presence of sin in their lives. When this happens, and they contrast this feeling with the feeling of what they fantasize a "graced person" must be thinking and feeling (I deliberately use the word *fantasize* here), they come up short in the comparison.

As a scrupulous person begins to go through the list of what they presume this imaginary graced person must be feeling like they eventually stumble across the thought that perhaps they are so different because they have given up hope or something that is essential. Perhaps they are tormented with sin and doubt because they have not fully cooperated with the grace of God in their life. Perhaps, if they would have only tried harder, or prayed harder, or resisted harder or whatever, they would not be in the predicament that they now feel that they are in. (Remember, this is all a manifestation of the crooked-thinking fantasy of the scrupulous condition, out of control.)

When this thought first begins to take root the scrupulous person moves on to the next step. Immediately they search for an answer to explain this latest feeling of desperation and they inaccurately assume it must be because they have somehow sinned against the Holy Spirit. Why not, every other possible combination of sin has been explored and worried about up to this point, why not fall prey to the ultimate fantasy of the ultimate sin?

Now, at this point some of our readers may find themselves reacting to my use of the word *fantasy*. "How can something be a fantasy when it seems so real, when there is so much pain and suffering?"

The power of our mind, the power of our imagination is an awesome gift that has been given to us by God. Imagination is necessary and useful for the human person. It is because of the gift of our imagination that we are able to solve problems, that we are able to see a way out of a difficult situation. Our imagination permits us to perform a simple task, such as purchasing a new shirt or a new outfit, because we are able to imagine what we will look like when we wear it. Our imagination permits this simple task, while at the same time our imagination permits us to perform more complicated tasks. Every person who has ever purchased a new home or moved to a new job knows the power of imagination helps us make the decision to take such a big step: we see ourselves living in the new house or performing the task and so we make the decision.

Just as imagination is an awesome gift that serves us well, imagination can also contribute to persistent feelings of inadequacy, or incompleteness, weakness, or even sin. We can become, at times, almost paralyzed into not making a decision or taking a chance because we can imagine only the worst possible outcome. Just remember the time when you were young, standing against the wall of the gym, waiting to be asked to dance for the first time: all the possible scenarios of disaster you were able to imagine!

The combination of strong feelings of inadequacy, the incorrect assumption that somehow ordinary and graced people do not have feelings of anxiety or doubt, and finally, the conditions that are present in the person that encourages the imagination to consider the possibility of the ultimate doubt and fear, all contribute to the false conclusion that somehow the sin of blasphemy against the Holy Spirit has been committed.

My personal belief is that any person who struggles with scrupulosity, a person who desires so much to please God that he or she doubts constantly of being capable of doing so perfectly, is incapable of committing the sin of blasphemy against the Holy Spirit. The decision to commit this sin, the necessary components of the conditions of grave and serious sin, are simply not operable. At the same time I believe that many scrupulous people are capable of imagining that they have committed this sin and they are capable of assuming to themselves the fear and the anxiety that go along with this sin. However, that being said, there is a huge difference between the sin and the fear of sin.

I realize of course, after asserting that scrupulous people are incapable of committing the sin against the Holy Spirit that some of our readers have already dismissed the validity of the assertion. These readers are so gripped by the manifestation of their scrupulosity that when a positive and life-giving direction is provided, which should provide them with a sense of relief and freedom, they assume that it does not apply to them. Such people consistently see themselves as the exception to everything because they are so bad, so sinful, and misunderstood. For these people I repeat my earlier assertion. "Even you are incapable of committing the sin against the Holy Spirit!"

I also believe that there is very good news that can be shared with each of you in reference to our discussion about this sin, and this good news may very well surprise some of you.

It is my experience that when this scenario of the imagination is being played out, when all of this fear and anxiety is being experienced, there is an even stronger, although many times not seen or even understood, outpouring of grace that is simultaneous. A good and generous confessor at this moment can become invaluable, helping the scrupulous person see the presence of grace in their lives and learning to accept that God will not abandon them, has not abandoned them, and will never abandon them, even at the moment of the greatest fear and the greatest doubt.

A regular confessor will help you understand that even though you may be imagining that you have walked away from God, that you have committed the ultimate sin, God does not and will not accept this condition within you.

It is my hope that each of the readers of this book read this reflection again and slowly petition the Lord to help them realize that they have not committed this sin. I realize that it may be difficult to believe and to accept, but I assure you that it is a true teaching. There are so many doubts, so many questions, but the fear and the anxiety that is associated with the sin against the Holy Spirit should not be the source of your suffering. Accept the freedom that the Lord desires to give you in this matter!

THE DYNAMIC OF IMPULSE AND COMPULSION, OR, ENERGY NEEDS FUEL

Every year in the western United States, there is a season that is called the "firefighting season." This is the time of year, after the winter water runoff and before the rains of the late summer and early fall, many of the great forests that cover this part of the country become very dry. Lightning is a common occurrence, as is the careless camper, and as a result forest fires become a major concern. Some of the fires are very dangerous, consuming literally hundreds of thousands of acres of forestland.

What makes a fire dangerous, and what enables the fire that starts out in a very small area to become one of the monster fires that we read about in the paper, is fuel. A fire needs fuel in order to be energized and the fuel that these great fires consume very quickly is the underbrush, the fallen needles and leaves from the trees, and the accumulated debris that lies on the floor of the forest. This is the fuel that makes the fire hot, that enables it to spread, and there seems to be a never-ending supply of this kind of fuel available to the fire, and

186 QUESTIONS AND DILEMMAS

as a result, a seemingly never-ending firefighting season, at least until the great rains and the cooler weather arrives.

We are not primarily concerned with land management of our national forests in this book. However, I am interested in the illustration that the reference provides. I am interested in the illustration because I think it may be helpful to understand what scrupulosity is all about.

Scrupulosity needs fuel, just as forest fires need fuel, in order to thrive and to wreck the havoc that each of us understand is part of the scrupulous condition. The person who suffers from the scrupulous condition provides the "fuel" that scrupulosity feeds on: the questions, the doubts, and the anxieties that seemingly dominate them. But it doesn't have to be this way, there is a way to deprive scrupulosity of the fuel that it needs, but again it is the person who suffers from the scrupulous condition who has to make this choice.

How can a person who suffers from scrupulosity deprive their scrupulous condition of the fuel that it needs? A few strategies come to mind as extremely helpful.

Act Against the Impulse

This means that we choose, when faced with a question or a doubt or anxiety about a choice or decision that we have made, that we try and not "give in" to the doubt or the question. As we know, more often than not when we are struggling with our scrupulosity one of the manifestations is that we are overwhelmed with a thousand questions and anxieties. If we direct our attention of a particular question or anxiety, as soon as we have answered that particular concern, another question or anxiety takes its place. When we act against the impulse, we choose not to give anymore attention to the questions that we have. We "steel ourselves" for the onslaught of questions that seemingly bombard us, calling out for attention, but we refuse to give them anymore of our attention. This is something that needs to be done again and again; it is most certainly not a one-time event, but it does get a little easier each time we choose to act against the impulse.

Accept the Fact That It Will Be Initially Frightening

This strategy serves as a caution and a warning. When we act against our fears and our anxieties we are going to initially become even more fearful and anxious, the doubts and the questions will at first seem even more powerful, crying out for attention. This initial onslaught should be understood as a powerful moment of grace because it means that we are, with the help of God's grace, actually beginning the process of healing. Nevertheless, it is a very painful and a very frightening experience but it simply has to be endured in order to turn the corner and begin the process of healing.

Choose a Confessor Who Can Encourage You

What is meant here is that we do not, and in fact it is not a good idea, try and enter the healing process from scrupulosity without some kind of support and encouragement. A scrupulous person has to stand alone with his or her fears and anxieties, no one can take them away or experience them for you; but at the same time, a scrupulous person needs help and support. An encouraging confessor, or for that matter a spiritual director and/or therapist, can be invaluable in the process, especially if you give him permission to help you. It might come as a surprise to some, but it is in fact necessary to inform your confessor that you are actively trying to get better and that you would welcome his support and direction. Often, if you do not inform the confessor that you are actually trying to do something about your condition, he may assume that all you want is a listening ear and a comforting word or two.

Read Something Each Day That Gives You Hope

Read something from the lives of the saints, or something from the sacred Scriptures. All of this effort is important because it will widen your perspective, and it will help you recognize the finger of God at work in the life of another person and lead you to an understanding that the same finger of God is actively working in your life. If you do not read something hopeful each day, you limit your perception and you therefore limit the possibilities in your life.

Imagine a Time in Your Life
When You Will No Longer Be Scrupulous

This might at first glance seem like silly advice, but it is actually very important. If you cannot imagine yourself living a life without scrupulosity, how will it ever happen? Every important decision and experience in your life has taken place because you were able to imagine yourself actually enjoying it or participating in it. If you cannot see yourself as a person that is free from scrupulosity, how will you ever know when the event occurs, how will you be able to recognize the grace of the moment?

Pray in Thanksgiving for the Healing That You Will Receive

This strategy is related to the point above about imagination, but it is perhaps the most important point of all. You need to anticipate the healing power of God in your life. Anticipation leads to faith and hope and it makes the possibility of God's grace active in your life a reality. If you do not truly believe that you will be healed, and if you do not live in hope for the day that it will happen, chances are that it will not. It is not that God does not want you to be healed but rather that you are not ready to accept it. I know this might sound a little startling, but perhaps if you reflect on it for a moment some of the truth of what is contained here might begin to make sense.

Scrupulosity is a negative energy in our lives. It does not lead us to growth or to happiness and is in fact very destructive to ourselves and more often than not to the people we love and who love us. If we desire to remove this negative energy from our life, we have to be willing to deprive it of the fuel that it needs.

RESPONSIBLE CITIZENSHIP

Every few years people who live in a democracy have the opportunity to go to the polls and register their preferences and make their choices known about who will lead and form the government. As we do so we are undoubtedly aware of the fact that it is a great blessing to be able to participate in the process. We are also aware of the fact that not all people enjoy the freedom that we enjoy and, even less— if we believe the commentators—are willing to accept the responsibility of freedom by participating and choosing to cast their vote.

For a scrupulous person participation in the elective process can be an experience of anxiety and stress. Decisions are always difficult, but decisions that have the potential to have far reaching consequences present a unique challenge. Although I do not intend to counsel anyone about how they should vote or for whom, I thought it might be useful to examine some general concerns that might make the process less stressful.

Searching for the Perfect Candidate

Although each political party will do its best to present its candidates in the best possible light, there is no one candidate who will perfectly be able to represent all of your values and your concerns. In addition, unless you personally know the candidate you will have to rely on how the candidate is presented to make your decision. As a result of the fact that you cannot possibly know everything about a candidate, there is always the possibility that you may be surprised after he or she is elected and a decision is made that you might not agree with.

For a scrupulous person it is important to recognize the fact that despite your best efforts you may well vote for elected officials who might later disappoint you. Although it may be disappointing, it is not sinful and you are not morally responsible if they later make a choice that you do not support or which you find offensive.

All Good or All Bad

Part of the political process is intended to cast a particular candidate as "good" and to cast their opponent as "bad." The belief is that if you can succeed in clearly defining your candidate as the "good" candidate then this will ensure a favorable outcome. There are many different ways that this can be accomplished, even by candidates who espouse the commitment to not "conduct a negative campaign," but to remain "focused on the issues." Particular candidates hope that you will view them favorably and, at the same time, they hope that you will view their opponent unfavorably, and then cast your vote accordingly.

For a scrupulous person, who may well be vulnerable to the suggestion that someone may be "good" and that someone else may be "bad," it is helpful to remember that things are seldom as simple or as black and white as they may be presented. It might be worth the effort to try and move beyond initial reactions and first impressions.

One-Issue Voting

The truth is that unless a person is participating in a specific referendum where the question is clearly defined between point A and point B, few other choices can easily be made based on one issue only. However, that being the case, political parties will attempt to convince voters who feel particularly passionate and committed to a specific issue, to cast their vote for them based solely on that single issue. There is of course some appeal and a sense of satisfaction to making a choice in this way because you can easily determine if you "won" or if you "lost" as soon as the election process is completed. However, once elected, each candidate will face not only the one issue that you consider important but a host of other issues that they will have to make a decision about. For a one-issue voter the determination needs to be made whether a candidate's position on the issue that you care about will also translate into positive decisions about other issues.

For a scrupulous person "one-issue voting" can seem to be a very appealing way to make a decision, especially if the one issue that you are concerned about is related to an issue that you may be personally struggling with. There can be a great sense of satisfaction and accomplishment if your candidate wins. On the other hand, if your candidate loses, there can well be a feeling of loss and disappointment. It might be worthwhile to consider if you really want to put all of your "eggs in one basket," thus risking either satisfaction or disappointment.

Responding to the "Hot Button" Issues

Certain issues that will be part of a campaign are also issues that are clearly defined as issues of morality and these issues are often identified as "core" issues within the electorate by the press and other commentators. Such issues are also the issues that more often than not produce the most passionate response and generate both emotion and excitement. In recent times "hot button" issues have included abortion, the death penalty, gay marriage, stem-cell research, issues concerned with such things as homeland security, and so forth. Each of these issues have a way of engaging people in conversation and debate, which can become both vigorous and heated and lead to judgments and opinions being formed about others, depending on their point of view.

For a scrupulous person the "hot button" issues are often a source of anxiety, not only for the individual person but also because of the perceptions and judgments that are formed. On more than one occasion I have been asked if it is necessary for a person to "challenge" or "correct" another persons opinion on these issues, especially if the person that is holding the opinion is a member of their family or a close friend. The answer of course is a strongly worded caution to proceed with care, if you proceed at all. The consistent advice of the priest/directors of SA over the years has been to avoid the impulse to correct and admonish another person, even on the occasion when you may well be convinced that they are in error. This advice has nothing to do with avoiding responsibility or giving scandal but rather has everything to do with prudence, discipline for the sake of the kingdom, and trust in the will of God being accomplished through grace.

What Does the Church Teach?

The Church has very clear and unambiguous teachings about every conceivable moral action or decision that may effect the human person. For example, the Church defends and promotes life from the moment of conception, speaks of the dignity of the human person in every time and place, and counsels respect and love of all human persons. Obviously the teachings of the Church can be used in the individual discernment process of choosing a candidate and the teachings and interpretations of the moral law can prove to be quite helpful. That being said, the Church, as an institution, does not promote the candidacy of any one person over another person. Individual leaders in the Church may well have an opinion and a preference, and may even express that preference in one way or another, but it is a preference and not an official teaching or endorsement. If someone claims that the Church has in effect declared a preference or made an endorsement of a particular candidate that would not be the case.

Although by no means the final word on preparing for an election, I hope that these five points may help you in your preparation and in your discernment. The freedom that we all enjoy to be able to participate in the elective process is a wonderful blessing, a blessing that we should never take for granted and use with the greatest respect.

Chapter Eleven

Questions Asked and Answered

In the first chapters of this book, I presented the main areas of concern that scrupulous persons often deal with on a daily basis. In a sense, the first nine chapters attempted to provide some insight and direction on the "big questions" of life. However, as we all know, not all the questions we have to deal with in life are concerned with the big issues. More often than not, it is the little things that demand even more of our attention and concern.

As I reviewed the archives of the *SA* newsletter, there were a significant number of questions that seemed to appear again and again. These questions, while dealing with a variety of subjects, are not material for distinct or extended treatment, although they are important to answer and reference.

In this chapter the questions and the answers provided are listed in no particular order and with no additional comment or direction from me. Encompassing several categories of concern, they are presented because they have been consistently asked, and they have been asked because someone suffers and is tormented by them. By including them here it is my hope that we complete the picture and that we fill in the blanks as we come to a greater awareness and understanding of the scrupulous condition.

UNSOLICITED MAIL

QUESTION: I receive letters of appeal from places like the Indian missions and other worthy causes, and I feel bad that I can't respond to all of them. I worry that they might be waiting for me to send them help. And sometimes they send a little crucifix or something, and that makes me feel worse when I can't do anything for them. What should I do?

ANSWER: First of all, don't feel badly that you can't respond to all the appeals made to you. The missionaries who need help send letters to thousands of people, and they understand perfectly well that perhaps only a small percentage of these will be in a position to help them. But they have to reach out to a great many people in order to get help from the few who are able to give. And a mail appeal is the only way many of them have of seeking funds. I suggest you pick out a few of these worthy causes, the ones that appeal to you most, and send what you feel you are able to give. For the rest, just ignore them. Someone else may be disposed to help in the cases that you pass up. And if they send you a little cross or some souvenir, keep it in good faith.

Father L. Miller, C.Ss.R.

QUESTION: My mother is eighty-six, and she gets begging letters from dozens of organizations, not to mention Christmas cards and other pious items that she hasn't ordered. What am I supposed to do with all this stuff? I have been sending it back, but this is becoming too costly. Is it OK to pitch these begging appeals, even though there are holy cards involved?

ANSWER: You certainly do not have to respond to every begging appeal, nor do these organizations expect everyone they contact to respond. This may be their only way of publicizing their good work, and if only a small percentage of those contacted respond, they are happy. You and your mother, I am sure, have a few favorite charities. Send what you can to them and ignore the rest. And if you don't want to keep the holy cards they send, just discard them. There will be no sin involved.

Father L. Miller, C.Ss.R.

QUESTION: Somehow my name and address have been put on the mailing lists of many religious organizations. I get Christmas cards, Easter cards, special calendars, little booklets with words of inspiration, and so on. Now what I want to know is this: Do I have any obligation to send a donation to these worthy causes?

ANSWER: Every Christian has the general obligation to use generously for others what God has given him or her. I am sure that you support your own parish, the local community of Christians where you participate in Mass each weekend. You help many diocesan and nationwide special collections. You also help various charities that do work for needy people. But you cannot help everybody unless you are very, very wealthy. So you must pick and choose. In answer to your specific question, you did not solicit any gifts and thus are not obliged to send a donation. These religious orders get enough response from people so that the gifts are paid for and a profit is made for the charitable works to which they are dedicated.

Father Santa, C.Ss.R.

QUESTION: Every time I receive an envelope in the mail asking for money for the poor, I feel that I must send a donation because God may have caused this request to come to me, and I dare not refuse to send the donation. I really believe in helping the poor, but I am getting loads of mail from many organizations. I try to send a small donation to each, but it seems it is a losing game. If I selected a certain number of them to concentrate on, do you think God would be pleased or not? The gospel story about "the sheep and the goats" is a frightening thing.

ANSWER: I am glad that you raised this question because I am sure many other members of SA would also like an answer to it. The first thing I want to stress is that there is absolutely no moral obligation to respond to all the requests you receive through the mail. Direct-mail campaigns have multiplied in recent years and there is no end in sight! It is true that we all have some obligation to help the poor, but we can't do everything. The Church has always encouraged us to well-ordered charity, that is: helping to take care of the needs of our family, our parish, our local community, the larger Church, the world community—but always and only according to our means. The second thing I want to emphasize is that there is no reason why you should feel guilty because you cannot respond to all appeals. You cannot take all the problems of the world on your own shoulders and lose your peace of mind because you cannot solve all of them. I suggest that you try to decide what you are able to give to charity. Choose a few charities that seem especially worthy, help these according to your ability, and leave the rest in the hands of God. This approach will help you fulfill the law of the gospel and at the same time give you peace of mind.

Father Lowery, C.Ss.R.

QUESTION: Would you kindly address the issue of donating to charities? I'm sure others receive requests for money from many different organizations. I feel guilty discarding letters with pictures of starving children when I eat well. Just how much more than my tithe to the parish should I give? Are there any guidelines one could follow to know that they are giving their honest share, short of living like Mother Teresa?

ANSWER: You ask a most difficult question and a very personal one at that. To be perfectly honest, I find myself in a dilemma to answer it. The reason for my dilemma, suggested by your reference to Mother Teresa, is my awareness of the fact that I live in the richest country in the world. I know I could choose to live much more simply and dispose of all my income that I do not need to live on. To do so would require a substantial change in lifestyle and would undoubtedly be viewed by many as irresponsible.

Certainly, some are called to live a life of radical giving and radical poverty. Others—and I think most of us can be found in this second group—are called to live life simply, according to our circumstances and needs. We are called to be generous and to be giving. At the same time, we are expected to plan for the future, to provide for our families, and to seriously accept the other responsibilities before us. In your situation, I feel it is not necessary to respond to every particular need for which you receive an appeal, no matter how needy or worthy it may be. Choose a representative sampling of charities that you feel you can support, and discard the other appeals. Do so in good conscience. If, in the future, you find yourself to be in a situation where you can be even more generous, then by all means choose to do so. God bless.

Father Santa, C.Ss.R.

RESTITUTION

QUESTION: Must one make restitution for each and every transgression against the seventh commandment, even if it is a venial matter? If one makes restitution for something, must the loss of interest accrued be added in when the money is sent?

ANSWER: If only a small amount of money is involved, a scrupulous person should not worry about restitution. Restitution is made in small matters when we give to the poor or to some worthy cause. As to lost interest accrued, only in the case of very large amounts of money would this be a consideration.

Father Kaler, C.Ss.R.

QUESTION: Could you tell me more about restitution? I have a number of questions about it. For example, if it is owed to a large company, is it OK to give it to charity instead? Also, can restitution be done anonymously?

ANSWER: First, I would like to say that oftentimes scrupulous people tend to think they are required to make restitution when no such obligation really exists. Second, I hesitate to answer detailed questions about restitution unless I am directly talking to the person. The reason is that some of these cases involving justice can be very tricky. The really complex ones can hardly be handled without a face-to-face consultation. That's why I suggest that individual questions be brought to the confessor. However, there are some general remarks that can be made:

1. Restitution should be made to the person whose right was violated. If that's not possible, make it to the person's family. If the person's identity is unknown, make it to charity.
2. One's good name doesn't have to be endangered—that is, restitution can be made anonymously.
3. Restitution should be made as soon as possible.

Father Kaler, C.Ss.R.

QUESTION: When does a person have to make restitution?

ANSWER: Because this is a general question about restitution, I'll try to provide an answer. Questions that are more detailed and specific should be taken to one's confessor. Here are some general guidelines. Restitution must be made when (1) we have unjust possession of another's property, or (2) we have caused unjust damage to another's property.

Concerning unjust possession, note the following examples:

1. If I knowingly have in my possession another's property, I must give it back at once.
2. If I have used it, destroyed it, or given it away, I must give the equivalent to the proper owner.

Concerning unjust damage, restitution is called for when the following conditions are present:

1. My action was the real and effective cause of the damage.
2. My action was deliberately unjust (it was not an accident).

Father Kaler, C.Ss.R.

QUESTION: I have been told that if it is impossible to make restitution to the person you owe something to, then giving to a charity would be an acceptable way to make restitution. What exactly does the word *impossible* mean here? I have become consumed at times with trying to locate people who live in other states, who are not in the phone book, and so forth. Part of me says it is impossible to find them, another part of me says there are ways, if only I was more courageous. What should I do?

ANSWER: I want to congratulate you on your insight into your problem and your awareness that you may well be consumed by the situation in which you find yourself. Recognition and awareness are the first steps toward healing. At the same time, may I suggest that it is exactly the fact that you are sometimes consumed and often anxious about the issue of restitution that should be a warning to you that your scrupulous voice is speaking. In other words, the issue is not that you do not understand the difference between what is possible and what is impossible, but rather that your scrupulous self refuses to trust what you know. Yes, it is very true you are permitted to make restitution to a charity if it is impossible to make restitution to an individual person. However, you are obligated to make restitution only when directed to do so by your confessor; you are not required to do so because you think it is necessary or because you feel compelled to do so. God bless you! Be at peace!

Father Santa, C.Ss.R.

PROMISES

QUESTION: If, after being in an automobile accident, you said you would not ride in a car again, would it be a sin every time you did?

ANSWER: No sin at all. To say such a thing under the nervous stress of an accident is understandable, but it is not a reasonable pledge to make, and God does not hold us to what is unreasonable.

Father L. Miller, C.Ss.R.

QUESTION: I said I would not go past a certain house because of being afraid of a dog that lived there. Now he is friendly. Do I still have to keep my promise?

ANSWER: No. If the dog wants to be friendly, give it a pat on the head as you pass by.

Father L. Miller, C.Ss.R.

QUESTION: I made a promise not to eat meat on Tuesdays in return for a favor. My trouble is that I was under stress and I said, "I promise sincerely and I vow never to eat meat on Tuesdays." I will resume this practice but I am very upset, lest I've committed a grave sin because I said, "I vow." Was my vow like that of a priest or nun?

ANSWER: No, your vow was not like the public vow of a priest or nun. You have not committed a grave sin. Scrupulous persons like you should forget about making private or personal vows. They usually add another burden of guilt to what is already there—and that's enough!

Father Lowery, C.Ss.R.

QUESTION: In the early stages of my scrupulous condition, I made a promise to God that I would become a nun and also say two rosaries daily if I were cured of my scrupulosity. These promises were made to bind for life under pain of serious sin. Am I obliged to become a nun and to say the rosaries?

ANSWER: No. You are never bound to keep foolish promises. Foolish because under the emotional stress of the scrupulosity you were not able to see clearly and were not fully free in your decision. Hence, these foolish promises do not oblige you. In general, it is a good idea before making any promise to ask your confessor so that you may have the proper advice and perspective.

Father Kaler, C.Ss.R.

QUESTION: I have a question about vows and promises. I was wondering if a person could bind himself or herself under pain of mortal sin in a small matter?

ANSWER: No, to pledge oneself to God to do something or to live a particular way—all these things by their very nature demand a certain seriousness. Trivial matters simply wouldn't bear the weight. Moreover, to me it looks a lot like superstition. It's like saying, "If I do this little action in a specified way, then a certain momentous event will take place (or a particular catastrophe will be avoided)." If we fall into that type of thinking—placing strange restrictions on ordinary actions, or having a set of esoteric mental rules binding us—we would surely have a breeding ground for many scruples, wouldn't we?

But what about the time of crisis? Sometimes people wonder whether they have made a vow, a promise, or a pledge when they were under great stress. For example, a person might say, "If I get out of this, I'll do such and such!" But there is no need for worry. Vows, pledges, and promises cannot be made in this way, without full consciousness of what is happening and full freedom to act. The desperate nature of the crisis situation would certainly preclude complete awareness and/or freedom on your part. Anything less would not be binding in God's eyes. What this means is that this worry can be put aside completely.

Father Kaler, C.Ss.R.

QUESTION: My question concerns promises, pledges, and vows. I have difficulty telling if I have made one or not. Intending to do something, thinking about something, makes me question: Did I make a promise or a vow? Would this be binding under sin?

ANSWER: No, clearly these "promises, pledges, and vows" are not binding under sin. The mere presence of a thought or the intention "to do something" does not constitute a vow in any sense. Determine right now that none of these kinds of promises—no matter how solemn or how sincerely made—will be valid in God's eyes or binding under sin unless it is first fully approved by your confessor.

Father Kaler, C.Ss.R.

RELIGIOUS ARTICLES

QUESTION: What do I do with my worn-out religious articles? Somebody told me that I should burn them. But I live on the fifth floor of an apartment building. I have no stove in my rooms, and I can't start a fire on the lawn. I have a drawer full of broken rosaries, blessed palms, and even a broken statue. What should I do?

ANSWER: Simply break up the statue or rosary until it no longer has its original shape. Then throw it away without worry or scruple. In general, as far as religious articles are concerned, remember that they are only signs and symbols. The material out of which they are made is not especially sacred. So, put aside your worry about throwing away religious articles when their usefulness has come to an end.

Father L. Miller, C.Ss.R.

QUESTION: How should one dispose of religious papers and magazines that contain pictures of our Lord, the Eucharist, and the saints? Must all these pictures be clipped out and cut into minute and unrecognizable pieces?

ANSWER: Do not confuse these religious pictures with the holy persons whom they portray. To throw away such literature is not an insult or slight to these holy people or to God. Cutting them up into little pieces before discarding them is unreasonable and uncalled for.

Father Farnik, C.Ss.R.

QUESTION: When we receive new blessed palms on Palm Sunday, I never know what to do with the old ones. What do you suggest?

ANSWER: Crush them in your hands and drop them in the wastebasket. If they end up in the incinerator, this implies no disrespect, since your intention is not disrespectful. Blessed palms are religious symbols meant to remind us of the saving events of Holy Week. Since you are replacing last year's palms with new fresh ones, the symbolism can and should continue. Certainly the usefulness of the dried-up old palms has come to an end.

Father Kaler, C.Ss.R.

QUESTION: At times I receive catalogs of religious goods in the mail. These contain pictures of Jesus, Mary, and the saints. Also there are photos of liturgical vestments, chalices, altar decorations, banners, and so forth. Is it wrong to throw away these catalogs? In the same line, sometimes missionary groups will write me asking for a donation and for prayers. They might include in the envelope a prayer card or a picture of a saint. I don't mean to be disrespectful, but I don't know what to do with all these "holy" things that I have accumulated. Is it all right to discard them?

ANSWER: Yes, it's perfectly all right to discard those catalogs of religious goods and also the individual "holy" pictures and prayer cards you have received in the mail. No disrespect is intended, and I'm sure none would be taken by the good Lord or his saints. Say a little prayer for the missionary groups that they will be able to continue their good works.

Father Kaler, C.Ss.R.

QUESTION: I was wondering if you could help me with what might look like a minor problem but one that really bothers me. What should I do with old religious articles such as broken rosaries, crucifixes, medals, candles, and so forth? It really bothers me to have these old things around the house, but I am really worried about committing a sacrilege. What should I do?

ANSWER: I have answered this question many times in the personal letters that I sometimes write. In addition, we have answered this question countless times in the pages of the *SA* newsletter. It seems that the advice I have given is not that helpful, so I asked around. I asked other priests what they would advise, and this is the answer that we all agreed on. Go through your house and gather together all those religious articles that you no longer want. Gather them all together into a box or an envelope or some container that they will fit in. Take the box that is filled with your collected items, along with a copy of this answer from the *SA* newsletter, to the rectory or the convent. ANONYMOUSLY leave the package at the rectory (but don't forget to include this answer). Father or Sister will understand immediately the dilemma that you have and they can be trusted to dispose of these religious articles for you. God bless you!

Father Santa, C.Ss.R.

HOROSCOPES

QUESTION: I faithfully read my horoscope in the daily newspaper. Is there anything wrong in doing this? I don't take what it says seriously, but sometimes the predictions do come true.

ANSWER: A number of people enjoy reading their daily horoscopes. It's a form of recreation for them. Like you, they don't take it seriously. When it's approached in this lighthearted way, there is certainly no sin involved. There are other people, however, who do take their horoscopes very seriously. Perhaps they don't realize what might be behind their fascination with astrology. Could it be the desire to escape responsibility? "If the position of the stars made me act a certain way, then I'm not responsible for my actions." Let's be honest: That's a cop-out, isn't it? It doesn't acknowledge that God is the creator of these stars and their movements, that he sent them spinning out into space, and that he regulates their orbits. He is Lord of the entire vast universe. It is absurd to ascribe mystical powers to the stars themselves as if they could influence us independent of God's providence.

What about those predictions that come true? Reread the particular horoscope and you'll find that it was worded in such a general way that it would fit just about any situation that might happen. There's also the "self-fulfilling prophecy" phenomenon. I determine that it will be a certain kind of day, not because of some "outside force," but because of the way I approach the day. In other words, I did most of it myself, not the stars.

The future will always hold an element of the unknown. For the Christian, however, the unknown is cushioned by the belief that all things are in the providential hand of a loving God.

Father Kaler, C.Ss.R.

TOBACCO

QUESTION: The use of tobacco, when one knows how damaging it is (and in this day and age, who doesn't know?), must have some sort of morality involved with it. Tobacco companies, people in stores who sell tobacco, not to mention those who use it—surely there is much guilt. What can be done?

ANSWER: Yes, all decisions and actions of the human person have issues of morality attached. We are moral people; this is an inescapable fact. At the same time, however, every moral issue and decision involves freedom. Freedom to choose, and thus take responsibility for my decisions and actions, is a necessary part of the discussion. It would seem to be unwise for a person who does not use tobacco to freely choose to begin using the substance. For a person already using it, the whole question of addiction is involved. When addiction is present, there is at least the reasonable doubt that freedom is impaired. So you see, your question is not as cut-and-dried as you might perceive. All answers are not always simple. This, too, is part of the human condition. What we are called to do is to learn to be patient with our humanity. Hopefully, if we can learn to be patient with ourselves, we can also learn to be patient with others. God bless.

Father Santa, C.Ss.R.

GERMS

QUESTION: Lately I have been worrying about the possibility of harming other people's health. Although I seem to be healthy, I'm concerned about passing germs to people I come in contact with. Maybe I have a hidden contagious disease and I'm spreading it everywhere. Recently I've been washing my hands excessively and am worried about other aspects of personal hygiene. Have others mentioned this problem? What is my obligation in this matter? Am I committing sins? Can I still receive Communion?

ANSWER: Yes, I have heard of your problem before. What has happened is that your scrupulosity has taken a turn in the direction of germs and personal cleanliness. It happens quite frequently. But since you seem to be in good health, it's unlikely you have any serious contagious infection. All of us are carriers of a whole range of "ordinary" germs and viruses. We spread them to one another all the time. After all, God made us social beings. He wants us to live together in families, neighborhoods, and nations. He wants us to work together, to depend on one another, to do good for one another. Very few people are called to be hermits. In all our social contacts, we are at the same time spreading germs to all the other members of the group, and they are doing the same to us. All this is normal. It cannot be helped.

So what is your obligation in this matter? You must take common-sense precautions to minimize the spreading of your "ordinary" germs. You should be using similar safeguards for yourself regarding other people's germs. An obvious example would be the use of a handkerchief or tissue when sneezing or coughing while suffering from a common cold. There are also recommended practices for the use of public facilities. If the possibility exists that a more serious infection might be spread, then proportionately greater care must be taken. The amount of precaution should equal the seriousness of the ailment. That, again, is common sense, isn't it?

Sometimes people become overwhelmed by the thought of germs. This is the direction in which you are heading. Frequent hand washing is classic OCD (obsessive-compulsive disorder) behavior. Please see a professional who is knowledgeable about this illness and get help.

Meanwhile, I would like to state that you are not sinning. Your worries are simply coming from scrupulosity; that is, they are exaggerated and unreasonable. Do not let them get a grip on you. And certainly do not let them keep you from holy Communion.

Father Kaler, C.Ss.R.

HYPNOSIS

QUESTION: Is there anything morally questionable about consulting a professional hypnotist? I am a law enforcement officer and have had serious problems with uncontrollable shyness and fear when facing groups of people. A friend told me hypnosis might help.

ANSWER: It is commonly agreed, I believe, that hypnosis can be a useful therapy for certain types of psychological problems. But it has its elements of risk, and you should make sure that you are dealing with a qualified professional.

Father L. Miller, C.Ss.R.

USE OF MEDICATION

QUESTION: I am a nervous person and, at times, a mental patient. In my last two stays at the hospital, the doctor put me on medication. But my question is, do I get as much benefit or grace from holy Communion and prayers under medication as I would if I tried to do without it? It almost seems that I am trying to find the easy way out.

ANSWER: You entrusted your case to a qualified and conscientious doctor, and he decided that you should use medication; therefore, you should have no hesitation in following his instructions. God sees your good will and, even though it is more difficult with medication to concentrate on your prayers, he accepts your prayers with the same divine love. A line from Saint Paul applies here: "Obedience is better than sacrifice."

Father L. Miller, C.Ss.R.

QUESTION: Is there anything wrong in occasionally taking sleeping medication? In Scripture Jesus said to stay "sober and alert." Does this mean that you can never use anything when rest is needed? My doctor has given me mild pills for nights when I can't calm down enough for sleep, but I'm concerned about whether to take them or not. I realize that there can be an abuse of such substances, but I'm talking about using them only when necessary.

ANSWER: In the Good Samaritan parable, Jesus has this caring man pouring wine and oil into the wounds of the half-dead victim by the roadside. This was a type of first aid or emergency medical treatment for those days. Also, the Holy Land is quite hilly and in some places the terrain is very rugged. Walking up and down the country would wear out anyone, so I'm sure Jesus knew what fatigue was. We have an instance of this in John 4:6: "Jesus, tired out by his journey, was sitting by the well." No doubt he enjoyed that little rest. The Lord also knew what it felt like to overcome physical tiredness by a refreshing good night's sleep. To answer your question, then, I don't see anything wrong with using sleeping pills when needed, especially if that's only occasionally and under a doctor's supervision.

Father Kaler, C.Ss.R.

PHYSICAL EXAMS

QUESTION: I have not been feeling well, and should go to a doctor for a physical exam, but I have scruples about this and dread such an examination. What should I do?

ANSWER: You should fight strongly against this scruple and go to the doctor and have whatever examination is needed for your case. God wants us to use reasonable means to preserve our health. This is surely one of them.

Father Kaler, C.Ss.R.

OBESITY

QUESTION: Am I sinning by being overweight? I've tried every diet in the book, and after an initial success, I gain back all that I lost. This is probably endangering my health, because there are cases of diabetes and cardiovascular disease in my family history. I'm worried about my health, but I'm even more worried about whether I'm sinning by being so fat. Can you help me?

ANSWER: You haven't been sinning, even though your diets have failed. The Lord knows you've tried! It looks to me that what we have here is more sickness than an occasion of sin. Concentrate your thoughts and energies on developing a weight-loss plan that'll really work. Experience says you can't do this by yourself. Avoid fad diets and seek professional help. Whether you have an eating disorder or some other sickness, you will be in the hands of the specialists, and I'm sure they'll be able to help.

Father Kaler, C.Ss.R.

LENTEN ABSTINENCE

QUESTION: The abstinence laws have been giving me a fit. I worry that what I'm eating might have had some contact with meat; for example, in the pan that was used to cook it, by its nearness to meat in the refrigerator, whether the cook had washed his or her hands after handling meat, because the same grill was used to cook both meat and later a cheese sandwich, and so on. Can you help me?

ANSWER: I fervently hope so. The abstinence laws were not meant to be the source of so much anxiety for you or for anyone. That's not what the Church or the good Lord intended for this holy season. The truth is, there is no danger of sin in any of the above situations. Follow this general rule: Whenever this worry comes up, act as if it hadn't come up; that is, go ahead and eat the apparently meatless food without worry. In other words, if what you are eating is a piece of fish or some peanut butter or a cheese sandwich or a salad—anything that is ordinarily accepted as "meatless"—then go ahead and eat it without worry about where or how it was prepared, what it might have come in contact with, and so on. Please try to do this without any anxiety. It's a perfectly safe way to act. By doing this you will find some peace and be very pleasing to our dear Savior.

Father Kaler, C.Ss.R.

CONTRACEPTION

QUESTION: Is it sinful to purchase other articles at stores that also sell birth-control products? I have noticed these products at discount stores that offer lower-priced household products and clothing.

ANSWER: No, it is not sinful. Unfortunately, it is almost impossible to find department or drug stores where these materials are not sold. According to Catholic theology, while one may not desire or intend to support the store in selling such immoral products, one may purchase other products as long as there is a reason for doing so. The reason here is that it would be a heavy burden for the average person to go in search of a store that does not sell them.

Father Lowery, C.Ss.R.

CHILDREN WHO ARE NOT
PRACTICING CATHOLICS

QUESTION: Our daughter and son-in-law are both Catholic high-school graduates, but they are not bringing up their children in the Catholic faith. The oldest is twelve, and neither she nor the other two younger children have been prepared for first Communion. I feel that I have an obligation to the children, but I don't know what to do.

ANSWER: I understand your concern and sadness. I would like to offer a few suggestions. We must always remember that the parents of these children have the primary responsibility for their religious education. Other people, such as priests, teachers, grandparents, and godparents can help but cannot usurp the role of the parents.

The kind of help you may be able to give depends a lot on the situation. If your daughter is truly alienated from the Church or has truly given up her faith in God, then anything you say or do will probably make her angry. In that case, your best approach is one of kindness to her and her family and regular prayer for her and for them. Often enough, however, young parents are not really alienated from God or the Church, but have just drifted away. As time goes on, they put their religious responsibilities on a back burner and "never get around to them." Then, if they decide that they should do something about the religious training of their children, they don't know exactly what to do or where to go or whom to contact. At such times, relatives and friends can be of great help. If this seems to be the case with your daughter and her husband, then I would suggest you gently inform them that you will be glad to be of help in getting the children started. You could contact your parish priest (or theirs) and obtain the necessary information. This can be a big help to people who have been away from Catholic practice for a long time.

Father Lowery, C.Ss.R.

PART THREE

Helps and Encouragement

Chapter Twelve

When Is
Professional Help Necessary?

In my ten years as director of Scrupulous Anonymous, I became accustomed to receiving many letters each day that ask a question or seek a clarification of something that I have written. The letters are usually respectful and begin with an admission of reluctance: "I know that you receive many letters each day and I have hesitated to write you, but..." The writer then asks a specific question, or possibly a series of questions, one question building on the presumed answer of the previous question, until every possible nuance and shade of gray has been addressed.

I am prepared for such questions, and I truly appreciate receiving the letters because it keeps me in touch with the members of SA and enables me to address their main issues and concerns. That being the case, I was completely caught off guard by a certain letter that I received some years ago.

The letter, if you can call it a letter, did not arrive in a standard envelope; it arrived in a box. When I opened the box and began reading the contents, I could not believe what I was reading. Neatly arranged, categorized, and computerized by commandment and rule, was page upon page of questions pertaining to the commandment or rule in question. The pages added up to 150! I had never received such a "letter" before, and frankly I was flabbergasted.

As I paged through the manuscript—there is no way I could think of it as a letter—I kept wondering what the sender's purpose might be. I was not prepared when I read the final question: "Father, I have sent you this partial listing of my sins in order for you to help me with my confession. I was wondering, do you think I may be scrupulous?"

I could not believe what I was reading, and I could not believe that the person who wrote me the letter would have any doubt he was suffering from scrupulosity. I was also convinced that there was much more than scrupulosity at work here.

What I struggled with, and to this day continue to struggle with, were the answers to the questions I had, after being confronted with such an obvious case of someone with scruples.

- How can I help someone with scrupulosity know and understand that the next step in their healing process may be to seek professional help?
- Are there any symptoms or warning signs that indicate it might be necessary for the person to seek the advice and counsel of a clinical psychologist or psychiatrist?
- When is it not enough to seek the help of a confessor or spiritual director?

Many, although not all, people who suffer from scrupulosity believe that if they can just "tough it out," if they are able to recite the right combination of prayers, or find the perfect confessor, or just improve their willpower, they will find peace and healing. For whatever reason, they are willing to pursue any option, as long as it does not include therapy or professional guidance. Where does this attitude originate? Why is there a reluctance to take the next step?

I believe that one of the reasons people are often afraid of turning to professional help is that they "misdiagnose" themselves. They think that because they are the person who is suffering, and have become "accustomed" to the suffering, there is a certain "normalcy" about what they may be feeling. It has been so long since they have felt anything other than what they are suffering, they just assume that "it can't be that bad." You often hear people say, "When I really get sick, I'll know it." The sad truth is that they do not know it, and may well need help in order to recognize their need.

Another reason people often choose to avoid professional help lies in the notion that "therapy doesn't really do anything." I have heard stories, in fact I think most people have, about people who have gone to a therapist for years and years and never seem to change. Of course, that is just an observation, but it might help someone understand how such an opinion can be formed. It also doesn't help our perception very much when we hear about famous people, such as movie stars, who freely admit that they are in therapy and we judge them to be "not that normal."

Yet another reason people may avoid professional help is the perception that such help is very expensive and not covered by insurance policies. When a person, unaccustomed to the legitimate costs of psychological health care, discovers that a therapy session, lasting 45 to 50 minutes, might cost $100 or more a session, and possibly even more, he or she may shy away from it "as a bit expensive for my needs."

Finally, yet another reason is the perception that scrupulosity has been given to a person as "a punishment from God because I have displeased God." With an attitude such as this, many times mistakenly identified as a type of humble acceptance of God's will, who would freely choose *not* to accept it? It would seem that a choice for therapy, with such a mindset, could not possibly be made or perceived in any other way other than an attempt "not to follow God's will." A person who suffers from scrupulosity could in no way make such a decision.

With all this in mind, and recognizing the seriousness of what is being discussed, and regardless of our feelings and perceptions, there may very well come a time when professional help is needed. How can such a moment be recognized?

Dr. Joseph Ciarrocchi, an associate professor of pastoral counseling at Loyola College in Maryland, and a clinical psychologist, lists five circumstances or symptoms that might suggest the need for professional help. These are found in his book, *The Doubting Disease,* which I have previously singled out and recommended.

- The symptoms have led to serious depression with thoughts about dying or urges to harm oneself physically.
- The symptoms interfere with a sense of well-being or happiness.
- The symptoms interfere with an occupation (paid employment, schoolwork, and homemaker).
- The symptoms interfere with interpersonal relationships (friendship, colleague, family living, and intimacy issues).
- The symptoms interfere with leisure time.

When we examine the listing provided by Dr. Ciarrocchi, I think we should be able to recognize immediately the seriousness of what we are faced with. This is no longer a matter of scrupulosity being an "inconvenience" or a "cross to bear," but rather an indication that something is not right. Each of the symptoms listed is an example of a state in life or circumstance that will not go away and cannot be ignored. Each symptom demands immediate attention.

It may also be helpful to recognize the fact that the symptoms provided by Dr. Ciarrocchi are *not symptoms of scrupulosity,* but rather symptoms of psychological illness. Scrupulosity, in and of itself, does not necessarily lead a person into depression or lead a person to contemplate hurting himself or herself. Scrupulosity does not necessarily interfere with one's happiness, occupation, and relationships: There is a difference between living with a scrupulous conscience and having life controlled by scrupulosity. The key difference, at least from my limited perception, is that in one instance *life is in fact being lived* and in the second example *life is being controlled and not lived.* May I suggest that if a person cannot recognize the difference, this might well be the first topic of conversation you may want to engage in with your therapist, or, at the very least, with a confessor or spiritual director who will then recommend a qualified and understanding professional.

Although what I am speaking about is very serious, I can also state that the majority of scrupulous people to whom I minister have no essential need for professional therapy. I can witness to the fact that they are living life, they are enjoying life, and they are successful in their relationships and occupations. But these people need to remain diligent and need always pay attention to the warning signs of scrupulosity. For them, this is all that is necessary. On the other hand, there are scrupulous people—a small minority—who, though working with a spiritual director or confessor, are in need of professional help, and should be encouraged to seek such help. They need to take the next step to professional therapy so that they may one day arrive at a point in life where they can live their lives and pay attention to their scrupulosity, but not be dominated by it. There is a difference.

Chapter Thirteen

Ten Commandments
for the Scrupulous

I n 1968, Father Don Miller, C.Ss.R., the founder of Liguori Publications, first proposed some basic rules that could be helpful for a person who was suffering from scrupulosity. Those basic rules are today known as the *Ten Commandments for the Scrupulous.* Of all the resources that we publish and of all the helps that we have for the scrupulous, these ten commandments are the single most requested helps. As a result of their popularity, these commandments have frequently appeared in the *SA* newsletter, and previous directors have made many references to them.

Several years ago, in the pages of the *SA* newsletter, I attempted an update of the commandments. The format I chose was to state the commandment, as first proposed by Father Don, and then follow it with a short commentary. The commentary was my own reflection on the commandment, but it was informed by the reflections and wisdom of both Father Dan Lowery and Father Pat Kaler. For my reflections I relied on their wisdom and direction as it has been collected over the years in the pages of *SA*.

THE TEN COMMANDMENTS

1. You shall not repeat a sin in confession when it has been confessed in a previous confession, even when there is a doubt that it was confessed or a doubt that it was confessed in a sufficiently adequate and complete way.

Almost every scrupulous person experiences anxiety and doubt about past sins. Older people have a natural tendency to reflect back on their younger years, and in doing so, often remember something that triggers a doubt. More often than not, such a doubt has to do with impure thoughts, desires, or actions. As a result of the combination of remembering and doubting, it is not unusual that the scrupulous person then experiences great anxiety and is robbed of a sense of peace. This is why this first commandment is so very important: Do not go back over past sins, and do not repeat the confession of them! Such an exercise is not at all helpful and must be resisted.

2. You shall not confess doubtful sins in confession, but only sins that are clear and certain.

Of all of the correspondence I receive, I would say this issue is the one that occurs most often. "What does a person do if they are not sure that they committed a sin?" For this reason, this is a very important commandment to remember because it clearly states the truth: *Doubtful sins don't count*! There is no need to confess something that does not clearly and certainly exist. In fact, it is harmful to one's self to confess that which is doubtful. Again, such a practice is not at all helpful and must be resisted. Now I can almost hear some of you saying, "I am not sure if I doubt that I sinned or if I am just trying to fool myself to believe that I am doubting that I sinned." This thought in itself demonstrates that you are in fact doubting, and so, therefore, the commandment comes into play: You shall not confess doubtful sins.

3. You shall not repeat your penance after confession or any of the words of your penance because you feel or think that you had distractions or may not have said the words properly.

The temptation to repeat prayers is a constant one for the scrupulous. You may feel you need to repeat them, again and again, until you "get them right." Unfortunately, such perfectionism is never satisfied, and so you will remain in a constant state of anxiety and fear. This situation becomes all the more distressing because many times the scrupulous person will argue that the fact they feel anxious or fearful is a sign they did not correctly perform their penance. "If I did it right I would be peaceful." This commandment is, therefore, very important because it is the only solution to the dilemma in which you find yourself. Father Miller is right: Do not repeat your penance.

4. You shall not worry about breaking your fast before receiving Communion, unless you actually put food and drink in your mouth and swallow it in the same way that a person does when eating a meal.

Much of the anxiety that is present in reference to breaking your fast before Communion centers on extraneous matters. It is helpful to remember that lipstick is not food. Snowflakes are not food. You cannot break your fast unless you deliberately choose to eat in the same way that you would choose to eat a meal or a snack. The commandment clearly suggests that no hesitations are allowed regarding accidental swallowing of things that are not considered food.

5. You shall not hesitate to look at any crucifix or at any statue in church or at home or anywhere else because you may get bad thoughts in your mind and imagination. If such thoughts occur, they carry no sin whatever.

Although this commandment deals with a situation that is not necessarily a problem for all scrupulous persons, it is nevertheless a real burden for some. If you try to avoid the problem by not looking, the problem will tend to become more severe. It is a much better choice to meet the problem head-on. Thoughts and imaginations that occur in this situation are simply not sinful. One should try and confront fear, not give in to it.

6. You shall not consider yourself guilty of bad thoughts, desires, or feelings, unless you can honestly swear before the all-truthful God that you remember clearly and certainly consenting to them.

This is a very important commandment. The whole area of impure thoughts and desires causes scrupulous people much anxiety. Unfortunately, scrupulous persons often believe that the very appearance of certain thoughts or desires in their mind or imagination means that they have committed a sin. This is most certainly not the case. In fact, it is humanly impossible for us to have absolute control over our interior faculties. Such thoughts and images are going to happen, whether we like them or not. Because we simply do not have absolute control over our interior faculties, the emphasis of the commandment is on clear and certain consent. Only a free consent, that is clear and certain, constitutes a sin. You cannot accidentally or involuntarily be guilty of sin.

7. You shall not disobey your confessor when he tells you never to make another general confession of past sins already confessed.

It is not unusual for the scrupulous person to desire to make "just one more general confession." The desire to do so is prompted by a wish for inner peace and calm. However, more often than not, what happens is the exact opposite. The anxiety generated by the process of examination and preparation, the actual confession, and then the review of the confession produces no inner peace or calm. There always has to be "just one more." The wisdom of this commandment is found in two simple words: No more! If the scrupulous person will follow the advice of his or her confessor on this matter, they will have a chance of finding peace. Otherwise, there is only turmoil, anxiety, and stress.

8. You shall believe and act accordingly, so that whenever you are in doubt as to whether or not you are obliged to do or not to do something, you can take it for certain that you are not obligated.

This commandment underlines the basic moral principle that doubtful laws or obligations do not bind the scrupulous conscience. The great saint and our patron, Saint Alphonsus Liguori, teaches: "When there exists in a scrupulous person the habitual will not to offend God, it is certain that he or she acts in doubt and there is no sin...." I find it very reassuring to read the words of Saint Alphonsus in reference to this matter. It is good to know that the teaching of our very wise patron and model, a saint whom you might recall also suffered greatly from scrupulosity, is so clear and straightforward. "There is no sin" are the words we need to hear and recall as often as necessary.

9. If, before you perform or omit an act, you are doubtful whether or not it is sinful for you, you shall assume as certain that it is not sinful and shall proceed to act without any dread of sin whatsoever.

Saint Alphonsus also supports this commandment. In his advice to confessors he says, "Scrupulous persons tend to fear that everything they do is sinful. The confessor should command them to act without restraint and overcome their anxiety. He should tell them that their first obligation is to conquer their scruples. They should act against their groundless fears. The confessor may command the scrupulous to conquer their anxiety and disregard it by freely doing whatever it tells them not to do. The confessor may assure the penitent the he or she need never confess such a thing."

10. You shall put your total trust in Jesus Christ, knowing that he loves you as only God can love, and that he will never allow you to lose your soul.

We often reflected in the pages of *SA* that the scrupulous person, for one reason or another, has a negative image of God. A negative image of God does not inspire trust but rather fear and dread. In Jesus Christ we are able to glimpse the true image of God: a God who loves and heals and saves. It is in that God, the God revealed to us by Jesus, that we can and should place all of our trust. It may very well be helpful to review some scriptural passages, which may help you change your image of God from a negative to a positive one. May I suggest you spend some time reviewing the prophet Isaiah, chapter 43, verses 1–4. In this passage you will hear the words of the Lord speaking to you and reminding you that "you are precious in my eyes." You might follow up Isaiah with a reading from Paul's Letter to the Romans, chapter 8, verses 26–39. In this reading we are assured that the Holy Spirit helps us in our weakness. You might finally end your reflection by reading from the first letter of the apostle John, chapter 4, verses 7–19. In this reading, John reminds us that love consists in knowing, "not that we have loved God but that God has loved us."

A HELPFUL PRAYER FOR THE SCRUPULOUS

I behold the Christ in you.

I place you lovingly in the care of the Father.

I release you from all anxiety and concern.

I see you as God sees you, a spiritual person,
    created in the image of God,
      endowed with qualities and abilities that
        make you needed,
      and important—not only to me but also to God
       and His plan.

I believe that you have the understanding
    you need to choose life.

I bless you.

I have faith in you.

I behold Jesus in you.

—Author unknown

Chapter Fourteen

Ten Commandments
for Peace of Mind

The original contribution of Father Donald Miller, C.Ss.R., and his *Ten Commandments for the Scrupulous,* continue to be pastorally useful and effective. However, as I reviewed the commandments, I realized that they are intended specifically for the celebration of the sacrament of reconciliation. Because they are specific to the sacrament of reconciliation they are not commandments particularly useful when the sacrament is not the main concern or focus.

I believe that it might be useful to offer a set of commandments that might be helpful in the day-to-day struggle with scrupulosity. I have designated these commandments as "Ten Commandments for Peace of Mind." I do not expect that these new commandments are anything more than just a small contribution and perhaps a helpful tool. It is my hope that they may prove to be as useful as are the original commandments.

1. Understand that scrupulosity can be a temporary condition or a persistent and seemingly unyielding condition, which is most often a manifestation of obsessive-compulsive disorder (OCD); in either case, it is not a punishment from God.

It is possible to speak of scrupulosity, and to understand the manifestation of scrupulosity, in two distinct ways. It is important for people struggling with scrupulosity, and those who counsel and minister to them, to understand and know the difference.

The first manifestation of scrupulosity, a manifestation understood and easily diagnosed by a gentle confessor and/or therapist might be best understood as a "tender conscience." In this manifestation the scrupulous person experiences doubt and anxiety about certain and specific sins, more often than not it is a scrupulosity that can be healed through a proper and consistent catechetical education. Once a person clearly understands the difference between a mortal sin and a venial sin, and grows in confidence in their ability to distinguish between the two, the scrupulosity will slowly heal and eventually not be a problem. This kind of scrupulosity is most often experienced by recent converts, people struggling with a specific and or habitual pattern of behavior that is distasteful to them, people experiencing a spiritual awakening, and many times during the experience of adolescence and the process of becoming a mature sexual person.

A second manifestation of scrupulosity, which is much more serious than the first type, is the manifestation that has been described by reputable authors as "a thousand frightening fantasies," or "the doubting disease." This manifestation might also be understood as a religious or sin focus of a psychological disorder, which is both obsessive and compulsive. The focus is the key; it does not necessarily have to be religion or sin but could just as easily be concerns about cleanliness and germs, or issues of safety and observance, or for that matter countless other possibilities. When the obsessive and compulsive focus is on sin we routinely identify it as religious scrupulosity. Catechetical education, even it is consistent and useful, will not heal the obsessive compulsion, although it may well help provide some relief. The only certain path to healing and wholeness is professional therapy, including ideally some cooperation between the psychological professional and the spiritual professional (in some cases it may be one and the same person).

In either manifestation of scrupulosity a person needs to understand that their scrupulous condition is not a punishment from God, it is not a cross that God has given them to carry, or God has not singled them out for a special reason. We do not fully understand how people become who they become; we do not fully understand how a person becomes scrupulous or how a person acquires OCD. We do know that is has nothing to do with their basic goodness, their acceptance by God, or their ability to love or be loved.

2. Acknowledge your need for help and guidance and accept that you cannot effectively pursue a path of healing and wholeness by yourself.

The consistent advice of all of the saints, such as Saint Alphonsus Liguori and Saint Ignatius of Loyola, is that the most effective remedy for the scrupulous conscience is an understanding confessor. Certainly this advice is most important for a person who is struggling with what we understand as a "tender conscience" and who is in need of consistent catechetical education and guidance. It is all the more important for a person who is struggling with OCD, and in such a case, the confessor may not initially be as important as the trained psychological professional.

Do not expect that the saints will refer you to a psychologist for the necessary help that you need, and then use this as an excuse not to seek the help that is required. It is unreasonable to expect sixteenth- and seventeenth-century saints to direct you to seek psychological help since they knew nothing of them.

The scrupulous person needs the help and the guidance of another person to effectively pursue a path that will lead to healthy and wholeness because the disorder robs a person of the ability to clearly reason and understand their choices. A scrupulous person consistently focuses on the smallest part of the decision or the question, and as a direct result, looses the perspective of the bigger picture. It is in the narrow focus that the condition is manifested and the role of the confessor and/or therapist is to help the person see clearly the entire picture and not get tangled up in the details.

3. Accept and understand that the presence of fear and anxiety is the condition of scrupulosity and not the indication or warning of the presence of sin.

Fear and anxiety are normal feelings that are experienced by all kinds of people, scrupulous people and people who have never experienced scrupulosity. Fear and anxiety are normally present in people when they are confronted with something that they do not understand or which is unknown. Fear and anxiety are also present when they are confronted with something that challenges them and which has not been previously experienced, or when something familiar and comfortable may change. For some the presence of the feelings of fear and anxiety can be exciting and pleasant, for instance when riding a fast roller coaster, while for others it is usually an experience that they never associate with the pleasant or the exciting and which they prefer to ignore. For some scrupulous people the presence of fear and anxiety is often misinterpreted and they conclude that the feelings indicate that God has somehow been displeased and they have sinned. The stronger the feeling, the bigger the sin, or so it is assumed.

With the help of a confessor and/or therapist, a scrupulous person learns that the presence of fear and anxiety is many times an indication that the opportunity to actively and effectively act against the scrupulous impulse is present. It is uncomfortable, it does challenge the person to accept something new, but it is also the only way to eventual healing and wholeness. The fear must be confronted and the anxiety must be experienced. Each and every time the fear and the anxiety are confronted and a healthy decision is made, the grip of feelings is lessened. Unfortunately the opposite is also true: each and every time a person does not confront the feeling it just makes the binding grip all the tighter, making it even more difficult the next time to choose to "act against the impulse."

4. Always remember and never forget that discipline is essential if you wish to become healed. Choose one helper and resist the urge to seek many different helpers and a variety of different opinions.

Recall often that what we are talking about is a disorder that is obsessive and compulsive. Realize that although the primary manifestation of the obsessive compulsiveness may well be focused on sin, for example, it is by no means the only possible manifestation.

Scrupulous people must accept a primary discipline in their life that freely limits their ability to choose. It is difficult, and at the same time humbling, to accept the fact that a variety of opinions and options is not at all helpful. What is necessary is one, clear, firm, and loving voice to guide a person on the path to healing. All other voices will only succeed in distracting and postponing the wholeness that we seek and which has been promised to all of us as the children of God.

It is counterproductive to go from therapist to therapist, confessor to confessor, friend to friend. It is counterproductive to read one book and then another, to ask one question and then another and another and another.

What many scrupulous people forget is that by seeking the advice and the help of one singular person means that there will be extended moments in the relationship where the helper is not accessible. Believe it or not, the nonaccessibility of the helper is an essential component in the healing process. It forces you to confront the obsessiveness, to resist the compulsive choice, and to sit and learn to be comfortable with the presence of both feelings, learning in the process of the sitting, how to effectively become a whole and a healed person. To flee from the uncomfortable feeling is to resist the potential healing.

5. Learn to be very patient with yourself, your confessor and spiritual director, your therapist, and with family and friends.

The healing process is very slow and delicate. There will be many days, weeks, months, and even years in which you may feel you are making no progress. Often when a person feels this kind of frustration, a frustration that is associated with the healing process, there can be a growing perception within him or her that "nothing is happening." If you experience this feeling, and perceive your healing process in this way, you might also experience occasions when you are not patient with the people who are trying to help and support you. You may have strong feelings of anger, rising anxiety and impatience, and even at times convince yourself that you are not really cooperating with the grace of God.

Do not complicate this kind of reaction to the healing process by immediately identifying it as sin. It is not sin, neither venial nor mortal, but is rather a normal reaction to a process that is slow, difficult, and at time frustrating.

It is also important to understand that we do not necessarily understand the healing process in its entirety and can make false and unhelpful judgments about it.

I remember that, when I was a small child, I would often pick at the scab that had covered the scrape I had on my knee. My mother would tell me that the scab was on my knee in order to promote the healing process and that I should leave it alone. Even though I knew my mother was very wise in these matters I was still intrigued by the scab and would continue to pick at it nonetheless. Needless to say, there where times when I picked it completely off my knee, interrupted the healing process, and had to start the process all over again. What I was doing was not at all helpful. It was understandable, but it was not a help but rather a hindrance to the process.

It is also important to realize that in the healing process from scrupulosity, since it is the doubting disease, that we may have a tendency to doubt the advice and the direction of the people who are very important in the healing process. The compulsion to doubt the directives and the insights of your spiritual director/confessor or therapist may by very strong. There are times that the compulsion to doubt will even seem to make "more sense," even more sense than what you have been directed to do. At such times it is important to strengthen your resolve and remind yourself of the importance of listening to the direction of the person who is trying to help you in the healing process. It may be difficult to resist, you may want to pick their advice and counsel apart, but it is much better to resist and to trust.

6. Discover and recognize your success and learn to celebrate your effort.

In the midst of the healing process, in the day-to-day living that is necessary for all people, even those who suffer from scrupulosity, it is important to recognize your progress. Scrupulous people have a tendency to recognize failure, to worry about imperfection, and to be less than patient with their failures, imagine if some of that energy could also be devoted to celebrating your good effort?

No matter who you are, no matter how strong a particular doubt or compulsion may be, every person is also cooperating with the grace of God in his or her life. It is only in God, through the power of the Spirit of God, that "we live and move and have our being" (Acts 17:28), and it is because of the grace of God that we are able to make progress in our daily living. The progress that we make on some days will be very distinct and important, for example we might be able to clearly recall a specific choice to "act against the impulse," while on other days it may not be so obvious. Regardless, it is helpful every day to remind yourself of God's love for you and to celebrate that love in some small way.

Your celebration may be as simple as a silent prayer to God—"Thank you, God, for being with me this day, this moment, even when I don't recognize it"—or it may be something a little more complex, such as sharing with your spiritual director-confessor and/ or therapist a specific example of how you made some progress. Regardless, choose each day to find something for which you can be grateful. It will make all the difference in the world and it will make the moments when you are not making as much progress as you desire seem to be not so discouraging.

7. When you fail, or feel that you have taken two steps backwards, pick yourself up and try again. Do not give in to feelings of failure.

Every single person, even people who seem not to have a care in the world, experience failure and disappointments. One of the major differences between a person with scrupulosity and a person that does not suffer with scrupulosity may be found in their perception and interpretation of the failure. A scrupulous person many times, when faced with failure, immediately fear the worst and interpret the experience in the most serious way possible. On the other hand, people who are not inclined to scrupulosity can experience the exact same kind of failure or disappointment and put it easier in perspective. Scrupulosity admittedly lends itself to a feeling of living on the edge; a feeling of impending catastrophe, but it does not have to be this way. A person can choose to fight the impulse to immediately think the worst or imagine disaster.

One strategy that is very helpful, when faced with the compulsion to become overwhelmed with fear, is to take a deep breath (sometimes more than one deep breath is required) and to say a little prayer to God. The prayer can be very simple, such as "Help me remember, God, that you and I together can accomplish great things," or it might be a little more complex, such as a favorite prayer that you simply enjoy praying. Regardless, taking the time to not react but rather redirecting your attention and your energy, taking the time to try and postpone the impulse, is often very useful.

8. Never underestimate the power of grace.

Saint Paul said, "Where sin abounds, grace abounds even more" (Romans 5:20). For a scrupulous person there is an almost overpowering recognition of sin. Sin can be seen in literally hundreds, perhaps even thousands of manifestations, but is there always the same conviction that grace is also powerfully present? I think not, and this is most unfortunate especially in moments of great suffering.

Because some manifestations of scrupulosity are so persistent, and there seems never to be a moment of relief, the condition can literally wear a person down. Discouragement is perfectly understandable, the presence of which is most definitely not a sin, either venial or mortal, but with the discouragement can also come something even more insidious.

Persistent discouragement many times contributes to a feeling or a belief that the person has been somehow abandoned by God, or if not abandoned seemingly punished by God. Such feelings can be very strong, and because they are so strong and because they produce a certain amount of anxiety and feelings of guilt, the person who is suffering with this manifestation begins to believe that it must somehow be true. The rational part of the person cries out that he or she loves God and that God returns the love, but there is just enough doubt present, mixed up with the fear and the anxiety, seemingly confirming the experience.

It may sound almost unbelievable to assert at this junction the following: although you may feel unloved and even abandoned because of the strong feelings associated with this fear, this is not a moment of sin but is rather a moment of profound grace. God, whom you love, and the God who loves you, will not abandon you, does not desire to inflict punishment upon you, is not the cause of your fear and your anxiety, but is rather completely and totally present to you at this moment. God is totally present to you, loving you, forgiving you, and trying to calm your fears and your anxiety. God is with you at this moment, even if you feel that God is so very far away.

Sin abounds, the great apostle reminds us, but even more truthful is that grace abounds even more. It is helpful to recall this truth often, not only when the suffering might be the greatest but also at all other times. It can be a great source of comfort and encouragement.

9. Pray, pray, pray. Try and live a life of thankful praise.

One of the positive signs of progress and healing, not only from scrupulosity but also from many other trials and burdens, is the moment when the suffering can become redemptive. This transition, from viewing the affliction as a burden to accepting it as a reality but refusing to see it as somehow limiting our human potential, is possible only through prayer.

This statement is intended to be a positive statement about the power of grace and the power of prayer. It is not intended in any way to suggest that God has somehow inflicted a person with a particular kind of suffering in order to make him or her a person of prayer—this would be an example of twisted and/or crooked thinking and very far from the truth of the matter.

Prayer, and the actual grace that comes from the practice of prayer, helps a person to perceive life in a different way. Prayer doesn't necessarily take away suffering or anxiety but prayer does help refocus the attention of the person onto someone other than self. It is in the communication, the relationship between the individual person and God, that the transformation takes place. When the transforming power of God's grace begins to be acknowledged and accepted, the wonderful and the miraculous becomes a reality.

10. Imagine yourself living free from scrupulosity.

As a spiritual director, especially in moments when I am trying to help a person discern the will of God in their lives, I often ask a question: "Can you imagine yourself living in the manner which is necessary to fulfill this vocation?" Many times this question actually surprises the person and they are unable to immediately answer while at other times an answer is very quickly offered.

I believe that when a person is unable to answer the question, if they are unable to describe the experience they seek in a realistic way, they might not have arrived at the real point where a decision can be made or a transition may be accepted. It is essential to be able to imagine yourself actually living, performing the everyday tasks and functions of that which you may believe is God's will for you. If you are unable to imagine it, chances are it will not happen.

It is a good question to ask a scrupulous person: "Can you imagine living your life free from the effects of scrupulosity?" If you can imagine such a life, can you also imagine the choices and the decisions that you made in order to enable this transition in your life? Can you recall specific moments when you "acted against the impulse," or lived with the anxiety of not performing or thinking about the specific compulsion that seemed to have you in its grip? When you are able to easily recall such moments, when you are able to easily celebrate such moments and see the progression of grace in your life, you will be firmly on the path to healing and wholeness.

If, on the other hand, you are unable to imagine a life lived free from scrupulosity, you might ask yourself some difficult questions. What is it about scrupulosity that I find appealing, for example, do I use my scrupulosity as an excuse not to change? Why am I unwilling to seek out a confessor and/or spiritual director, or for that matter a therapist, who can help me and direct me? Am I comfortable (as strange as that might sound) with fear and anxiety, the doubts and the questions, and am therefore unwilling to risk the necessary steps to live my life differently? Is there something in my image and experience of God that may need to be challenged, even if it is a very fearful thing to do, in order to take the necessary steps that I need to take?

Chapter Fifteen

This Helped Me:
Members of SA Speak

pproximately once a year we ask the readers of the *SA* newsletter to share with us anything they might have discovered that has been useful to them on the road to recovery. This simple invitation has resulted in an outpouring of personal witness and encouragement from the members of SA. Their response is always immediate, heartfelt, and prompted by no other reason than to try to offer some type of help and support to others who may be suffering from the affliction.

We have received written responses from all over the world. Some of them are just small notes of encouragement; others are quite extensive and complete, reflecting a concern with detail, which is not completely unexpected. What each response has in common is that it is reflective of something that has been tried, maybe as a result of a suggestion from a confessor or spiritual director, or even from some unknown source, and has somehow helped.

The wit and wisdom of our readers is collected here under the title "This Helped Me."

From Dorville, Georgia

In response to your request in the newsletter, I would like to offer an answer that came to me when I was becoming obsessed with an unhealthy thought. When I have the grace to recognize my thinking is off base, I now simply say, "I am dwelling on this, Lord, help me to dwell in you." It has given me peace of mind and helped me to redirect my thoughts.

From the Philippines

I would like to share with you and the SA members a guideline that my confessor has given me. It has helped to make my life a little less tense. "Believe that even if your heart condemns you, God is greater than your heart."

From McClean, Virginia

The main help for me has been finding the right confessor and strictly adhering to his advice. Nothing has been more useful. It took me a while to firmly believe that God speaks to us through our confessor, but this is a fact. Therefore, when he gives me any guidelines or advice, it is as if our merciful Savior was addressing me in person. I keep in an easily accessible place Saint Alphonsus Liguori's reminder, "Obey in all things your spiritual father, for by the practice of obedience you will always be secure, and doubt not that if you practice you will become a saint."

From Kalamazoo, Michigan

I want to be completely candid. I have made a veritable pest of myself to every priest who has time to listen to me. I can only repeat, "I want to be with Jesus, my mother, and all the angels and saints forever." This prayer gives me peace.

From St. Louis, Missouri

We must seek the help of trusted professionals who can help us see things more clearly. One of my friends, who is a priest, told me that because it "makes good people think that they are bad," scrupulosity is one of the devil's most powerful tools. While we are obsessing and dwelling on sins, past or present, we are unable to use that energy for God's work, or to progress in our spirituality. I am sorry that we scrupulous people tend to be overly critical of others and ourselves. It seems to me that you get a lot of undeserved criticism. I pray for you daily and hope that more people will realize there is wisdom in what you write.

From Truth or Consequences, New Mexico

What has helped me is getting help and reaching out to people who can help me. I don't believe in suffering in silence.

From Syracuse, New York

I would like to mention something, which I find so helpful for life in general—and probably especially for us scrupulous persons: Live in the present moment. I mean, for example, when you are eating, eat. When you are sleeping, sleep. When you wash, wash. When you walk, walk. When you listen, listen. Be where you are. I work at it often, and I often fail, but it is wonderful when it actually happens.

From Cresson, Pennsylvania

I would suggest that your readers continue their spiritual journey by reading (if they like to read), by listening to tapes, diocesan programs, prayer, retreats, support groups, and so on. Don't stop believing or looking—God loves us more than we can imagine.

From Kalamazoo, Michigan

What helped me in my quest for normalcy, or peace of mind, was to find a regular confessor who understood scrupulosity and to stick with him. I resisted the temptation to switch confessors or to keep looking for another answer. I achieved peace of mind, and my illness was arrested (I will not say cured because you have to keep constantly vigilant). It has worked for me for the last twenty years.

From Anaheim, California

My healing started when I joined an anonymous 12-step program. I was struggling, and I thought my only problem was that I weighed too much. What I discovered was that I needed spiritual and emotional help. Your publication provides me with joy, help, and hope. We need it to sustain and protect us from all that we are exposed to every day.

From Ocala, Florida

Thank you for all that you have done. I think I am ready to come off your list. While I still wonder about things and occasionally have a stab of fear over something that I have done, I try to go back logically and enumerate the three things required to commit a mortal sin. I also review some of your lessons.

From Indianapolis, Indiana

I no longer stop and try to figure everything out. I have learned that God wants me to serve him in joy, in the present moment, now and in love. God wants me to live without worrying. In the past year I have been to Communion almost every day. Praise and thank God; in the Holy Trinity, through Mary.

From Shawnee Mission, Kansas

Pray, pray, pray. I know that this is a source of distress; however, I have learned to hang in there. Most of the time I get past all the junk and move on. I am practicing centering prayer, and I do a lot of traditional praying. The main thing to remember is that the more you run away or fear the thoughts, the worse they get. They have to be faced. Then they are not so frightening.

From St. Louis, Missouri

It seems to me that scrupulous thoughts, especially thoughts about sinning against the Holy Spirit, come when I am worn out and tired. I think that is why they are so hard to shake, at least for me.

From Atlantic Highlands, New Jersey

I pray this prayer: "I am sorry, Lord. That thought came up again, but I am not letting it separate me from your love. You died for my sins—sins that I know I shouldn't do but choose to do anyway. This thought that I just had, I discard it and choose not to listen to it. I choose to listen to you. I choose to believe in your love and your protection and your mercy. I choose to rest in your care, knowing that you know my fear of losing you and also knowing that you will do everything in your power not to lose me. You trust that your love is perfect, even though I am not. Perfect love casts out fear. Thank you, Lord, for your peace. Thank you, Lord, for loving me at this moment and every moment."

From Metairie, Louisiana

Your article, "The Thoughts That Cannot Be Shaken," has given me the most comfort than I have known in a lifetime of scrupulosity. I thank you for your understanding of our pain and constant struggle. Never before have I felt so truly understood. I take comfort, too, in your suggestion that we who suffer scruples pray daily for one another. It helps knowing that we join with others suffering the same plight.

From St. Louis, Missouri

I have had trouble getting rid of unwanted thoughts. One method that proved useful to me was to picture a blackboard full of words. Then in my mind I get an eraser and slowly, mentally erase everything. Then, if an unwanted thought tries to come back, I say to myself, "It is gone, I have erased it all."

From Santa Clara, California

After having written you a rather negative letter earlier, I feel it is only right to write a more positive message this time. I find this prayer very helpful: "Lord God, you alone are the great healer. When our minds and bodies are weak, we look to you for strength and reassurance. Surround us each day with your presence of love and compassion. Quiet our spirits so that we may know your goodness and be filled with your peace. Help us, Lord, according to your plan for our lives. This we pray through Jesus Christ our Lord."

From Fenton, Missouri

I heartily recommend the Divine Mercy Devotion, available from the Marian Helpers in Stockbridge, MA 01263. In particular, I recommend the daily praying of the Chaplet of Divine Mercy. According to what I have been able to discover, Saint Maria Faustina received the Chaplet in 1935, in a vision. Saint Faustina was praying when she suddenly felt the power of Jesus' grace within her. At the same time, she found herself pleading with God for mercy with words she heard interiorly: *Eternal Father, I offer you the Body and Blood, Soul and Divinity, of your dearly beloved Son, our Lord Jesus Christ, in atonement for our sins and those of the whole world; for the sake of his sorrowful Passion, have mercy on us and on the whole world.* Unfortunately, I am not able to provide you with more information because of a lack of space. However, if this appeals to you, please write the Marian Helpers at the address given above.

From Wayne, Nebraska

I sometimes ask my guardian angel to enlighten me, and he often does help me. His answer comes as a sort of interior conviction. It is usually a brief, subtle sort of experience. I have found that what I need to do is simply take the advice and go with it and not hash it over in my mind. Then everything seems to be OK.

From Kingston, New York

By the grace of God, I found AA and Recovery, Inc. These two groups have changed all aspects of my personality regarding my scruples.

From Springfield, Illinois

I save every *SA* newsletter and reread them in times of stress. The Al-Anon program and its twelve steps are a godsend. These are my survival tools.

From Duluth, Minnesota

(1) Walking and low-impact aerobics on a regular basis; (2) deep breathing exercises daily; (3) going to communal penance services once or twice a year. Unlike many scrupulous persons, I tend to avoid this sacrament because I have difficulty speaking to priests and panic. Practicing the following goals: objectivity, courage to make mistakes, and the will to bear discomfort.

From New York, New York

The *SA* newsletter and spiritual directors paved the way. Then I read a quote from the Bible to the effect that not by meticulously keeping all the commandments do we reach heaven, but by faith in Jesus Christ. So I changed my focus.

From Cleveland, Ohio

What helped me most was teaching religion classes, which I did for ten years. I was not very knowledgeable about the Bible or official Church dogma, so I had to teach myself as I taught the children. I studied through courses at a local Catholic college, courses offered by the diocese, and by reading materials connected with Confraternity of Christian Doctrine teachers' manuals. In my youth I learned of a strict, threatening, punishing God. Fortunately, the youth today learn (and all of us should) about the love of God, the love that surpasses understanding. God offers us his peace and his love, and all we have to do is accept it. Whenever I am tempted to think of some terrible sin, I remind myself that God loves me, he knows I love him, and he has forgiven me "seventy times seven." Through these reminders I am able to be at peace with myself.

From Cedar Rapids, Iowa

I have been scrupulous most of my life. I'm now getting close to forty. A year or so ago I was put on medication by a psychiatrist. Along with this medication, I receive counseling from a priest in a nearby mental health hospital. I see my priest and psychiatrist on an outpatient basis. The medication seems to calm down my anxieties. Between that and the counseling, I am getting along very well. I can't believe the difference the medication has made. It was hard for me to call the mental health hospital because I thought that meant I was admitting there was something wrong with me. I also suffer from OCD. But with the medicine and counseling, things are going well. I do think if you suffer from OC scrupulosity you should see a psychiatrist and tell him what you're going through. I also recommend getting counseling from a priest.

From Portland, Maine

My confessor told me to "make my decision and stick to it." Prior to this, I used to go to morning Mass on my way to work. There were six confessionals and I would go from one to the other because I didn't feel I had made myself clear. I finally chose one confessor, and he advised me as above.

From Toronto, Ontario

(1) Talking to my spiritual directors; (2) the book *Helps for the Scrupulous* by Father Abata, and especially the pamphlet *Crippled by Fear* by Father Daniel Lowery, which I use as the first-aid kit when scruples come; (3) the book *The Boy Who Couldn't Stop Washing: The Experience and Treatment of Obsessive-Compulsive Disorder*

by Judith L. Rapoport, MD. This book enlightened my whole family about what is wrong with me.

From Amarillo, Texas

I tried everything to overcome my scrupulosity, but failed. I was frustrated a lot, cursed myself, and feared a lot. But now I devote myself to reciting the rosary when I am driving, eating, walking, or working. How wonderful this spiritual medicine is! You should try this and find out for yourself the real GOOD the rosary is. Reciting the rosary is so simple, so easy, but you should focus your own mind on the rosary. Please do not ridicule this practice...I am a highly educated person. Remember that Saint Alphonsus Liguori was a doctor of the Church, and he recited the rosary continuously.

From Albany, New York

For the last several years a young priest with compassion and patience has answered many far-out questions for me. He has seen me through a lot of pain and sorrow and has been my spiritual advisor. I started going to other confessors when I felt better, partly because I felt I was overburdening my own confessor, and partly because I felt I had to take responsibility for myself. One priest told me he would answer questions if he felt they should be answered, but the questions I did ask he wouldn't answer. He said he was sorry, but answering would just feed my problem. This made sense and also made me start answering my own questions and trusting in God. My sister has also become my secular spiritual advisor (with the approval of my regular spiritual advisor). This has also helped.

From Colorado Springs, Colorado

What helped me the most was an organization called Recovery, Inc. The program does NOT contradict anyone's religious beliefs. It is a mental-health organization open to all. There is no cost, although they do accept "freewill offerings." It was started by a prominent Chicago psychiatrist, Abraham A. Low, MD. I learned, using their technique, to be an AVERAGE person in many phases of my life and, through my own initiative and common sense, have applied it to scrupulosity. It's terrific—a lifesaver for me.

From New Paltz, New York

(1) Regular reception of the Eucharist; (2) the support of a faithful confessor and doctor; (3) Recovery, Inc.—a self-help support group; (4) your own *SA* newsletters, which have provided encouragement and direction. Regarding Recovery, Inc., one thought pattern I've developed from their meetings is referred to as "secure thoughts." A "secure thought" would be any peace-giving idea that would counter fearful feelings. Examples are as follows: (a) "Bear with the discomfort and comfort will come" [from Recovery]; (b) "objectivity [for example, reading a book] overcomes panic [from Recovery]; (c) "he who prays will certainly be saved" [from your own Saint Alphonsus]; (d) "no child of Mary is ever lost" [Saint Bernard].

From London, England

"When in doubt, do!" is my philosophy, and it has worked wonders in my life. Other helps: seeing God as a loving God, not out to get me for every little thing; a wonderful priest's sermons on the fact that God made us human, so love the fact, don't hate it as we were taught to do; your newsletter, which I've been receiving from the first issue.

From Saskatchewan, Canada

I finally found a sympathetic, knowledgeable spiritual advisor, who leads me to good readings on the matter of neurosis/scrupulosity.

From Streator, Illinois

Very slowly, and with the help of two understanding priests who spent many long hours talking to me, I have come to know a God of love, understanding, mercy, and forgiveness. Knowing that God has and always will love me, even with my faults, helps me to control my scruples.

From Plano, Texas

I pretend I am another person talking to me. I can see my troubled look, my nervous gestures, and my overall uptightness. This other person I pretend to be is also my best friend and knows my deepest fears and greatest strengths. She gives me the best advice, and she's never as hard on me as I would be on myself. By getting out of myself like this, I can cut the problem down to size. I try to limit self-destructive thoughts. Funny thing, I am more likely to take my own advice than anyone else's, because it really fits me. I can remind myself that I am a terrific person who deserves to enjoy life—not sit around worried sick over some matter I probably have no control over anyway. It doesn't work perfectly every time, but it works well most of the time. And this "friend" is always available.

From Atlantic City, New Jersey

Talking to my confessor has helped. Also your newsletter has explained problems I never understood and helped me realize I wasn't alone or crazy!

From Wonder Lake, Illinois

I married an alcoholic and, strangely enough, I found the answer to my scrupulosity through the twelve steps of Al-Anon. I truly believe these twelve steps are a gift from God.

From Bangkok, Thailand

Despite my fears, I turn to prayer each day and feel that God will not abandon this struggling soul.

From D. B.

Thank you for your wonderful newsletter about scrupulosity. Although I don't believe I am an extreme case, I have always been told I worry too much. I never really paid attention to this comment because it was such a part of my life. Recently, however, I've really been tested by my anxieties. There are times I've really felt as though I was addicted to worrying, when, in all honesty, I believe it was the easy way out. I think that facing up to decisions I've made, letting the past be, and getting on with my life was a harder responsibility. It has to be my decision to turn my life around, with the help of God. Last year, my son was preparing for his first holy Communion. As he prepared for reconciliation, he would constantly ask me, "I'm sorry I looked at my brother in a mean way," or "I thought about something bad. Is it a sin? Do you forgive me?" Exasperated, I would say, "Look, you didn't sin. Of course I forgive you, but get on with it and forget this. Do something to help others, and have fun. You're missing a great time of your life." Well, it hit me like a ton of bricks. Here I was acting like God, but I couldn't even accept my own advice. I really began to miss feeling happy and enjoying life. I felt as though my worrying took time away from myself in trying to be a better and more fulfilled person. As I taught my son about the sacrament he would receive, I taught myself to trust in God's love and healing power. A priest at confession gave me a wonderful piece of advice: "Just say to God that you know that he knows you've tried your best. He knows it's finished and he wants to see you happy and looking to the future." I still falter. I'm a little anxious reading the "Dilemma Department." But I think I'm making progress. I just wanted to give you my new address for the newsletter, but my heart wanted to hug you, too. Thank you.

From N. Z.

The single most helpful idea I ever derived from a sermon was one priest defining "mercy" as God being right in the thick of everything with us, of his feeling and enduring all of our lives with us. He's not just an observer; he's right with us, experiencing our joy and heartache in everything that happens. Our feelings, hopes, discouragements, and pain are his, too. We must simply go together with him through it all.

From P. F.

For scrupulous people, "God" is always that small voice saying, "That's not quite good enough." He's a very domineering God, ready to punish if we don't do the right thing at the right time. We know the true God is different. Read the stories of the prodigal son, of Mary Magdalene, Matthew, Zacchaeus, and Peter. Christ never demanded that these persons earn their forgiveness and fellowship with him through some of the formalisms and tortures a scrupulous person puts himself through.

From T. S.

I've made great strides in overcoming my scrupulosity, and I would like to share my ideas. First, realize that freeing yourself from scrupulosity takes time. Take positive action; prayer alone isn't enough. Find an understanding confessor, even if it means going outside your parish, and follow his advice. Don't trust your own feelings, at least not until you have developed better judgment. Read Catholic literature to learn all you can about confession and forming a correct conscience. I've found question-and-answer columns very helpful. Send in a question occasionally. Realize that God loves you, even with your failings. He loves you as you are, and he knows that you are trying to do the right thing. Know that the sacrament of reconciliation is meant to be a positive experience that brings peace of mind. If you agonize over it, you should seek help. Pray to the Holy Spirit for the guidance and courage needed to overcome scrupulosity. Then do your best and leave the rest in God's hands.

From G. N.

Whenever I start to feel anxious, I remember these words of Saint Alphonsus Liguori: "God is all-powerful; he can help. God is all-good; he wishes to help. God has pledged his word; therefore, he will help." The good saint was bothered by scruples himself in his old age and would repeat this act of faith over and over again.

From P. K.

I am presently 98 percent cured of scrupulosity. I would like to tell the members of SA some advice I have found helpful. When you are "hit" by a particular scruple or worry and feel the need to "analyze" or think about it, resist the temptation. In the past I felt that I might resolve the situation if I analyzed it enough. This "compulsion" to analyze resulted in the particular worry becoming greater in my mind. I eventually found that if I ignored whatever it was I felt so compelled to worry about, when I thought about it later, it didn't bother me as much. In fact, it often didn't bother me at all! I would recommend to individuals to resist the temptation to analyze until they can see their priest or spiritual counselor. Mine used to tell me, "Don't analyze until you're here with me." That was darn good advice. If someone doesn't have a spiritual counselor, I would recommend this: When something hits you, give yourself time out before you think about it. If possible, wait a few days to think about it, but do not write it down! That will only make matters worse! Someone may say, "What if I die before I analyze my problem or see my counselor about it?" All I can say is life has its risks. If, by risking this, you may be able to live with a little less anxiety, a little less worry, and possibly move toward curing yourself of scrupulosity, then I believe it is worth it. My own experience showed that 99 percent of the time I was worried over nothing more than a scruple.

From K. L.

One afternoon while paying a visit to a church, I picked up your pamphlet *Scrupulous Anonymous*. I'm twenty-nine years old. I've constantly been plagued by scruples since an early age, feeling I've lost out on so much as a result of these scruples. Lately I've managed to get above some of these worries, but many linger on. Your little pamphlet was to me both a medicine and a comfort in knowing that others have suffered greatly and have found a way out. Up until now I've felt alone with this problem.

From T. C.

For me personally, fighting scrupulosity has turned into a lifelong affair. I am nearly sixty-five and still struggle at times. In my mind, though, I am confident that with God's help I will win out in the end. The kind words and the examples illustrated in your monthly publication have been a real assistance. Thank you so much. You know, sometimes when I read the Dilemma Department's questions and answers I think to myself, *What weird questions*—that is, until I look into my past. I then realize that while some of the specific questions may be different from mine, the thrust of the questions is no different.

From J. C.

I have suffered with scrupulosity for many years. I recently attended a charismatic renewal service and asked Father to pray for me. I am not healed completely, but I know that Jesus did touch me and I am on my way to recovery. Your prayers would be greatly appreciated, as I consider myself one of the really bad cases. My scrupulosity began in my teenage years, and I am now sixty-four years old. I do know that the Lord has been helping me. I have felt like a different person in the past five or six weeks. Still, it is going to be a while before scrupulosity is completely gone from my mind.

From A. C.

I have suffered from scrupulosity and feel that I have now overcome it. I still sin, of course, but who doesn't? God accepts my weaknesses and knows I myself will try to find strength to overcome them. And, yes, I will continue to try. Heaven is a beautiful place, and what makes it beautiful is a compassionate, loving God who does accept our weaknesses as well as our strengths. God invites us to look past our weaknesses and look at the potential that we all have. I will continue to pray for all people afflicted with scrupulosity. Heaven is obtainable for all people!

From A. G.

I have saved every one of the *SA* newsletters for future reference, they are so helpful. I seem to make great strides and then get set back once again. It sure has been a great struggle. I keep asking God to help me. One positive side to my scrupulosity is that it keeps me close to God because I need him so much to get through life. Keep up the good work, we need all the encouragement and positive feedback we can get.

From J. F.

To believe is to trust fully in God's endless mercy and to return again always to that mercy. But often we hold on to our sins, our guilt, and our shame, and act as if we were too bad, too ugly, or too dirty to be forgiven. The greatest act of faith—that is, of trust—is to let God be for us who God is: a God without hatred, revenge, anger, or resentment; a God who is love, mercy, compassion, and forgiveness.

From D. S.

It is important to unbend the bow occasionally in some way, that is, to relax and to play. It is especially important for people who are inclined to be scrupulous. Don't feel guilty when you are enjoying needed recreation. Throw yourself fully into play, just as fully as you throw yourself into work. The more you can work out a healthy balance in this regard, the more likely you will be able to achieve that sense of well-being and peace that God surely wants us to enjoy.

From F. L.

Let's look at parents teaching a baby to walk. They put the baby down, back up, and say, "Come on, honey," and the baby takes a step in their direction…and falls flat. What's the next thing the parents do? Do they spank the baby for falling? Of course not. They run over, gently pick up their little one, kiss the spot and make it well, put the baby down again, back away, and say, "Come on, honey, try it again." Now, the plain truth is: God loves you as much as parents ever loved a baby, so take a deep breath and say, "God really loves ME! Nothing else matters."

From K. K.

My child, you are not to fight the power in a stormy sea. The "you" that is not attached to anything is a cork. The smaller the cork, the easier it rides the waves. You are a very small cork, and no matter how high the waves become, you will ride buoyantly over all of them, without any talent of your own. The worst that will happen will be a little spray or a foamy wave will top over your head for a moment or two. No matter how mountainous the seas become, you need have no fear at all. A cork is buoyant because of air cells trapped within the enduring bark. The air in your cork is the wind of my Spirit. The bark is the fabric of your faith in my Son, Jesus. Your cork will weather all storms. Take heart, my child, and allow yourself to float.

From Sister Karen Berry

"As clay is in the potter's hands, so you are in mine" (Jeremiah 18:6). We need a reminder that we are still in the hand of the Potter, and if the Potter chooses to smash us (or seems to), that's because he has a better vision than we of the new creation we can still become. Watch a potter some time. The smashing is not done in anger, in order to destroy. The smashing is simply part of the process, part of the creating, part of the unfolding of potential. It isn't bad being a clay pot. Someone has a vision for us. Someone holds us to shape us. Someone will create us anew again and again.

From R. B.

John 6:37 states, "I will not reject anyone who comes to me." What a consoling passage this is for those scrupulous persons who fear God's wrath and rejection.

From P. M.

I recently read in a pocket calendar some useful information about first aid and units of measure. I found the word *scruple* as a unit of measure, symbolizing something very small and minute. I had to chuckle to myself because it is funny and true. What foolishness to think we actually are or ever will be perfect in what we do. We are only human. The important thing is to try and to keep trying. When we fall, let's stand up and try again.

From D. F. W.

I only wish I had put myself in the hands of a mature and good priest whom I trusted a long time ago. Years of unnecessary suffering would have been saved. I do exactly what he tells me, especially concerning the reception of the Eucharist; and confession, which used to make me physically ill, is now a joy.

From M. S.

I was ninety years old on December 9. I would like to pass on to you something I have always told my children, grandchildren, great-grandchildren, and great-great-grandchildren: Never hold a grudge. Get it out in the open and talk about it. Don't make mountains out of molehills. I believe in confession in the Catholic Church because I think it helps to not make mountains out of molehills, if we are sincere.

From K. M.

I would like to tell my fellow SA members that I pray for them constantly. When I hear about their worries and doubts I can relate to their sufferings, even when my own scruples might be somewhat different. At heart, every one of our scruples is about our relationship with God. Once we are assured that that is all right—that God still loves us despite everything—then peace and happiness can come into our lives. That's my prayer for all who are afflicted with scrupulosity, myself included.

From A. L.

Advice for confession—three B's: Be Blunt, Be Brief, Be Gone.

From S. W.

You can find enough trouble in the world without going out of your way to find it. But no matter where you go, you can find happiness if you look for it.

From A. P.

People worry about many things, when only one is necessary—and that is their love of almighty God.

From L. M.

I try to remember that God does not give us a cross heavier than we can bear, and when he sees fit he will lift it, I'm sure.

From T. R.

Get the most out of each day and don't worry about yesterday's mistakes.

From J. P.

If God is good enough to you to forgive you your sins, be good enough to yourself to forget them.

From S. F.

The greatest troubles we have are generally the troubles that never happen. Imagination makes fools of us all.

From G. S.

Through the goodness of God, and with the help of the *SA* newsletter, I have been enjoying peace of mind more than I ever have in my life. I live a happy life and have started to pray for other scrupulous people so they will find the same peace that I have.

From C. W.

When I go to confession, what helps me to say the prayers assigned to me as my penance is not to say them all at one time. I will say one prayer, and then in about an hour I will say another, and so on. This gives me a fresh start and a new outlook.

From S. B.

I am scrupulous and would like to share with your readers a message that has helped me very much. It is from Archbishop Helder Camara: "There is no single definition of holiness. There are dozens, hundreds. But there is one I am particularly fond of: Being holy means getting up immediately every time you fall, with humility and joy. It doesn't mean never falling into sin. It means being able to say, 'Yes, Lord, I have fallen a thousand times. But thanks to you I have gotten up again a thousand and one times.'" That's all. I like thinking about that.

From D. D.

Just a note to share on the blessings of confession. One time I went to confession heavily burdened with my sins. After confessing "monumental" sins, the priest said, "Is that all?" and then, "Go in God's peace!" This sacrament has deepened my concept of God's infinite mercy and forgiveness.

From G. H.

After morning coffee, I read over one of my old *SA* newsletters. As a morning person I can take in new ideas then which won't go in at other times.

From R. F.

This is a Worrier's Prayer that I learned a long time ago: "Dear Jesus, please help me to be patient all through the day. My heart is troubled by little but vexatious trials. Dear Lord, please help me to see things as they really are, not as my distorted mind sees them. From neglect of thy holy inspirations, Lord deliver us."

From C. S.

When I am troubled with a particular scruple, I first give the problem over to the Lord: "Let go and let God." I just know that if I trust him totally he will bring the present matter out for my good and his honor and glory, providing I do not take it back—no matter how much it hurts. He knows what's best for us and will bring us the peace that surpasses all understanding.

From J. S.

I have suffered from scruples for many years, but have found that by going to one confessor and staying with him and doing exactly what he says has helped very much.

From K. M.

I would like to share a "tool" that has really been a wonderful help to me. Perhaps other scrupulous persons will also find this helpful. I purchased a small notebook, one which fits nicely into a purse or glove compartment. I have labeled each page with a date for each day of the year. I am entering a sentence or two for each day. For instance, on one day I have written: "The benefit of the doubt is in my favor. Should I be wrong, it does not matter. God will not hold me responsible" (from *Helps for the Scrupulous* by Father Abata). Another day: "Act against scruples. Make this your intention today" (from the *SA* newsletter). Or: "Fear is useless. What is needed is trust" (Jesus; in the Gospel). Each day upon awakening, during my prayer time, I will read a page from my *SA* "meditation book" and use my daily reading as a weapon against my scruples. This has been the best help I've found, after prayer, to combat my daily struggle with scruples.

From J. G.

One day a thought occurred to me. It has helped me a great deal and I'd like to pass it on to others. When I am troubled or worried about past sins or whether I made a bad confession, I simply say to myself, *I would do whatever God wants me to do, and God knows I am telling the truth.* With that, the trouble ceases.

From P. C.

Once there was a woman who lived near a dam. One day the heavens opened and the dam overflowed and flooded the town. The woman climbed on to her roof. A neighbor came by in a small wooden boat and shouted, "Come into the boat!" She answered, "Oh no, the Lord will save me." A few hours later the Coast Guard came by in a motorboat and shouted, "Come on, get in!" She refused saying, "Oh no, the Lord will save me." The water continued to rise. At last a helicopter came, and the pilot shouted over the megaphone, "This is your last chance! Please get in!" She refused again, repeating, "The Lord will save me." So the woman drowned. She went to heaven and met the Lord. "Why didn't you save me?" she complained. The Lord answered, "What do you want from me? I sent you two boats and a helicopter!" I believe this little story shows how we scrupulous often overlook God's ways of helping us, simply because his ways are so ordinary. We need to see that God is very efficient. He doesn't spend lots of extra energy doing fireworks when all that is needed are a few small candles.

From B. McG.

It is so important for us scrupulous people to realize that God loves us. He's not waiting for us to make a mistake so that he can send us to hell on a technicality!

From D. B.

I am entering my second year of theology in preparation for the priesthood. I would like to offer this letter of advice and consolation to the scrupulous. I have suffered from scrupulosity for years. Now I find that I am much more confident and that my scrupulosity has decreased greatly. There is great hope for the scrupulous. Things can get better. Use the cross of scrupulosity to get closer to Jesus. As you get more wrapped up in the love he has for you, especially through the Eucharist, you will become less scrupulous and more free, more like Jesus. By increasing your spirituality—through participation in the Eucharist, daily prayer, reading holy Scripture—you will kill two birds with one stone. You will get rid of scrupulosity and at the same time become a new person in Christ....Also, get a regular confessor/spiritual director. Always obey his advice, even when your feelings tell you not to. At such times, you are called to go against your feelings, to walk on the water toward our Lord, trusting that the Lord is working through your confessor. It will hurt to do this, but as time goes on it will get easier and you will be glad you obeyed. Remember that God is a tremendous Lover, a loving Father, and not a policeman seeking to catch each little mistake you make.

From J. D.

After rereading some back issues of the *SA* newsletter, I decided to share my feelings with you. I suffer from scruples, of course, and admit to being a perfectionist and a self-centered person. Through SA my perfectionism has been toned down; I also have a gem of a spiritual director who has helped me view life more realistically. My particular brand of self-centeredness (blue moods) does not mean I do not care for those around me. For myself, it is just a matter that there are times when I take too many things to heart. As I'm slowly taking charge of this area of my life, many self-created hurts are going away. Being a sensitive, creative, and affectionate person makes this twice as difficult for me. One practice I have made in my life is to be as thoughtful as possible to others. Also, my spiritual director suggested I be considerate toward my own needs when I see someone becoming selfish toward me. I went through a period in my life when I was extremely strait-laced and austere. All this achieved was a heightened degree of anxiety to the point that I got hives! My life is much more relaxed now and it is easier for me to accept my limitations on a day-to-day basis, while leaving the rest in God's hands.

From D. H.

I also struggled with impure thoughts and images and feelings. The harder I fought against the thoughts and images, the more they came. What really helped me was to remember that since I didn't want these thoughts in the first place, they were not sinful. Many times I felt doubts that I was letting these thoughts come or letting them stay or even making them come, but I knew it was all part of my working so hard against them. When I began to relax a little in regard to this problem, it eventually stopped bothering me. In regard to the person who is worried about thoughts and desires to curse people, what helps me is to remind myself that I don't really wish that on them or at least I don't want to wish it on them, and then forget about it.

From M. A.

It is awful to be scrupulous and to worry about everything. But I try to give it all to the Lord and put it in his hands. I find that when I give a situation to the Lord Jesus, he always takes care of it. I know he really loves me and all of us. But sometimes I forget. And I don't remember everything that the priest tells me in confession. But God has been good to me.

From M. L.

It helps me when I keep in mind that God loves everyone whom I love—only infinitely more so. So I say this prayer many times: "Dear Lord, I love all the people who are worried right now, tortured in their minds and hearts by scrupulosity. I love them, but I know that you love them so very much more than I do. Help them all, dear Lord. Fill them with your consolation and peace. Make them all remember that you are our Father. No power can tear us away from you. All our trust rests in you, O Lord."

From C. P.

Communion time has always been the hardest time for me. I feel so unworthy. Then I came upon this prayer that has helped me so very much: "Jesus loves me, accepts me, redeems me, and forgives me as I am this moment." I repeat it over and over as I approach Communion. I use a shorter version, too: "Jesus loves me as I am this moment." Now my lack of perfection and lack of holiness do not make me think that Jesus does not love me. I realize that he loves me as I am, and I love him. Now I am more relaxed and more at peace, and I think of Jesus, not my faults, at Communion time.

From J. I.

When some particular fear is troubling me, I find this procedure helpful:

1. I tell God, in my own words, what I am troubled about and ask his help.
2. I imagine the fear disappearing and leaving me.
3. I think about what the Church teaches to be true or what I know to be true.
4. I thank God for helping me.
5. I make sure that I am doing my work or helping my wife, even though I am suffering from this anxiety and fear.

From L. B.

This prayer to Saint Anthony helps me: "Blessed Saint Anthony, faithful servant of Jesus, God has granted so many favors through your intercession. So many lost and mislaid things have been recovered through your prayers for us. I pray that you find for me peace of mind. Help me find the right and prudent way to act. Find for me the path out of my scruples and darkness and uneasiness and doubt. I want to faithfully serve my God and Savior with peace of mind and fullness of love in my heart. Through your prayers, dear Saint Anthony, I hope one day to be with you and all the other saints in heaven forever. Amen."

From H. C.

If you are worried with scruples or any other trouble, and trying on your own to be a good Christian, but not sure you are winning the battle, try this: Believe in Jesus Christ, the Son of God. He said, "Ask anything in my name." So ask him, "Jesus, Son of God, come and live your life in me. I'm sorry for my sins. Come and reside in my heart that you may live your life through me. I praise and thank you because I believe in your word, and you are the truth that sets me free."

From L. O.

Father, I come to you humbly, and ask you to let the Holy Spirit have complete control over me and my life—all of my thoughts, each word spoken by my tongue, my temper, my attitudes and feelings toward my fellow men. In every phase of the work I do, let it all be done for your honor and glory; let the Holy Spirit have absolute control over all my life. Amen. Praise, honor, and glory are yours, almighty and loving Father.

From E. T.

With a strong faith in God
Much can be done,
From fighting a war,
To seeing it won.
To bearing a hurt
That can never be cured,
To finding a way
Where vision was blurred

Yes, battles are won,
And loneliness fought
And sickness is cured,
Where God is first sought.
And remember this saying,
Whate'er you shall do,
"Take one step toward God,
And he'll take two toward you."

From R. T.

I was the lost lamb in your flock of sheep,
And you've found me and carried me home.
You guide me in everything that I do,
And I know that I'm never alone.
After all the pain that I've given you,
You've given to me only love.
And now I know that wherever I go
You'll look after me from above.
A wise man once said that those who seek
The Lord has already found him.
I believe it's true, for in seeking God,
I have built my world around him!

From F. T.

During recent years I have found it quite helpful to write down on a slip of paper, which I keep in my wallet, the advice the priest gives me after my visit with him. Reviewing my notes when a problem or situation recurs usually helps me to avoid another visit to the priest. I thought I would mention this for what it is worth.

From H. M.

> I like myself, accept myself, quite unconditionally.
> With all my scruples, faults, and fears,
>   there's no one else like me.
> I know my happiness depends on what's inside of me.
> It can't be purchased at a bank, or at a pharmacy;
> God is good and God is kind, and thus he did decree.

From J. R.

Some lines from a hymn we used to sing console me:

> Lord, for tomorrow and its needs I do not pray;
> Keep me, my God, from stain of sin just for today.
> Guide me, guard me, keep me, Lord, just for today.

From R. M.

With regard to the holy fear of God, this helps me: the words of Mary in her prayer the *Magnificat*, as recorded in the Gospel of Luke: "His mercy is from generation to generation toward all those who fear him." Therefore, even as I fear God, so his mercy is upon me. This knowledge and this experience of mercy upon me is a big help. Also the Book of Ecclesiasticus contains many words about God's reward toward those who fear him. Fear of God is very real in my life, but not a problem. I am being rewarded for having this gift of the Holy Spirit.

From P. N.

> I cannot dwell forever on things of the past,
> I cannot hang on tightly for they will not last.
> I must progress, not only remember,
> From the first little flicker to the last dying ember.
> The good of the past is all that remains;
> May the good of the present blot out its pains.
> May the Lord give me strength to see it all through
> As he does when we ask him,
> through old times and new.

From J. N.

> O Jesus, pardon and mercy and grace to accept the burden
>   laid on my shoulder by the merits
>   of the wounds of thy sacred shoulder.
> O Jesus, pardon and mercy and grace to accept
>   the sorrow sent us
>   through the merits of the wounds of thy sacred hands.
> O Jesus, pardon and mercy and the help to walk
>   the straight way
>   through the merits of the wounds of thy sacred feet.
> O Jesus, may our hearts leap with joy when we
>   hear thy name
>   through the merits of the wounds in thy sacred side.
> O Jesus, help us all.

From M. W.

I believe that the scrupulous person, by his very worrisomeness, is constantly living in the presence of God and is growing in the love of God through his constant petitioning for relief, or at least for the grace of patient acceptance. For many of us, growing up in the fear of God, instead of the love of God, has made so much difference. We have to change this around. But regardless of counseling, some things have to be dealt with by the individual directly with God.

From R. P.

I will try to be happy under all circumstances. I will make up my mind to be happy within myself right now, where I am today. Let my soul smile through my heart, and let my heart smile through my eyes. O God, let me scatter your rich smiles in sad hearts.

From S. O.

The other day I went to the park to sketch trees. I took up painting to use up some of my overactive imagination, and it really helps! Maybe this will help some other scrupulous people. Looking at the trees, I thought:

> A newness, a new beginning,
> Thank you, God, for spring.
> Help me, Lord, to renew.
> To throw off hate, to put on love.
> This is my Good News:
> God loves me!

From M. M.

Jesus loves me! What a mighty truth to give strength to my living; to give beauty to my loving; to give courage to my doing! He loves me whether I am alone or with others; at work or at prayer; tried by temptation and discouragement or happy and at peace. Then how much can I love him in return simply by giving myself to him, because he loves me!

From A. N.

Being scrupulous, we are lovers of truth, and this is truth, God is love; God loves us; God loves you. Be confident in the acceptance of that unshakable fact.

From F. C.

> Even as the light
> Descends on darkness,
> Even as the rain
> Descends on the parched earth,
> So your peace, Lord,
> Descends on our anxiety.
> Grant us your peace.

From Saint Alphonsus Liguori

Let scrupulous persons suffer this cross of theirs with resignation and not perplex themselves about it. God himself sends it to them for a number of good reasons: so that they may be more humble; so that they may be on their guard against the occasion of real sin; so that they may more often commend themselves to the Lord in prayer and put their entire trust in the divine Goodness. Let them also often have recourse to the Blessed Virgin Mary, who is called and truly is the Mother of Mercy and the Comforter of the Afflicted.

If you want to be sure of not losing God, then give yourself to him without reserve. A soul which resolutely separates itself from everything and gives itself all to God will never lose him again; because God himself will not allow that a soul which has heartily given itself all to him should ever again turn its back upon him and lose him.

From D. C.

Do we receive crosses as a great deal less than we deserve? Do we take them in a spirit of resignation and a sense of their justice? Wouldn't we eliminate a good many altogether if we did this? Our limitations of nature, position, and intellectual gifts are very real mortifications and crosses; but, if we have some realization of what we have deserved for our sins, we shouldn't be lost in admiration of our patience, but we shall accept them quite naturally.

Appendixes

The History of Confession

Not everyone realizes that the sacraments have not always been practiced in the form in which we are familiar with them. Sacraments have undergone a development, a development influenced not only by the Church's understanding of what Jesus intended, but also influenced by the society in which the Church has flourished and by the needs and hopes of the People of God.

In the pages that follow a very condensed history of the sacrament of reconciliation is presented. Perhaps you might be able to recognize, not only the details of the sacrament as it has developed over time, but even more important, the gentle prodding of the Holy Spirit, constantly present in the Church and in each of us. It is this same Holy Spirit that is present to each and every one of us today —guiding, directing, and forming each of us into the people that will be the "Lord's own" (Deuteronomy 7:6).

I also hope that as you read this history of confession, you will recognize that God's love and mercy in what has been a consistent way in which the Church has asked for and celebrated that mercy and love. I hope that, as you let this truth grow in your hearts and influence your appreciation of the sacrament, it may help each of you feel a little more at peace, especially in those moments when you feel that you have made a mistake in your confession or perhaps omitted some detail or explanation. It seems that God has found a way to forgive his people throughout time, and that is what is the most important.

JESUS AND SINNERS

Even people who do not believe that Jesus is the Son of God are nevertheless left with the impression that he was a person with an unusual capacity for forgiveness. Not only was he able to forgive sinners, he was also able to forgive those who had sinned against him (Luke 23:34). The gospels are filled with illustrations of his forgiveness in action; the story of the Prodigal Son (Luke 15:11–32), the story of the Lost Sheep (Luke 15:3–7), and the story of the Woman caught in adultery (John 8:3–11) are some obvious examples.

The message that Jesus preached, a message preached by John the Baptist (repent and believe) but completed by Jesus (because the Kingdom of God is among you), was a message that called people to *metanoia*, the Greek word that means to change your life and your heart. It was more than a message of calling people to repentance, which means to be sorry for what you have done; Jesus wanted people to be sorry, but he also desired that they be fundamentally changed by their sorrow and their personal experience of forgiveness. This fundamental change, the reordering of their life and their decisions was to be understood as *gospel* (good news) because it would usher in a new way of life and a new way of living, which he called the kingdom of God.

Jesus was so insistent on *metanoia* and the ramifications of this life-changing decision that when his apostles asked him for further clarification, "How much more do we have to forgive?" he answered them, "not seven times, but, I tell you, seventy-seven times" (Matthew 18:22). In other words, in the kingdom of God there was no limit to what could be forgiven and no limit to what needed to be forgiven: "Forgive us our sins, / for we ourselves forgive everyone indebted to us" (Luke 11:4).

After his resurrection, Jesus appeared to his disciples, and spoke to them in the words that have traditionally been understood as the words that instituted the sacrament of penance and reconciliation: "If you forgive the sins of any, they are forgiven them; if you retain the sins of any, they are retained" (John 20:23). Within the context of his life and ministry it can be understood that, although the power to "bind someone" is certainly a prerogative, the intention of Jesus was to not bind but rather to loose, to free people from that which held them fast and set them firmly on the path to the kingdom of God.

THE PRACTICE OF THE EARLY CHURCH

The primary sacrament of forgiveness in the early Church was baptism. The apostles preached the gospel as it had been given to them by Jesus and invited people to turn away from their lives of sin and to embrace the good news. It was understood by all that baptism reconciled a person to God and forgave all their sins, but it was also understood that it could be received only once. There was a problem with those people who had already been baptized and who did not live up to their baptismal promises. What could be done on their behalf?

The early Christian community looked first, as might well be expected, to their Jewish roots and heritage for an answer. Jewish rabbis had a practice that was known as "binding and loosing." If a member of the community somehow offended the community the rabbis would bar them for the community, and if they later repented of their offense, the rabbis would welcome them back. This practice was a practical application of the admonition of Jesus, if all else fails between you and a brother and a sister, "take it to the Church" (Matthew 18:15–18) for judgment. Saint Paul may well have been referring to this practice when he instructed the community in Corinth that they should have done this when a certain member of the community had violated the marriage laws by "living with his Father's wife" (Leviticus 18:8; 1 Corinthians 5:1–13). Paul expected that the community would expel the man, and then later accepts him back into the community if he reformed his life (see 2 Corinthians 2:5–11).

The practice of binding and loosing was useful, but by the second century the Church had developed a practice by which a person, who had fallen into serious sin (that is, murder, adultery, idolatry), could become a *penitent* (from the Latin *paenitentia,* which means repentance). Penitents formed a special group within the community who would spend an extended period of time in fasting, prayer, and giving alms, all the while asking for the strength to be faithful to their baptismal promises. The Christian community would join them in prayer during the period of penitence. When the bishop of the community determined that they had indeed reformed their lives he would welcome them back in the name of the community, lay his hands on their head as a sign of reconciliation and forgiveness, and invite them once again to join the community in the celebration of the Eucharist. A person was permitted to become a penitent only once in their lifetime; to be admitted more than once, in the words of Clement of Alexandria, "Would make a mockery of God's mercy."

The group of penitents was very small, because most people did not commit the kind of sins that were considered serious enough for this type of public penance. Others, aware of the fact that they could seek public forgiveness and reconciliation only once in their life, postponed entrance into the group of penitents for as long as possible. For most people, however, forgiveness was something that they routinely asked for, and received, from their brothers and sisters in the community or something they asked God for at the beginning of the Eucharistic liturgy. As long as the Christian community was small, this form of public penance and reconciliation worked well; but as the community grew larger and larger, the practice became more and more strained and seemed not to fit the needs of the community.

A further strain was put on this particular form of the practice of sacramental reconciliation by the persecutions suffered by the Christian community in the third century. Some members of the community went to their death as martyrs, while others chose not to accept martyrdom. Those who did not become martyrs performed the required sacrifices to the gods and renounced Jesus, and then later, when the furor of persecution had settled down, asked to be re-admitted to the Christian community. Some bishops freely accepted these returning apostates but other bishops and communities were not so inclined. Apostasy, according to one bishop of the time, was the "unforgivable sin" (Matthew 12:31) and could not be forgiven. A consistent and pastoral approach to this situation was never agreed upon.

Eventually, the practice of public penance and reconciliation slowly died out. It was replaced by a different practice, a practice with roots in the burgeoning monasteries and monasticism that were beginning to flourish throughout the Mediterranean and across much of Europe, into England and Ireland.

BEFORE THE COUNCIL OF TRENT

Monastic training often included the concept of what today might be called a "mentor." A new recruit in the monastery would be as-signed an older monk who was entrusted with the task of teach-ing him all about being a monk (from the *Greek* meaning, "to live alone"). The younger man would visit the older man once a week. In their conversations the younger monk would often confess his faults and failings to the older monk, and ask for the direction and the advice that might be helpful in overcoming them. At the end of their session, they would pray together and ask for the forgiveness of any sins that they may have committed.

In the fifth century, at the direct request of the papacy, the monks, who up until this moment were centered in their monastic compounds, were entrusted with the task of converting to the Chris-tian faith the Germanic tribes that were migrating into former ter-ritory of the Roman Empire. These monks, particularly the monks from Ireland, brought with them the practice of confessing their sins to another and they urged their new converts to do the same. The monks understood the practice as a way of keeping the new Christian faith alive and vibrant in the lives of their new converts. The practice seemed to be well accepted and popular among the people because it spread very quickly.

When this new penitential practice reached the parts of the former empire in southern Europe, the first reaction of the bishops of that place was to condemn it, but eventually the practice took root, even in those places where it was vigorously opposed. People wanted some assurance that they were loved and forgiven by God and the traditional practice of public penance did not fulfill their needs. They also preferred to confess their sins directly to the priest, which this new practice permitted, and not to the bishop, which was required in the more traditional practice. By the seventh century private confession of sins had taken root in most places and within a few centuries it was accepted throughout the Church.

During the Middle Ages the practice of private confession of sins continued to be both practiced and developed. For example, the penance assigned for the remission of sins at first needed to be completed before a person was accepted back into Communion, perhaps a concept adopted from the old practice of public penance. Eventually, however, it was understood that the penance could be performed and the person could return to Communion at the same time. The penances themselves also changed. Originally the assigned penance would be closely related to the sin; if a person stole one goat, they would have to return two goats to the aggrieved party, but eventually the recitation of certain prayers were all that was normally required, as long as proper restitution was made.

The other development was that the role of the priest evolved more and more into the role of a judge, and the keeper of God's mercy. This was a distinct development because it seemed, in the original format popularized by the monks, that the priest would simply assure the penitent that their sins had been forgiven by God, but eventually this evolved into the practice where the priest would absolve the penitent from their sins. The absolution was given in the name of God but it could be surmised, and at least for some people it was assumed, that the forgiveness was dependent on the priest and not on God. This became the primary "fuel" that powered the Protestant Reformation's insistence that people seek forgiveness directly from God, and not from a priest.

Other developments during this period of time impacted the Church's understanding of the sacrament even more profoundly. These developments included the distinction between mortal sin and venial sin, perfect and imperfect contrition, and the punishment of sins.

Mortal Sin and Venial Sin: There had been a long tradition in the Church that distinguished between serious sin (sins which required public penance) and less serious sins (which were forgiven in the Eucharist). Serious sin was understood as sin that was so grievous (murder, adultery, idolatry) that it was "deadly" to the soul and to the life of grace within a person. It was understood that if a person died in this state that he or she would be denied heaven. Other sins were considered less serious and very pardonable. In the Middle Ages a listing of mortal (serious) sin and venial (pardonable) sin was never detailed, but there was agreement among theologians of the time that it was possible for a person to deliberately reject God through their choices and actions. It was understood that such a rejection of God and the law of God would bring a person to the everlasting fires of hell for all eternity.

Perfect and Imperfect Contrition: Sorrow for sin that is motivated by fear of punishment is understood as imperfect contrition; it is considered imperfect because even the most hardened criminals might regret that they will be punished but might not regret their choices and actions. Perfect contrition, on the other hand, is contrition that is based on the recognition within a person that the life of sin has no place in their life if they are trying to live their baptismal promises; this kind of contrition is necessary for a life of conversion and repentance.

Punishment of Sin: Sin, because it was understood as an offense against God, needed to be punished. People understood the consequences of breaking the civil law, for example, and recognized that even if forgiven, there were still consequences as a result of their actions. Sin was understood in much the same way; God would forgive sin, if the sins were confessed and absolution was received and the penance was performed, but there was still the consequence of sin. Theologians of the time differentiated between the *temporal* punishment due (punishment for sin after death, but for a set period of time) and the *eternal* punishment due (forgiven in the sacrament, but if not forgiven, punishment that would last for all eternity). The place where temporal punishment was experienced was *purgatory* and the place where eternal punishment was experienced was *hell.*

THE COUNCIL OF TRENT

The Council of Trent, in direct response to the Protestant Reformers who saw little need for the confession of sins to anyone except directly to God, issued strong directives and teachings about the sacrament of penance and reconciliation. The complaints and challenged issued by Martin Luther were particularly signaled out, and in his excommunication by Pope Leo X in 1520, twelve of his ideas concerning penance were condemned.

The Council reaffirmed that it was the will of the Lord and the constant tradition of the Church that the "integral confession of sins" was necessary after baptism for the forgiveness of sins. The Council understood that this integral confession would include the specifics and the particulars of all mortal sins committed; venial sins could be confessed, but it was not necessary to do so since they were forgiven in the sacrament of the Eucharist. This integral confession of sins was necessary so that the priest could judge the severity of the sins committed and assign the necessary penance.

The end result of the teaching of the Council of Trent was that most Catholics continued their practice of going to confession once a year, in preparation for their annual reception of holy Communion. This remained the common practice in the Church until early in the twentieth century when Pope Pius X encouraged the frequent reception of holy Communion. Catholics responded to his request, but because of their training and understanding also assumed that it was necessary to go to confession before the reception of Communion. As a result of this assumption, practically unchallenged and perhaps even encouraged by the clergy, Catholics would go to confession once a month or once a week, depending on how often they went to holy Communion.

CONTEMPORARY PRACTICE

By the time of the Second Vatican Council, it could be argued that there was general agreement and understanding that the sacrament of penance and reconciliation needed reform. Although for some Catholics the celebration of the sacrament was certainly an opportunity to deepen their relationship with the Lord and experience the Lord's abundant mercy, for many others confession was an obligation, a rule or requirement that needed to be fulfilled so that they would meet the minimal requirements of the law. It was for this reason that the Council emphasized that the purpose of the sacrament was an opportunity for conversion, confession, and forgiveness (*CCC* 1423–1424) and not a test of discipline.

The reforms of the Second Vatican Council reaffirmed two basic principles about sacramental confession and reconciliation, principles that were considered as essential to the *fundamental structure* of the sacrament. The first principle is that contrition, confession, and satisfaction are the graced action of the Holy Spirit, calling the individual person to ongoing conversion of life. The second principle is that the action of God is manifested through the ministry of the bishops and priests, through which the person is healed and restored to ecclesial communion with the Church (*CCC* 1448). The Church affirmed that it is only God who can forgive sins, but also reaffirmed that the Church is a sign and an instrument of the forgiveness and reconciliation of God (*CCC* 1441–1442).

The contemporary practice of the sacrament begins with the premise that the celebration of the sacrament is primarily a liturgical action that contains the following elements: a greeting and blessing, proclamation of the word of God, exhortation to repentance, the confession of sins, the imposition and acceptance of penance, and finally, absolution along with a prayer of thanksgiving and praise (*CCC* 1480). Understanding of the sacrament reaffirms the necessity for individual and integral confession and absolution (Council of Trent) but also introduces two new forms of the sacrament: communal celebration of the sacrament (with individual confession and absolution) and a communal celebration of the sacrament with general confession and general absolution (in cases of grave necessity) (*CCC* 1482–1483).

THE SA EXPERIENCE

Certainly the members of SA have experienced at least some of the changes in the practice of confession that resulted from the actions of the Second Vatican Council. We now experience the celebration of the sacrament in a completely different way than we did before the Council; but despite the changes, there are still some lingering attitudes that may not be helpful and which make our full participation in the spirit of renewal at best difficult. The most obvious attitude seems to be a continuing struggle to understand the difference between *metonia* and discipline. Many members of SA continue to emphasize specific elements of the sacramental practice, such as exact number of sins, performing the correct penance, being in the correct state of mind, and so on, over the primary purpose of the sacrament, which is the opportunity for the celebration of conversion, confession, and forgiveness. Discipline continues to receive the attention and the emphasis and celebration seems so far away and perhaps even unattainable.

There are probably few members of SA that are surprised by this assertion, because we know well that the manifestation of scrupulosity has always been found in the details. I think it may also be true to state that although it is the details that seem to consume us and hold our attention, each and every one of us hope for the day when we will be able to embrace the true spirit and purpose of the sacrament and be freed from the burden of guilt, anxiety, and worry.

Two specific actions may positively contribute to each of us reaching the goal that we all hope for. The first is the unmerited gift of grace and the second is a regular confessor.

Unmerited Gift of Grace: The Council makes it very clear that the forgiveness of sin is the action of the Holy Spirit, the activity of grace, that cannot be earned or demanded, but rather comes to each of us as a free gift from God. Each of us would do well to daily remind ourselves that it is God who is the provider of the grace that we need. Not that we should sit back and simply wait for something to happen, but perhaps it would not be a bad idea to remind ourselves each day that the grace that we need is a gift, and then prepare our hearts to be receptive for the gift that God desires to give us. Many members of SA are surprised to discover that some of the efforts that they consider to be essential and important are in fact blocking the power of God's grace working in their lives. That which blocks grace most effectively is fear, anxiety, worry, and guilt and so perhaps we are called by God to work actively against these impulses.

A Regular Confessor: We again repeat it here. The single most effective help to becoming open to the gift of God's grace and to overcome our scrupulosity is to work together with a regular confessor. Every one of the saints is in total agreement with this advice and recognizes the necessity of making this the primary emphasis. We have discussed it many times before, and we have also discussed the difficulty that many of us experience in our search for this kind of relationship, but despite the difficulty and effort demanded, it is worth the struggle.

Note: This section on the history of confession originally appeared in The Essential Handbook of the Bible, *Thomas M. Santa, C.Ss.R. (Liguori, MO: Liguori, Publications, 2001). Used with permission.*

A Letter From a Priest

few years ago, after the first edition of this book was published, I received the following letter from a priest. The letter was completely unsolicited and arrived in my normal stack of correspondence. As I read the letter I was immediately struck by the true pastoral concern expressed by the priest. I was also moved by his desire to be of help to the scrupulous person who had asked for his help and direction. With his permission I shared the contents of his letter and my response with the readers of *SA*. I include it here because I believe it effectively illustrates the dynamic that is often experienced between the confessor and his penitent.

QUESTION: I have been recently asked to hear the confession of a person who wants to go to confession every week. Well and good, but the person rattles on from a grocery list of sins and never shows any improvement. The person claims to be scrupulous and never seems to improve on the faults confessed. I am not sure if it is scrupulosity or ignorance of how to make a good confession. The person resents any corrections or suggestions. How would you handle this? I have been hearing confessions for fifty years but never ran into anything like this. Any suggestions?

A frustrated confessor

ANSWER: Father, thank you for taking the time to write your letter and for the pastoral concern that you have demonstrated seeking a response to this important dilemma. I appreciate the effort. I am sure the people who receive your pastoral care also are appreciative that you are willing to continue to learn and to seek the best advice and counsel possible. I hope the little bit of insight that I have to offer you will be helpful and might shine some light of understanding on the pastoral challenge that you face.

The person who has approached you with a request for you to become their regular confessor is perhaps scrupulous—there are many different manifestations of scrupulosity—but I believe this person is more than likely obsessive and compulsive. The difference between the two is important and essential to understand for both the person who is experiencing the difficulty and the confessor who encounters him/her within the sacrament.

A person who is scrupulous is a person who experiences what might be called a "tender conscience." Such a person experiences anxiety and frustration during his or her examination of conscience and within the celebration of the sacrament of penance because he or she desires, more than anything else, to please God and to receive the fullness of the sacramental grace. When confronted with a scrupulous person a patient confessor will discover the person's willingness and openness to pastoral direction and care. It is possible for both the scrupulous person and the confessor to observe and chart substantial progress in addressing the manifested anxiety and frustration. It will perhaps be a long process, and at times it will be very painful and difficult, but there will be progress nonetheless.

A person who is suffering from an obsessive and a compulsive disorder, a disorder that also has many different manifestations, is something completely other than what we might understand as scrupulosity. A person with obsessive and compulsive disorder might routinely identify himself or herself as scrupulous, but this identification is in fact misleading and not at all helpful. It is not helpful because as long as the emphasis remains on sin, or fear and anxiety about sin, or any of the other conditions that are routinely considered within the sacrament of reconciliation, there will be no progress and no healing.

What is at the core of the obsessive-compulsive disorder might best be understood as experiencing "a thousand frightening fantasies," or as another author once described it as "the doubting disease." What needs to be addressed is the impulse to doubt and not the doubt itself. The doubt, in the case of the scrupulous person the doubt about sin, is the manifestation, it could just as easily be about something else. It is the impulse itself that is at the root of the condition.

The person who is coming to you for confession, seemingly rattling off a list of sins and who is not open to questions or suggestions, is mired into a pattern of behavior and acting out that is indicative of obsessive-compulsive behavior. I do not believe the confessional experience that you describe is reflective of their ignorance of how to make a good confession, in fact my guess would be that this person knows well all of the rules and the requirements. I also believe that this person, in their heart of hearts, is motivated by the love of God and the desire to do good. Unfortunately, what you are encountering on a weekly basis is a person who is suffering terribly and who has made so many decisions and choices, not a single one which is sinful or deceitful, that has brought him or her to this point: it is a point of helplessness for the person and also for you.

That being said, I might also observe that the person who approached you, although suffering from a terrible illness, is nevertheless misusing the sacrament of penance, and by extension, you as his or her confessor. I use the word *misuse* deliberately in this reference. The person is misusing the sacrament and the confessor as an opportunity for reconciliation, not primarily to be healed or graced, but rather to seek relief from the anxiety and the fear that he or she is experiencing. This person is fooling oneself, again not deliberately or sinfully, but nevertheless misusing the sacrament of penance is not at all helpful. In the process of going to confession, performing the action that he or she has deemed essential, will not experience any relief, or at best a momentary relief, and will directly contribute to the progression of the illness instead of the possibility of becoming healed. This is one example of what makes obsessive-compulsive disorder so painful: instead of addressing the obsession and the compulsion this person is concentrating on the manifestation, and in the process, simply making matters complicated.

The situation that I am describing, as terrible as it sounds, is in fact even worse than you might imagine. The person who is misusing the sacrament and you as his or her confessor is at least somewhat aware of doing so. It is not a sinful action and it is not a sacrilegious action, but is rather an act of desperation, reflective of either the unwillingness or inability to engage his or her obsession and compulsion in a healthy manner. More than likely other confessors, members of the family, and close friends, not to mention professional psychologists and doctors, have all tried to intervene and help break the spiral of desperateness; but, in each instance, they have been rebuked and faced the same kind of resistance that you have experienced. Every time you suggest some sort of change or a new approach, you tap into the emotion, the anxiety, and the frustration that has been growing within. It is not that this person does not desire to listen to you and follow your advice, but rather that he or she is unable to do so.

With all this being understood, what can a confessor do? What can your response be? Unfortunately the answer that you seek will be much more nuanced and complicated than you might first imagine.

When a person comes to confession and he or she launches into the barrage of supposed sinfulness, understand that there is really nothing that you can do but listen. Don't question, ask for any detail, comment about any of the particulars, or make any other response other than that which is required. Realize that you are not doing anything more than participating, perhaps even unwillingly, in a ritual energized by fear and anxiety. This might seem cold, uncaring, and perhaps not even a pastoral response that is helpful. I assure you that it is the best pastoral response that you can offer.

However, that being the case, as you listen—sometimes for weeks or even months—to the ritual that is being performed for you, listen with a discerning ear. Every once in a while there will be a moment, a pause in the ritual, in which the opportunity to offer hope and understanding is present. Again do not judge, fix, correct, or admonish. It is much more helpful to share something like, "I understand something of the fear and the anxiety that you are experiencing. Would you accept some help?" There may be a response to your question, there may not be. Sometimes it will have to be repeated more than once, and on different occasions, before the person will respond to you. Wait patiently and when the opportunity finally presents itself be prepared to (a) distribute a copy of this *SA* newsletter and suggest that he or she requests a subscription; (b) suggest a name of a confessor and/or spiritual director who has some expertise in obsessive-compulsive behavior if you feel inadequate or unprepared; and (c) prepare yourself to be ignored or your advice not accepted. Above all, try to not be discouraged. The frustration that you feel is minor compared to the frustration of the person you are trying to help.

Father, the priest/confessor is many times the only person who experiences the full manifestation of the obsessive-compulsive ritual. Within the privacy and the sacredness of the sacrament, the person exhibits the depth and the emotion of his or her suffering. If you forget everything else that I have written, please remember at least this much. The person who is coming to you has suffered enough. He or she needs, more than anything else, at least a moment of understanding and acceptance. The person understands that you cannot "fix" the situation and that you as priest/confessor may feel helpless as well during the ritual. Be that as it may, each person who comes to you desires a patient, accepting, and a listening ear. This will be more helpful and more beneficial than you can possibly imagine.

Appendix Three

Collected Prayers, Inspiration, and Words of Wisdom for the Scrupulous

WORDS OF WISDOM

Saint Alphonsus Liguori

When God sends us crosses, let us thank him, since it is a sign that God means to pardon all of our sins.

Pray, pray, never cease to pray, for if you pray, your salvation will be secure.

When we are in danger and tempted to disobey God's law, prayer will obtain for us God's help and we shall be preserved from sin.

Those who love God also love all those whom God loves; they eagerly look for ways to help others, to comfort them, and to make them as happy as possible.

Remember that God is always present within you. You do not have to go to heaven to find your God: You will find God within your soul. If you think of God as some distant being when you pray, you will easily become distracted. God is everywhere....God is present within you.

Edward Everett Hale

Look up and not down; look out and not in; look forward and not back.

Renee Bartkowski, *Our Family Prayer Book*

How unwise it is to worry, to waste our time and energy so uselessly. How often do we look back and worry about the past—and look ahead to worry about the future? Teach us, Lord, that the only thing we can possibly do anything about is the present. Call us into the present—to live one day at a time, fully and well. Bless us, Lord, with the faith and confidence we need to know that you are always available to help us face tomorrow—when tomorrow arrives. Amen.

Helen Steiner Rice

Remember, God is ready and willing to help you. All you have to do is reach out your hand and you will find him. He's only a prayer away.

If I do my best, God will do the rest.

O, God, what a comfort to know that you care, and to know when I seek you, you will always be there.

Author unknown

We must come to see the blessings of God in all things. Then the sorrows we experience become opportunities to grow in love, faith, and compassion.

There are so many happy, hopeful things in life to hold onto—a baby's finger, an honest compliment, a pleasant memory, a smile, and a song.

Let go of your old, cold grudges and latch on to the warm feeling that can come only from a generous, forgiving heart.

Make tomorrow another day and not today's sequel.

Lord, help me to remember that nothing is going to happen to me today that you and I together cannot handle.

John Watson

Be kind—everyone you meet is fighting a hard battle.

George Eliot

What do we live for, if it is not to make life less difficult for each other?

Helen Keller

The best and most beautiful things in the world cannot be seen or even touched. They must be felt with the heart.

W. D. Gough

God takes life's pieces and gives us unbroken peace.

Victor M. Parachin, *Scripture Pathways to Inner Healing*

Through God's grace, I dissolve all negative, limiting beliefs. Through God's grace, I am letting go of all accumulated pain, guilt, and fear. Through God's grace, I am moving toward wholeness and peace.

Saint Teresa of Ávila

Let nothing disturb you, nothing cause you fear. All things pass; God is unchanging. Patience obtains all: Whoever has God needs nothing else. God alone suffices.

Philippians 4:6–7

Don't worry about anything, but in all your prayers ask God for what you need, always asking him with a thankful heart. And God's peace, which is far beyond human understanding, will keep your hearts and minds safe in union with Jesus Christ.

Appendix Four

Glossary of Terms

ABSOLUTE AUTHORITY The authority that belongs to God and to God alone. Since God is the creator of all things, all authority comes from God and all true authority accurately reflects the will of God. The *Catechism of the Catholic Church* (1899) states, "There is no authority except from God."

ABSOLUTION The sacramental form, or words, that are prayed by the priest, within the celebration of the sacrament of reconciliation. When prayed by the priest these words complete the sacrament of penance and God grants pardon to the sinner. The actual words of absolution are: "God, the Father of mercies, has reconciled the world to himself and sent the Holy Spirit among us for the forgiveness of sins; through the ministry of the Church may God give you pardon and peace, and I absolve you from your sins in the name of the Father, and of the Son, and of the Holy Spirit. Amen" (The Rite of Penance, #46).

ACT OF CONTRITION Contrition is understood as heartfelt sorrow for sin and the firm intention of not sinning again. An act of contrition is a prayer that may be prayed, that expresses heartfelt sorrow for sin and which expresses the firm intention of not sinning again. Any prayer that includes words that express sorrow and words that express the intention of not sinning can be understood as an act of contrition. A traditional act of contrition is: "Oh my God, I am sorry for having offended you. I firmly resolve, with the help of your grace, to sin no more and to avoid the near occasion of sin. Amen."

ACT OF PERFECT CONTRITION Perfect contrition is understood as sorrow from sin that comes from the heart because of a love for God. Imperfect contrition is understood as sorrow for sin that comes from the heart because of some lesser motive, such as fear of hell, or some other desire. Within the celebration of the sacrament of reconciliation, imperfect contrition is all that is necessary for the forgiveness of sins.

ANXIETY A feeling or state of apprehension, fear, worry, or lack of peacefulness. People who suffer from scrupulosity often identify themselves as "being very anxious" when thinking about sin, in their relationship with God, or before the reception of the sacraments of reconciliation and Eucharist.

BLASPHEMY Freely and deliberately choosing to speak or act against God or against people and objects that have been consecrated to God, for the purpose of showing a lack of reverence or respect. The *Catechism of the Catholic Church* (2148) defines it as "directly opposed to the second commandment."

CHOICE Implies the opportunity to choose and implies the opportunity to choose between more than one option. In moral terms it is commonly understood as the opportunity to choose between that which is reflective of the will of God and that which does not reflect the will of God. For scrupulous people it is often the experience of choosing that presents the most difficulty. Scrupulous people desire, above all else, to choose to do that which reflects the will of God, but they are plagued with the notion that they have not chosen the will of God and are somehow displeasing God.

COMPULSIONS Behaviors that are repetitive and intentional, that are performed in response to an obsession. Common compulsions include repetitive hand washing, touching, or counting. A person experiences anxiety and tension when they attempt to resist the compulsion and experience immediate relief if they yield to the compulsion.

CONFESSION The acknowledgment and praise of the holiness of God, by the act of admitting to God our faults and our failings, in the certain hope of receiving God's plentiful forgiveness. Understood in the sacramental sense, it is the act of celebrating the sacrament of reconciliation by recalling God's mercy, confessing our sins to a priest, and receiving absolution.

CONFESSION OF DEVOTION A type of confession that a regular confessor may suggest to a scrupulous person as the preferred form for their celebration of the sacrament of reconciliation. A confession of devotion includes a renewal of sorrow for sin and the resolution not to sin again. It generally does not include the listing or numbering of sins.

CONFESSOR An ordained priest, who represents the forgiving Christ within the sacrament of reconciliation. It is the role of the confessor to offer absolution for sin, spiritual help and guidance, and to celebrate with the penitent his or her full restoration to the Body of Christ.

CONSCIENCE A dictate of practical reason or a personal judgment which decides, on the basis of general moral values and principles, that an action is morally good or evil, as reflected by the law of God.

CONSCIENCE, DELICATE A descriptive word, often used to refer to a person who struggles with scrupulosity or any kind of moral decision making. A person with a delicate conscience is often perceived as a person who is comfortable with events or circumstances that are clearly black or white, good or bad, but often uncomfortable with any deviation, no matter how small, from that which is understood as God's will or God's law.

CONSCIENCE, SCRUPULOUS Describes people who doubt God's love for them and who doubt their own ability to be loved by God. People who are possessed by a thousand frightening fantasies, who suffer from recurring or intrusive thoughts that seem never to go away. People who need a regular confessor to assist and guide them in their spiritual journey. People who may suffer from OCD (obsessive-compulsive disorder) and who may need some form of professional therapy.

DISPENSATION A relaxation of the ecclesiastical law in a particular instance by a person who has the authority to do so; for example, a dispensation from the obligation to fast and abstain during the designated days of Lent.

DISTRACTION A thought or idea, an action or reaction to an outside stimulus, that seems to divide attention or prevents concentration.

DOUBT To be uncertain about, to question, to hesitate to believe. There are two kinds of doubt: voluntary and involuntary. Voluntary doubt disregards or refuses to believe what God has revealed or that the Church teaches. Involuntary doubt refers to hesitation in believing or difficulty and anxiety in overcoming objections connected with faith.

DOUBTING DISEASE A reference to scrupulosity.

EASTER DUTY A popular term for the obligation to receive Communion at least once a year. Canon 920 requires that this obligation be fulfilled during the Easter season unless it is fulfilled for a just cause at some other time during the year. The Easter season has traditionally been understood to extend from the first Sunday of Lent until Trinity Sunday (a week after Pentecost).

EUCHARISTIC FAST The obligation to abstain from food or drink (not including water) for a period of one hour before the reception of Communion. The obligation to abstain does not apply to prescribed medicine or to any substance that may be accidentally ingested, such as toothpaste or mouthwash. The obligation does not apply to those who are sick or who have another just reason for dispensation.

EXAMINATION OF CONSCIENCE A prayerful review of a person's relationship with the Lord. The examination is usually a preliminary to the celebration of the sacrament of reconciliation. For the scrupulous person the examination should follow the rules that have been agreed upon with their regular confessor. For still others, who suffer great anxiety as a result of such an examination, a regular confessor may oblige them not to engage in this particular spiritual exercise.

FEAR A distressing emotion, usually brought on by pain, danger, evil, or the perception that something distressful may occur. For the scrupulous person a common fear is the fear of displeasing God or the fear of being deprived of heaven.

FORGIVENESS To receive pardon for an offense, to seek absolution, to be willing to extend an understanding and gentle heart to self or to another.

FRIDAY ABSTINENCE A penitential practice of doing without something, usually meat or some other food, on all Fridays during the year, including Good Friday and Ash Wednesday. The code of canon law extends to the National Conference of Catholic Bishops the authority to determine the actual penitential practice that is to be followed.

FULL CONSENT OF THE WILL A requirement for the commission of sin or for the performance of any immoral act. A person must be able to freely choose the action and fully desire to commit the sin. In reference to sin, full consent presumes the age of reason (usually seven years old), an informed conscience, and the desire to displease God.

GRAVE MATTER The *Catechism of the Catholic Church* (1858) defines grave matter as something "that is specified by the Ten Commandments." A person must consider the fact of the gravity of sin as more or less great, such as the sin of murder is graver than the sin of theft. A person must also consider who is wronged; stealing ten dollars from a poor man is graver than stealing ten dollars from a rich man.

GUILT A feeling of responsibility or remorse from some action performed. As a result of the action and the feeling that accompanies the performance, the person may well perceive (real or imagined) that the action was displeasing to God or to another.

MORTAL SIN For a sin to be considered mortal, three conditions must be present together: the object or action chosen must be grave matter; it must be chosen with full knowledge; and there must be deliberate consent. The effect of mortal sin is the loss of charity and the privation of sanctifying grace.

OBLIGATION Something that a person is bound to do because of a sense of duty or as the result of a law or a custom. For example, a holy day of obligation obliges a person to attend Mass. This obligation comes from law (the law of the Church) and from custom (traditionally the high holy days were celebrated with a special Mass).

OBSESSIONS Persistent ideas, thoughts, and impulses, which are usually resisted through the attempt to distract oneself by trying to think about something else. For the scrupulous person the most common obsession is the thought that he or she may have offended God, either by choosing to perform some particular action, or choosing not to perform some particular action that is perceived as pleasing to God.

OBSESSIVE-COMPULSIVE DISORDER (OCD) *The Diagnostic and Statistical Manual of Mental Disorders* (3rd edition, 1987, American Psychiatric Association) defines OCD in this way: The essential feature of this disorder is recurrent obsessions or compulsions sufficiently severe to cause marked distress, be time-consuming, or significantly interfere with the person's normal routine, occupational functioning, or usual social activities or relationships with others. OCD usually begins in adolescence, is considered to be chronic, and the impairment can become the major life activity of the person. There are no predisposing factors known to cause OCD, and although it is presumed that the disorder is rare in the general population, some studies have indicated that mild forms may be relatively common. OCD affects both men and women equally.

PENANCE Commonly understood as prayer, offerings, works of mercy, service to our neighbors, voluntary self-denial, or any other sacrifice that helps people understand their sinfulness and come to an appreciation and thankfulness for the mercy and forgiveness that they have received from God.

RESTITUTION Returning to the rightful owner whatever had been taken unjustly from them; restoring stolen goods or their equivalent. A sin of injustice cannot be forgiven unless the penitent intends to make restitution to the best of their ability. For scrupulous persons restitution should not be assumed or attempted unless directed by the confessor.

SACRAMENTALS In imitation of the sacraments, sacramentals may be understood as sacred signs and symbols of God's action and intercession. Common sacramentals include blessings, holy water, blessed candles, blessed medals, and scapulars.

SACRILEGE Understood as the treatment of sacraments and other liturgical actions in a profane or disrespectful manner. All persons, things, or places that are consecrated to God can suffer sacrilege. Sacrilege committed against the Eucharist is always considered a grave sin.

SCRUPLES From the Latin, meaning "a small, sharp stone." If you walk with a sharp stone in your shoe, it can be annoying. Scruples should not be neglected.

SCRUPULOUS A person who is either not well informed about the moral law (they tend to interpret as sinful that which is not sinful) or not able to make correct judgments about what is right and wrong (groundless fears and nameless anxieties tend to interfere with correct judgments).

SEAL OF CONFESSION The secrecy demanded of the confessor in the sacrament of reconciliation; no reason justifies the breaking of the seal, and the Church reserves grave penalties for any confessor who would dare to do so.

SIN OF COMMISSION A sin that is actually committed; it may be mortal or venial in nature. An example of a venial sin of commission is the sin of swearing (the use of profane language).

SIN OF OMISSION An action that is omitted and not acted upon; but by its omission a sin results that can be mortal or venial in nature. An example of a venial sin of omission is not acting to stop gossip about another person when the opportunity easily presented itself.

SPIRITUAL DIRECTOR A trusted person, male or female, who is also in a spiritual direction relationship with another, who is willing to "walk with you on your spiritual journey." It is a person who has been to the place where you want to go and who is willing to help you arrive at that place.

SUFFICIENT REFLECTION The time that is necessary, the information that is essential, and the counsel that is appropriate in order to discern a particular choice. Sufficient reflection is dependent on the seriousness of the question that needs to be discerned.

SUNDAY OBLIGATION The serious obligation of all the faithful to attend Mass on Sunday. A person may be dispensed from this obligation because of advanced age or sickness or because of circumstances beyond his or her control that makes it impossible to safely fulfill the obligation; for example, bad weather, or no access to a vehicle that can transport you to the place of worship.

TEMPTATION An attraction or enticement to sin, arising from within a person or from without (the flesh, the world, the devil). Temptation is itself not a sin.

UNFORGIVABLE SIN AGAINST THE HOLY SPIRIT A sin considered repugnant to the third person of the Blessed Trinity. There are six sins against the Holy Spirit: despair, presumption, envy, obstinacy in sin, final impenitence, and deliberate resistance to the known truth. It is commonly understood that the sin of despair is the unforgivable sin against the Holy Spirit, because this sin makes it impossible for the Holy Spirit to work on our behalf. Many scrupulous people wrongly believe that they have sinned in this way, when in fact what they are experiencing is not the unforgivable sin, but rather the effect of scrupulosity.

VENIAL SIN For a sin to be considered venial the matter is not considered grave or serious, or when a law or standard prescribed by the moral law is not followed, or when a moral law is not obeyed, but without full knowledge and consent of the will. Venial sin does not destroy charity and does not deprive a person of sanctifying grace.

Appendix Five

Bibliography and References

A Thousand Frightening Fantasies, William Van Ornum, Ph.D. (New York: Crossroad, Revised 2004).

Answers to Praise: Letters to the Author of Prison to Praise, Merlin R. Carothers (North Brunswick, NJ: Logos, Revised 1993).

Catechism of the Catholic Church, Libreria Editrice Vaticana (Liguori, Mo.: Liguori Publications, 1994).

Following Christ: A Handbook of Catholic Moral Teaching, Daniel L. Lowery (Liguori, Mo.: Liguori Publications, Revised 1996).

Helps for the Separated and Divorced, Medard Laz (Liguori, Mo.: Liguori Publications, 1981).

Obsessive Compulsive Anonymous: Recovery Support Group (Obsessive Compulsive Anonymous, Inc., New Hyde Park, NY, 1990).

The Doubting Disease, Joseph W. Ciarrocchi (Mahwah, NJ: Paulist Press, 1995).

The Essential Catholic Handbook of the Bible, Thomas M. Santa, C.Ss.R. (Liguori, Mo.: Liguori Publications, 2001).

CPSIA information can be obtained
at www.ICGtesting.com
Printed in the USA
LVOW01s0752140116

470574LV00031B/411/P